TIKOPIA COLLECTED

First published in 2017 by
Sean Kingston Publishing
www.seankingston.co.uk
Canon Pyon

British Library Cataloguing in Publication Data
A catalogue record for this book is available from the British Library.

Printed by Lightning Source

ISBN 978-1-907774-39-3

Tikopia Collected

Raymond Firth and the Creation of Solomon Islands Cultural Heritage

Elizabeth Bonshek

Sean Kingston Publishing
www.seankingston.co.uk
Canon Pyon

Figure 1   'Tikopia natives aboard the mission ship "Southern Cross" bartering native products for fish hooks, knives etc from passengers'. Photographed by Anglican missionary Revd David Lloyd Francis, while based in the Solomon Islands between 1928 and 1930. Firth arrived in Tikopia on the Southern Cross in 1928 and departed with it in 1929. Lantern slide, 8.2 cm high, 8.2 cm wide (British Museum: Oc,G.T.2329).

ACKNOWLEDGEMENTS

The process of publishing a thesis some time after it was written demands the consideration of updates to the original or of leaving things, in terms of theory and approach, as is. I have chosen the latter: the process of updating would logically demand the contemporary view of the Tikopia. As this is now underway, by Tikopia themselves, it is an examination of the collection and the process of its making in historical context that I believe is the most valuable contribution I can make at this time.

When I was writing my thesis I received support from my advisors, Nicholas Thomas and Lissant Bolton. Jim Specht and Val Attenbrow from the Australian Museum also read the original manuscript and made valuable comments. More than a decade on, I am grateful to Michael Scott of the London School of Economics and Ben Burt of the British Museum, who have offered insights on how to improve the original manuscript for publication. I am also grateful to Ben Burt for editing the revised text at the commencement of this project and to Aedeen Cremin for her kind assistance in copy-editing the final manuscript. I would like to thank Anna Craven, who has generously donated her time to read through the manuscript; Julian Treadaway, who has assisted in circulating my original thesis to Tikopia undertaking work upon their own book; and Rhys Richards, for providing a copy of his manuscript on the early explorers to Tikopia.

My own photography of objects in the collection at the Australian Museum in 2013 was made possible thanks to the efforts of the collections staff, Dion Peita and Keren Ruki. I owe a big thank you to photographer Bob Miller for photo-editing assistance with these images (Figures 5, 10, 11, 15, 21, 22, 27). The remaining images of objects in the Firth collection were photographed by Paul Ovenden, and are copyright of the Australian Museum. Parts of Chapter 6 appeared in 'Ownership and a peripatetic collection: Raymond Firth's Collection from Tikopia, Solomon Islands', in *A Pacific Odyssey: Archaeology and Anthropology in the Western Pacific*. Papers in Honour of Jim Specht (2004), ed. Val Attenbrow and Richard Fullagar, pp. 37–45. Records of the Australian Museum, Supplement 29. Sydney: Australian Museum (dx.doi.org/10.3853/j.0812-7387.29.2004.1400) and have been reproduced here with the permission of the Records of the Australian Museum.

Images from the Dumont d'Urville expedition and by Augustus Earle are reproduced courtesy of the National Library of Australia. Permission to reproduce Firth's field photographs and include quotes from his correspondence, held in the London School of Economics (LSE) Archives, London, was kindly granted by Hugh Firth. Thank you to Anna Towlson and Catherine McIntyre, Archives, LSE for providing access to these materials and for arranging contact with Firth's descendants. And thank you too to Abraham Haurisi, General Secretary of the Anglican Church of Melanesia, for granting permission to make reference to the '1928 Synod Trip' diary of the Revd Richard Godfrey, priest of the Melanesian Mission, made available at the Project Canterbury's website (anglicanhistory.org). Thanks also to Nyree Morrison and Melanie Grogan, Archives, Fisher Library, University of Sydney and Patricia Egan, Australian Museum Archives, Sydney.

While many people have contributed to the development of my thinking about museum collections, objects and their manifestation as cultural heritage, I remain responsible for any errors and omissions that may become apparent in the book.

A final note on names: there are slight differences in the spelling of Tikopia names as they occur in various publications or archival documentation. I have not attempted to standardize these, but have simply used the spelling that appears in a particular source.

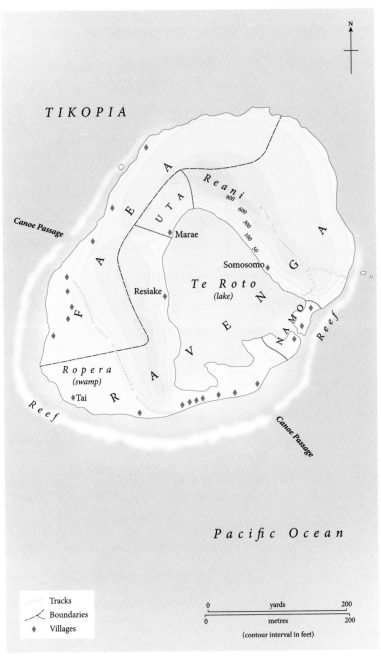

N

TIKOPIA

Canoe Passage

R e a n i
900
600
300
100
50

U T A

Marae

F   A   E   A

A

G

Somosomo

Resiake

Te Roto
(lake)

N

E

NAMO

Reef

A   V   E

R

Ropera
(swamp)

Tai

R e e f

Canoe Passage

P a c i f i c   O c e a n

Tracks
Boundaries
Villages

0   yards   200

0   metres   200

(contour interval in feet)

Map 1   The island of Tikopia

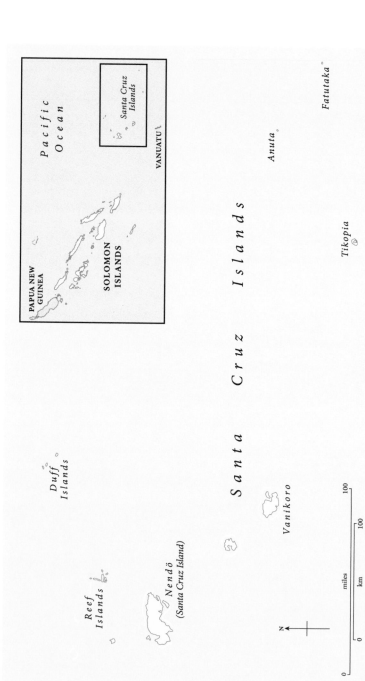

Map 2   The Santa Cruz Islands

CONTENTS

ILLUSTRATIONS

Figure 2   Raymond Firth, photographed by Sarah Chinnery in 1932 (image courtesy of the National Library of Australia).

INTRODUCTION

This book focuses on the objects collected by Professor Sir Raymond Firth (Figure 2) while he was carrying out fieldwork in Tikopia in Solomon Islands in 1928, and the subsequent history of these objects as a museum collection. I am interested in tracing the process by which the objects were transformed into an 'ethnographic' collection and then into 'cultural heritage': a transformation that took place between the time of collection in Tikopia and then in various museums or museum-like sites in Australia. This work emerged from my unpublished Master of Arts thesis for the Centre for Cross Cultural Research, Australian National University, in 1999, which in turn was born of a specific time and place. The thesis was an outcome of my work on the Melanesian collections[1] held by the Australian Museum in Sydney during the late 1980s and into the 1990s.

The predominant concerns for museums and policy makers in Australian museums at that time related to indigenous access to museum collections and the acknowledgement of the indigenous Australian voice. It was against this background that I was interested in what Melanesians thought about museum collections from their respective countries. Did Melanesian voices sound differently to indigenous Australian voices?

I hoped that Raymond Firth's collection from Tikopia would provide an opportunity to explore the Solomon Island voice, if not the Melanesian voice. Firth's Tikopia collection came to the Australian Museum in 1989 as part of a much larger acquisition (now referred to officially as the

---

1   The designation 'Melanesian' to refer to Papua New Guinea, Solomon Islands, Vanuatu, New Caledonia and sometimes Fiji is not without problematic associations (Thomas 1989a) but is accepted usage amongst people from these countries as well as anthropologists.

University of Sydney collection) which was transferred from the National Museum of Australia at that time. And indeed, this relocation itself forms an important part of my narrative about the construction of cultural heritage (see Chapter 6).

Firth's collection was attractive from a research point of view because it constituted a discrete collection: its acquisition date and place were well defined; often the names of donors were available; and, importantly, the collection of some 641 objects was supported by extensive ethnographic context. I wrote to Firth, who kindly granted me an interview at his London home in 1994, at which time he provided me with copies of his collection list to supplement those available in the museum's records. Fortuitously, and prior to my arrival, a Tikopia man, Moses Lonsdale (Figure 3), who was then attending theological college in Solihull, Birmingham, had made contact with Firth. And so shortly after visiting Firth, I boarded the train to Birmingham to meet Lonsdale and discuss the collection with him.

Lonsdale, at that time a well-travelled man in his 30s, was quickly interested in the collection. As a boy he had lived amongst the Tikopia community at Nukufero in the Russell Islands, on Tikopia itself and then on Vanikoro, Tikopia's island neighbour to the north-west (Map 1). By the end of 1981 he had moved to Honiara, where he joined the Anglican Church. Over the following years he attended a number of religious studies courses and worked in pastoral-care programmes which took him to other parts of the Solomon Islands as well as to Papua New Guinea and, in a timely fashion for me, Birmingham, England. In 1998 he enrolled at the University of Auckland in New Zealand to study theology.

From Lonsdale I learnt that the Tikopia referred to Firth as the 'Master Writer' (see also MacDonald 2000, 2002) and further discussion reinforced my hope that the collection would be of interest to Tikopia. In Lonsdale's words the collection was important, because the objects reflect 'what make us Tikopia'. But, while on one hand the objects 'constituted' Tikopia, the objects had also been given away to Firth as a gift: and as such they signified a relationship between Tikopia and Firth, the 'Master Writer'. Lonsdale said he thought it would be a good idea to have a museum on the island to display the old objects for everyone to see. A year later Lonsdale was in Sydney and I showed him the Firth collection at the Australian Museum. I met him again in 1996, in Honiara, by which time he had completed his studies. Lonsdale introduced me to several Tikopia who resided in Honiara, the nation's capital on Guadalcanal, and in Nukukaisi,

Figure 3   Moses Lonsdale, Honiara, 1996 (photo: Bonshek).

a Tikopia resettlement on Makira Island (established in 1962). During my brief one-month stay I also visited Lata, Temotu's provincial capital, which lies at the most eastern part of Solomon Islands in the Santa Cruz group. While my interviews do not constitute a record in the tradition of anthropological fieldwork, I do include some of the responses to the photographs of the objects taken in 1928–9, as a range of feelings were expressed and recorded. By including these comments I also acknowledge the assistance of those who took the time to talk to me and who, most importantly, offered their hospitality to me without hesitation.

Two people could recall meeting Firth in 1928: Joseph Manu-tai (Figure 4), an elderly man living in Honiara, said that as a boy he had cooked for Firth. Conversation took place in a mixture of Tikopia and Solomon Islands pijin translated into English by Frieda Tuki, the daughter of Ishmael Tuki, Firth's co-author of the *Tikopia-English Dictionary* (Firth with Tuki 1985). Remarkably, Manu-tai also recognized one of the bowls in the Australian Museum's collection. The bowl (Figure 5), which Firth noted had been made by Pu Resiake, had in fact been given to Firth by one of Manu-tai's brothers. Manu-tai added that the objects in the collection had been given

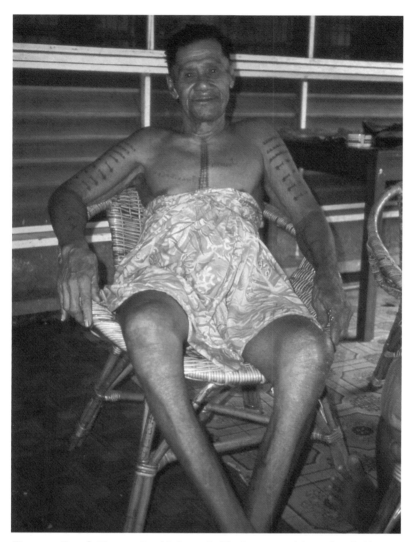

Figure 4   Joseph Manu-tai at his home in Honiara, 1996 (photo: Bonshek).

to Firth as presents and recounted that Firth was always following people
and taking pictures. He added: 'He knows everything, including women's
knowledge'. He observed, laughingly, that when Firth left Tikopia he had
objects sticking out all over the *Southern Cross*, the Melanesian Mission's
boat which travelled between the islands.

Figure 5 *'Kumete for holding coconut cream, unusual shape; made by Pu Resiake'. Firth no. 1.07. 26 cm (diameter) × 16.5 cm (high). AM registration no. E84376 (photo: Bonshek).*

The second person to have memories of Firth was an elderly woman, Mane (Figure 6). As a young girl she remembered that upon his arrival Firth had been carried ashore. This placed him in a commanding position in her eyes, as chiefs were carried in this way as a sign of respect for them. She remembered that, once ashore, Firth had been taken to see the chiefs, who had already agreed to his coming to Tikopia, and then he had visited every household. This was when she shook hands with Firth. She said that the Tikopia were happy for him to come and record *kastom* and to make a record of 'the history of the generations'. She remembered that waist-mats and barkcloth were presented to Firth as gifts and that objects had been exchanged with him. She made little comment on individual objects represented in my photographs, but noted instead that tattoo designs appeared on dancing paddles (*paki*).

These unexpected memories of Firth were supplemented by other commentaries about how certain objects were still in use or still made: for example, Lily, the wife of Ishmael Tuki (Figure 7), co-author with Firth of the *Tikopia-English Dictionary* (1985), was a weaver and named certain design features and techniques of manufacture of mats. In naming techniques and parts of objects, some made use of the Tikopia dictionary, using it as an authoritative reference. But some also commented that the Tikopia language had changed since Firth's time. Tuki remembered robust discussions with Firth about Tikopia language and language change while

Figure 6   Mane, Nukukaisi, 1996 (photo: Bonshek).

compiling the dictionary: he added that Firth had defended adamantly the usages from the old men that he had recorded in 1928. One young person raised language loss as a matter of concern.

Nukukaisi villagers had mixed responses to the photographs of the collection: some were very interested, others less so. Comments included whether or not certain object types were still made and who could make them: chiefs' headrests (Figure 8) were still made, but no longer by specialist carvers. Likewise, canoes could be made by whoever wished to make one. They also thought that Tikopia living on the home island

Figure 7   Ishmael Tuki, Nukukaisi, Makira, 1996 (photo: Bonshek).

would know more about the use and meanings of objects and could talk more extensively about *kastom* life. There was a sense that people living away from Tikopia considered themselves less knowledgeable of *kastom*, although some individuals were singled out as an exception. As a geographical place, Tikopia was talked about as the location of pre-Christian knowledge – the place where 'things were different'. Firth also referred to 'exchange nights' in his notes, and Tuki suggested that these might have occurred in the context of dances, as this was a time of non-ceremonial exchange. He suggested that people from all over the island would have visited and brought portable items to trade and exchange. Indeed, Tikopia men on board the Melanesian Mission boat, the *Southern Cross*, were snapped taking the opportunity to trade at around the time of Firth's arrival (Figure 1).

Some Nukukaisi villagers were quick to question whether I was intending to buy artefacts, others wanted to know if I was working with Firth. I replied in the negative to both questions, but added that I had met and talked to Firth, at which point I felt my status in Nukukaisi eyes had risen. Firth's reputation was deferred to: one man offered that it would be easier to ask Firth about the objects rather than ask the people I was then sitting amongst.

Both Tuki and his daughter, Frieda (Figure 9), who had assisted with translation with Manu-tai, were concerned to match the names of

Figure 8   Urunga nga ariki (chief's headrests). Left: Firth no. 4.19, given to Firth by Mairunga; AM registration no. E84637, 36.3 cm high; 41.4 cm at widest point between 'wings'. Right: Firth no. 4.9; AM registration no. E84639, 32 cm high; 35 cm at widest point (photo: Paul Ovenden, Australian Museum).

individuals on Firth's collection lists with family names and to identify clans and various branches of families, including where they were then living. In some ways, this was a more important task than discussions surrounding the objects. For one man, it was Firth's photographs, not the objects in his collection, that were the centre of his attention. He wanted to know if I carried a photograph of his deceased father; if so, he wanted a copy. The collection also prompted commentary concerning how things had changed since Firth's visit in 1928.

The late Bishop Lazarus Munamua of Lata had specific interests in the collection and spoke expansively about it. His father had been the first catechist on Tikopia. One of his uncles, whom he called a 'pagan' priest, had been an elder and spokesman for the chief. A second uncle had also been a 'pagan' priest, as was a third who died in Vanikoro, a small island to the north of Tikopia. In contrast, Munamua grew up in a Christian family. But after finishing school he spent four months with his first uncle at the time

Figure 9   Frieda, Honiara, 1996 (photo: Bonshek).

that the latter decided to become a Christian. Munamua was interested in the religious aspects of the objects, in terms of their association with both pagan and Christian religions. He told an anecdote about Firth, whom he referred to as 'Ray-mond'. Firth went to talk to an elder. The elder wanted an adze (a European one) from him. But 'Ray-mond' said he couldn't give him an adze, because he wasn't a chief. The elder told Firth to go and ask the chiefs who he was. So Firth did so, and came back with an adze. He then asked the elder to show him his gods. So the elder called out, and a lizard appeared and moved straight towards him. Apparently disturbed by this event, Firth left the scene, 'shaken'.

Munamua was interested in the designs on objects and their potential for revealing meaning. He drew comparisons between the presence of notches carved into the sides of headrests (Figure 10) and the notches which adorned sacred canoes, which in the latter case reflected associations with genealogies (cf. Feinberg 1988:50–1 on the association between people and birds on Anuta; see also Firth 1966b; Milner 1969). Confirming Mane's comment, he also noted that some designs on the *paki* (dance paddles, Figure 11) appear as women's tattoos. He suggested that certain designs and stories belong to families, and there were different levels of knowledge appropriate to a specific listener. A mother's family held a set of tattoos, which she passed onto her oldest daughter. Later it was the daughter's responsibility to pass these tattoo designs on to the next appropriate daughter. (Pendergrast 2000 describes the state of the art of tattooing in the 1970s and the overlap between motifs as tattoos and visual elements on a number of material objects, but does not mention family designs.[2])

He also spoke about the opposition between the terms 'left' and 'right', which, he noted, Firth had talked about in regard to houses. The Bishop explained that the left side, *sema*, was 'unclean', while the right side, *matau*, had various meanings: 'hook' or 'food', or 'woman's breast'. This division, he explained, continued into Tikopian Christian religious sensibility, where to move from the left to the right was to move to a place of honour. In another commentary, while contemplating photographs of *paki* (dance paddles), he added that *paki* also means 'to move on' and this was a metaphor symbolizing the way ahead: 'to think positively'. He did not extend the metaphor to the dancing in which the *paki* are used, but perhaps this is implicit.

Munamua too was concerned that the nuances of Tikopia language and cultural values were in danger of being lost, and the objects in Firth's collection could be used to identify and explore, and perhaps also to capture these changing values. He felt that knowledge was not being passed down to the next generation and was interested in a project which would investigate the meanings of objects. His purpose in understanding 'traditional' Tikopia motifs was to provide more relevant translations of the Bible and to mediate between 'pagan' and Christian beliefs.

The last person I want to make reference to is the late Fred Soaki, then Commissioner of Police, who was a member of Kafika, the highest ranking

---

2   'There are no restrictions on the wearing of tattoo and in the past the decoration was almost universal among the adults on the island (Firth 1939:85). It was considered a normal and desirable attribute to adult life. It does not indicate membership of any family or clan, nor does it show social status or hereditary privilege. It may be worn by anyone prepared to pay the artist for his work, the payment taking the form of a gift – barkcloth, mats and food being usual elements. The differences shown in various patterns indicate the personal preferences of the person being tattooed and/or the tattooist.' (Pendergrast 2000:15). However, later he comments: 'Religious sanction for one pattern, *te tau*, the line which runs down the front of the body on both men and women was mentioned by a few. They claimed that persons without this decoration so annoyed a spiritual being called Tenavanava that he punished them in the next world by forcing them to carry *te tunga*, the heavy wooden anvil on which bark cloth is beaten.' (Pendergrast 2000:15).

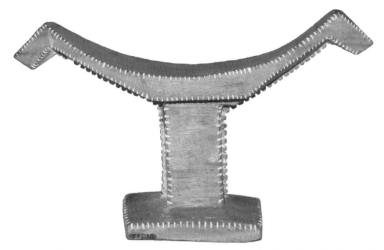

Figure 10 'Urunga – common type; new, made by Pa Rangifuri, notched ornamentation' (Wedgewood 1928:5). Firth no. 4.07; AM registration no. E84035, 18.8 × 31 cm (photo: Bonshek).

of the four chiefly clans of Tikopia. He was very supportive of the idea of research on the collections. Viewing the photographs of the collection also prompted him to talk about conversion to Christianity, though in the context of the burial of sacred objects in 1956, an act orchestrated, he said, by Tafua family members (the second-ranking chiefly clan) and an Anglican priest from Isabel island. At this time, all the 'old things' were buried. On a personal note, he also singled out some of the clubs and recounted how his own grandfather, who had worked as a plantation labourer in Queensland, was the first person to bring firearms to Tikopia. His grandfather had joined up with blackbirders three times. The association of the club (Firth no. 13.8, see Appendix 2)[3] with the gods prompted him to comment that the Tikopia still believed in spirit possession. For Soaki, as for Munamua, the objects were markers of a pre-Christian era and held the potential to reveal insights into the past.

These responses to the objects in 1996 revealed a high regard for Firth and a view of him as the recorder and possessor of greater knowledge about Tikopia traditional life than anyone else. Firth's work had been read by some and accepted as authoritative by the majority of people I met.

---

3   AM registration no. E84651-2.

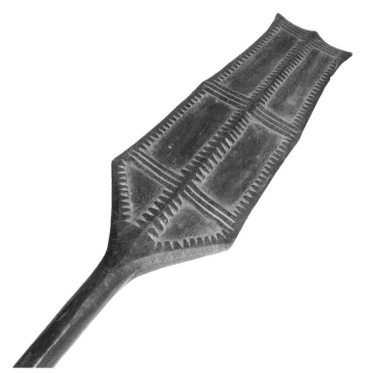

Figure 11   Paki: 'Dancing bat. Used by men, made from puka or mei wood'
(Wedgewood 1928:16). Firth no. 14.04, AM registration no. E84659, 92 × 19.5 cm
(photo: Bonshek).

Only two people argued with this, and both of these had been educated
in Western schools and lived away from the home island. However, most
people, if not all, were interested in the broader network of kin relationships
which the collection represented. They were excited when they discovered
a personal association with the people identified by Firth as the donors
or makers of specific objects. This interest reflected an interpretation of
objects which emphasizes the social associations of the collection, rather
than the functional meaning of individual objects.

They viewed Firth's collection and work as a record of *kastom*, that is,
pre-Christian behaviour. This interpretation of *kastom* is not inconsistent
with that of other countries in the Pacific (Keesing and Tonkinson 1982).
But for a few, Tikopia's pre-Christian practice was associated with negative
aspects such as devils and fighting (although the latter was not something

recorded by Firth at the time of his fieldwork). Many people accommodated a belief in the power of the old spirits within their practice of Christianity.

As I travelled from Honiara to Nukukaisi and then to Lata, the difficulty of getting to Tikopia became increasingly apparent. There is no airstrip on Tikopia, and visitors must travel there by boat from Honiara or Santa Cruz, either way a journey of considerable distance and uncertain scheduling. For this reason, from this point onwards my research was based on textual sources in libraries and archives, and I focused on the collector, Raymond Firth, and an exploration of the historical period and contexts through which the collection eventually arrived at the Australian Museum via the University of Sydney and the National Museum of Australia.

I learnt a great deal from the people I encountered during my short visit in 1996, and in addition to those mentioned above I would like to acknowledge Ishmael Tuki's family, Casper, Angamoa, John Rangikofe, John Marakei (Nukukaisi village, Makira) and the Dean of St Barnabas Church in Honiara. I hope that this book investigating Firth's collection will provide a meaningful resource for them and their descendants. While evidence of this interest was apparent in 1996, it has seemingly gained momentum, with some Tikopia actively seeking out information about Firth and the objects and photographic record that he has made. Assisted by Anna Craven, former Curator of the National Museum of Solomon Islands, who has devoted considerable energy to the preservation of cultural heritage in Solomon Islands, and Julian Treadaway, a long-term resident of Honiara, Tikopia are seeking funding to produce their own books drawing upon the collections housed in several institutions internationally, including Firth's photographs held at the London School of Economics. Copies of my thesis have been sent to this group and I hope that my work will contribute to their understanding of the museum world and the role of anthropology in the creation of cultural heritage, as well as to their reflection upon the unfolding of Tikopia history and the expression of the 'Tikopia voice' nearly 90 years after Firth's visit in 1928.

When I showed Moses Lonsdale the Firth collection at the Australian Museum in 1995 (previously he had seen only photographs), he was confronted with the volume of Tikopia material in the stores – he expressed amazement that Firth could have collected so much. He asked me why Firth felt the collection to be important enough to bring back to Australia. I hope that this book will contribute in some part to answering his question.

Dear Professor Radcliffe-Brown,

I expect that the 'Southern Cross' [the Melanesian Mission's boat] will be arriving in a few days' time and as this may be the only chance of communicating with you for about nine months I am forwarding some MS notes of my work which will probably be of interest. I hope that they will serve also as the Report to the Research Council and give some indication of Tikopian ethnography.

I have settled for some time in a leaf house built by the natives at the cost of an axe, five knives and some fishhooks, pipes and tobacco and find it very comfortable. My tent has not been unpacked as yet; winds here are extremely severe, and the advantage of being able to move quarter does not count for much in Tikopia where the two principal settlement areas are less than two miles apart...

Letter from Firth, dated 17 October 1928, written in the first months of his field work on Tikopia to Alfred Reginald Radcliffe-Brown, Chair of Anthropology at the University of Sydney (LSE Firth 7.10.4).

Figure 12   'Mission ship "Southern Cross VII" off Tikopia with natives & canoes'.
Photographed by Revd David Lloyd Francis, 1928 to 1930, 18.9 x 25.3 cm (British Museum, Oc,A4.56).

CHAPTER 1

Collecting Tikopia

To say that Professor Sir Raymond Firth was an important figure in Melanesian anthropology risks ignoring his stature within the discipline more broadly. Having gained his PhD from the London School of Economics under Bronisław Malinowski, a giant of the discipline, Firth came to Australia to carry out ethnographic fieldwork on Tikopia (1928–9), funded by the Australian National Research Council. He was based at the University of Sydney for three years, just as the first school of Anthropology in Australia was established under Alfred Radcliffe-Brown. After his fieldwork in Tikopia, Firth took up the Chair of Anthropology at the University of Sydney in 1931; his association with Australia continued, and between 1947 and 1948 he was Academic Advisor to the Interim Council of the Australian National University in Canberra (Firth 1996) and helped to establish the Research School of Pacific Studies. While Tikopia was his primary field site, he also carried out fieldwork with his wife Rosemary in Malaya between 1939 and 1940 (Firth 1966a, 1974) as well as in New Guinea in 1951 (Firth 1952b, c). He retired in 1968, was knighted for his services to the discipline in 1973 and lived in London until his death on 22 February 2002 at a hundred years of age.

During his first trip to Tikopia, a tiny volcanic island in the easternmost part of Solomon Islands (Map 1) with a population close to today's (about 1,300 people, Pendergrast 2000; Treadaway 2007:111), Firth made a collection of 641 objects, now housed at the Australian Museum, Sydney. Firth made a second collection with anthropologist James Spillius during a return visit in 1952, and this is now held at the Australian National University, Canberra. While both collections have significance in the history of museum anthropology and as cultural heritage, it is the 1928–9 collection that figures in this book.

The collection is important not only because of Firth's stature as an anthropologist, but also because of the wealth of his publications which can be drawn upon for an interpretation of the objects. Firth published a large body of work during the sixty years following his first fieldwork, and also extensively documented his acquisitions: the ways objects were used, and the names of people who made them and gave them to him. This depth of detail makes the collection remarkable: it is rare to find museum collections from this period which have been so well recorded. It was in the 1970s that the collection attracted attention within museum circles as the subject of a repatriation request – perhaps the moment of its creation as 'cultural heritage'.

Researching and writing in an era when scholars were moving away from museum-based comparative studies of material culture towards a concern with social behavior, Firth's theoretical framework was functionalist and largely dismissive of earlier 'armchair anthropology' and ethnological studies of material culture. He viewed the objects he collected as material evidence of the daily activities of Tikopia people, a society he characterized as both divided and integrated by a system of clans (*kainanga*), each with a chief (*ariki*) and ritual practices in which the chiefs used objects to mediate with their gods (*atua*). He made the collection not to illustrate the evolutionary and diffusionist theories still popular from an earlier period of anthropology, but rather to gather material data. While the detail presented in Firth's ethnography and supplementary notes (Firth 1928; Wedgewood 1930) allows the nuances of his interpretation of material culture to be teased out, I suggest the nature of the interactions between Firth and Tikopia people is also discernible. The acts and transactions in which Firth acquired the objects mediated his relationship with Tikopia people and through these interactions Tikopia agency can be deciphered.

Objects, museums and ethnographic authority

What might be called the conventional museum interpretation of an ethnographic object has centred on its context of use and manufacture. This approach stems from material culture studies, traditionally associated with museums, but which have undergone substantial revision since the 1980s. Recent work on objects as material culture encompass phenomenology, materiality, the body and senses and postcolonial theory (see Edwards *et al.* 2006; Miller 1994, 2005; Tilley 1990; Tilley *et al.* 2006). Studies on collectors and object acquisition have also burgeoned (for example,

Clifford 1988; Fabian 1998; Gosden and Knowles 2001; Gosden and Larson 2007; Lawson 1994; O'Hanlon and Welsch 2000; Pannell 1995; Peterson, Allen and Hamby 2008; Quanchi and Cochrane 2007; Schildkrout and Keim 1998, to name a few).

For museums, questions concerning cultural property and repatriation have long been issues to be dealt with (Anderson 1990; Clifford 1997; Edwards and Stewart 1980; Furst 1989; Kaeppler 1989; Kavanagh 1989; MacDonald and Alsford 1995; Mulvaney 1985; Pearce 1989, 1994; Prott and O'Keefe 1989; Saunders 1995; Specht and MacLulich 1996; Stanton *et al.* 1990), but perhaps today fall into the mainstream of museum business. This is especially the case for New World museums, which now have established policies and procedures with which to deal with requests for access and returns (for example, in Australia, Council of Australia Museums Association 1993). Artefacts held in museum collections today have become objects that reveal history, or multiple histories, and within museums they are often referred to as not just ethnographic collections but as 'cultural heritage'. As such, museums must negotiate issues around the ownership of and access to ethnographic and archaeological material, as well as those of ethnographic authority.

The literature commenting on museums' activities is large and absorbs issues such as the 'creation of tradition', colonial and post-colonial bias, the ethical responsibilities of museums and the epistemological status of analytical categories such as art, text and culture (some of these issues are reviewed by Jones 1993, but see also Anderson 1990, 1995a, b; Bolton 1993; Galla 1997; Layton 1989; McBryde 1985; McLear 1996; Specht and MacLulich 1996). The 'new museology' (Vergo 1989) embraces the democratization of constructions of history through multiple narratives and the relinquishing of curatorial authority, and may look to non-Western cultural practices for models for new curatorial techniques (for example, Kreps 2007; Stanley 2007). Revived material culture studies, often referring to 'materiality' (Miller 2005), embrace the agency of objects located both within the museum as well as without, in everyday life (e.g. Henare *et al.* 2007). This is the background against which all collections, regardless of their geographical and cultural origins, may potentially be judged.

This book contributes to the literature on agency and collecting by exploring the circumstances under which Firth obtained his collection, including the social relationships entailed in specific acquisitions. I first examine the collection from the point of view of the collector and of the givers (that is, the way the Tikopia regarded the transactions, although this necessarily depends on historical interpretation). Then I pursue the interpretation of the objects into the present by examining the meanings attributed to them in recent museum contexts. It is the juxtaposition of past and present interpretations which is particularly interesting, together with the implications of this contrast for the creation of a category of object commonly referred to as 'cultural heritage' and now largely in the care of museums.

However, it is anthropological perspectives which offer the best insights into the interactions between Firth and the Tikopia he collected from. Alfred Gell's (1998) *Art and Agency* examines the ways in which objects mediate activities and relationships, identifying the qualities or attributes that facilitate an object's effect on an individual or group. For Gell, this agency is made manifest in a number of different ways: in terms of the intentions of the maker of the object, the instigation or commissioning of the creative act by the patron, and the effect of the object on the viewer. Perhaps one of the most valuable contributions of Gell's approach for my work is the detour it makes around the discussion of what is and what is not art. His perspective can be applied to any object, not simply to objects the West labels as 'artworks'. His work was liberating in contemplating Firth's acquisition of objects, as it embraced the symbolic associations of objects in conjunction with, but not exclusive to, a description of their physical attributes. In this sense, Gell's work inspired my search for agency within the varied contexts of object acquisition and interpretation, although I did not adopt his formal expressions (active/passive creator and active/passive receiver).

Arjun Appadurai's (1986) approach in *The Social Life of Things* emerged from the field of economic anthropology, and examines not the objects themselves but the social activities that move objects between individuals and groups of people, prioritizing the transfer of objects as commodities between people. Gell's analysis, while overlapping to some degree with Appadurai's, moves away from the sphere of economics to the identification of agency, including that of the creative moment. Most pertinent for me is Appadurai's illustration of the potential for objects to stray out of their original contexts of use and have their social uses re-defined. Such 'diversions' (Appadurai 1986:16–29) from original contexts appear to be at first sight the very stuff of museum collections.

Nicholas Thomas' (1991) work provides a deeper understanding of interactions between Pacific Islanders and strangers encountered during European expansion in the region. He explores the 'entangled' relationships surrounding object 'diversions' when there was no or little common understanding of the original contexts of use of the objects being exchanged. Thomas emphasizes the agency of Pacific Islanders in their exchanges with foreigners, echoing Marylin Strathern's (1990) divide between frameworks of knowledge (the 'frame metaphor').

The approaches of Gell (1998), Thomas (1991), Strathern (1988, 1990) and Appadurai (1986) influenced my search to identify how the objects collected by Firth have mediated social relationships in the past. Concerned with the acquisition of objects, I begin with the collector. In Chapter 2, I examine Firth's concern to create a scientific record of Tikopia social practices through his collection of their material culture. I examine the theoretical framework in which Firth was working and his concern to distinguish between objects, technology and the social relations of technology. Firth's methodological concern was to transcend the work of 'armchair anthropologists' by investigating at first hand 'primitive' societies untouched by Western influence. In Chapter 3, I give an overview of European accounts of interaction with Tikopia prior to Firth as a counterpoint to Firth's own expectations of a 'pristine' society. In Chapters 4 and 5, Firth's ethnographies, removed from their theoretical framework as far as possible, provide material to assess the significance of objects to Tikopia at the time of the acquisition. Returning to the arena of the museum in Chapter 6, I examine the birth of the collection as the cultural heritage of Solomon Islands and Tikopia through a repatriation request made to the National Museum of Australia in the 1970s from the National Museum of Solomon Islands. Chapter 7 takes as its starting point the small conversation between Firth and Tikopia in the 1960s concerning a 'treasure place': a conversation which revealed nascent Tikopia consciousness of cultural change. In concluding that chapter I draw upon the work of Judith MacDonald (1991) and Julian Treadaway (2007) for their observations of more recent changes in Tikopia.

This book is a history of how Firth's collection has mediated a series of relationships: between an indigenous people and a colonial anthropologist; between the new National Museum of Solomon Islands and the National Museum of Australia; and, as cultural heritage, between the source community and the globalized world.

CHAPTER 2

Firth's scientific anthropology

It is extraordinary how one becomes enmeshed in one's social environment, despite one's struggles. I find that I am enormously susceptible to the opinion of Tikopians regarding my doings and my relations with them. I must assume a purely detached point of view but find that I become quite excited when a man tries to cheat me or offends my dignity, become ashamed when I unwittingly step over the line of good manners – or the like. I have not, that calm cool assurance of superiority that I am sure ARB [Alfred Radcliffe-Brown] would have under similar circumstances. I would like to know just how you took such matters.

(Extract from a letter from Firth to Bronisław Malinowski, Professor of Anthropology at the London School of Economics, dated 24 March [?] 1929. LSE Archives, Firth 7.10.4)

Firth's comment on what he perceived to be a failure, his inability to remain objective, 'detached' and not 'excited' perhaps betrays his desire to remain 'scientific'. How did Firth's scientism manifest itself?

Firth commenced his career as an economist. He was awarded a BA in Economics by Auckland University College in 1922, at the age of 21, and in 1924 he completed a Masters dissertation on the kauri-gum industry. Firth attributed the beginning of his interest in anthropology to his experience of learning Maori. At this time he also developed an awareness of indigenous issues in New Zealand: the 1840 Treaty of Waitangi and its long-term consequences; dispossession of land; and post-war land confiscations (Institut für den Wissenschaftichen Film 1993). Maintaining his original focus, Firth went 'home' to England in 1924 to continue his studies at the

London School of Economics (LSE) and to write his doctoral thesis on the frozen-meat industry in New Zealand (Freedman 1967:viii; Institut für den Wissenschaftichen Film 1993; MacDonald 2002).

But once at the LSE, Firth decided to supplement his study with subjects in anthropology. He was already familiar with Bronisław Malinowski's work on the Trobriand Islands, Papua New Guinea, and at the LSE he met the ethnographer. Within six months of arriving in England, Firth abandoned economics to begin his career in anthropology. He became a postgraduate student with Malinowski (Freedman 1967:viii), working as his research assistant in 1925.

However, it was Alfred Reginald Radcliffe-Brown who sent Firth to Tikopia. Based at the University of Sydney, Radcliffe-Brown was looking for researchers to work both in Australia and the Pacific. Firth heard of these positions, funded by the Australian National Research Council, from Alfred Cort Haddon (Cambridge) and Charles Gabriel Seligman (London School of Economics), and wrote to express his interest in working on Rennell Island in Solomon Islands (LSE Archives, 7.10.4: Firth to Radcliffe-Brown, 20 January and 10 April 1927).

> I have always been greatly interested in the outlying Polynesian settlements in Melanesia – Tikopia –Sikaiana, etc – and would like to investigate one of them, especially Rennell Island. As far as I can ascertain this is anthropologically fresh, and is comparatively unknown, even to the Island traders.
> (LSE Archives, Firth 7.10.4: Firth to Radcliffe-Brown, 20 January 1927)

Firth's prior knowledge of New Zealand Maori was seen as advantageous for work on the Polynesian outliers (Firth 1925a, b, c, d, 1926a, b, c, 1927, 1983:6 and pers.comm. 14 November 1994). However, at the time of his communication with Firth, Radcliffe-Brown had allocated another researcher to Rennell Island and Firth was subsequently sent to Tikopia, another of the Polynesian outliers in Solomon Islands.

Firth expressed regret at not being able to go to Rennell Island. 'I had hoped among this folk who have been so little in contact with the white man that the residence of one or even two years which I had planned would have produced some interesting results.' (LSE Archives, 7.10.4: Firth to Radcliffe-Brown, 21 September 1927). But he was also happy to go to Tikopia 'for much the same reasons'. And if Tikopia were not possible, he would elect to go to the Massim area, either Sudest or Misima. While Radcliffe-Brown had also suggested that he might work in Australia, Firth felt that his previous training better equipped him for Melanesia.

And so Firth went to Tikopia, a tiny island formed from the peak of a volcanic crater. Located at 12 degrees south and 269 degrees east, Tikopia is 3.5 km long by 2 km at its widest point, and 4.6 km² in land area. In 1928 the population was 1,281 people (Firth 1983:368).[1] Although politically part of Solomon Islands, it is closer to north Vanuatu than to Honiara, the nation's capital. Anuta, its nearest neighbour, lies 137 km to the north-east and Vanikoro lies 228 km to the north-west (MacDonald 1991:258). At the time of Firth's first visit Tikopia was considered to be the home of the last intact Polynesian culture surviving amidst damaging social change elsewhere in the Pacific (Anon. 1931:4; Rivers 1922; Speiser 1922:37).

Firth published little on his fieldwork experience from a personal perspective. However, a sense of this can be gained from a letter to Radcliffe-Brown written shortly after arriving:

> I am finding it fairly easy to work with the people, who temperamentally are of the usual Polynesian type – jovial, plenty of laughter and talk, good natured and ready to inform me about the details of most of their observances. They are very greedy for white man's goods but so naïve about it that the impression is not so disagreeable after all. A white resident is such a novelty that he is expected to conform to Tikopia custom in many respects as in matters of hospitality, making of gifts at appropriate times and – what comes hardest – eating heartily at any time and season. If I enter a house for a chat I have to eat first and if I attend any ceremony it is the same. Most ceremonies take place indoors so that there is no possibility of observing from outside the crowd of participants. One simply has to join the group.
>
> Readiness to give information stops short on matters connected with religion and the <u>kava</u> ceremony, the two being interdependent. The contrast between eagerness to inform on everyday matters and reticence on esoteric affairs is again I fancy very [...?] typical of Polynesians, too. All the ritual is centred in the chiefs and much of the knowledge

---

1   Firth recorded 687 males and 594 females in his 1929 census. Of this number 45.8 per cent were children and adolescents and 38.9 per cent were adults up to middle age. The remaining 15.2 per cent were above middle age.

is confined to them, and I learn that they have quietly made it known that nothing of this kind is to be divulged to me, or the consequences will be unpleasant. I have managed to get behind their guard to some extent and under pledges of greatest secrecy have induced three people, quite separately, to furnish me with various formulae used on different occasions. As my relations with the chiefs are very friendly on the surface, I think that in another few months I shall be able to complete my records. I have already been allowed to witness the <u>kava</u> ceremony twice, but the formulae and mention of ancestors are uttered in such low tones that it is impossible to hear a single word, or even to be sure if a formula is being said as the chief carefully turns his back to me at the crux of the ritual. But, though I may be too optimistic, I think that it is simply a question of time before getting the information from the chiefs.

I have been working entirely in the Tikopian language for the last 6 weeks or so: very painfully at first but now with some freedom as far as ethnographic work goes. Dealing with an informant is fairly easy, as the conversation has some thread, but ordinary small talk or casual questions often leave me floundering. Even so, I find its advantages over English are enormous.

As regards volume of work – I have fairly comprehensive notes on incision – the ceremony lasts three days with its feasting and reciprocal presentations – and death and funeral rites – these last from five to eight days. I arrived in Tikopia just in time to be present at the annual <u>renga</u> making (turmeric). This is fairly <u>tapu</u> and the most important operations take place indoors so that I had to join the chief's party and for several days lived and slept in his house and kept the taboos. Some of the turmeric turned out badly at first and had to be re-baked, but luckily a scapegoat was found, a man from outside who had entered the cook-house of one of the party and tainted it, so my presence was not held responsible! [...] I enclose a few photographs which give some idea of the strands of Tikopia culture.

(LSE Archives, Firth 7.10.4: Firth to Radcliffe Brown, 17 October 1928)

Firth was accompanied into the field by Vahihaloa, from Ontong Java (another of the Polynesian outliers in Solomon Islands). While Firth described Vahihaloa as his 'personal servant', the latter acted as a cultural intermediary, particularly with regard to determining the distribution of food into and out of Firth's house (Firth 1983:10). Reflecting upon his fieldwork some decades later, Firth said that he felt that the Tikopia people 'conformed to so much of the precipitate picture' of Polynesian society: they were bare to the waist, wore barkcloth skirts and waistbands and cooked food in earth ovens, but he had been frustrated at his own inability to communicate during the early days of his fieldwork (Institut für den Wissenschaftichen Film 1993).

Firth remained on Tikopia for a year. In March 1952 he returned, accompanied by anthropologist James Spillius, and stayed until August of that year (Spillius 1957a, b, c). Prior to their arrival Tikopia had been hit by a cyclone and a famine followed. The presence of the anthropologists was opportune for Tikopia, as the two visitors were able to make radio contact with the British authorities and negotiated for shipments of rice. Firth visited again with Torben Monberg in 1966 (Monberg 1971, 1975, 1996).

He began publishing about Tikopia in 1930, and his first major ethnography, *We, the Tikopia*, appeared in 1936, and in an abridged version in 1957.[2] In total he produced some 120 works on Tikopia, continuing to publish into the 1990s. The extended period of work complicates an analysis of the collection and of his approach to material culture. I have concentrated primarily on his accounts published in the period up until his second field trip in 1952. This is a somewhat arbitrary divide, and not one I adhere to strictly, but the earlier work is more relevant for an insight into the making of the collection of 1928.

Firth's work in this period reflected the functionalist tradition of the British school of anthropology and was concerned with the identification of social institutions, structures and organization (Harris 1968; Radcliffe-Brown 1952a, b, c; Stocking 1984, 1985). The intellectual influences of the time – functionalism, the idea of anthropology as science, the rejection of ethnology and the speculative history of small societies, the avoidance of psychological interpretations in favour of an examination of what is done, rather than what is said (Parkin 1988:333) – all affected Firth's interpretation of objects and of the process of their acquisition.

---

2   Firth excised sections on domestic life, food recipes, eating, linguistic data regarding kinship, dirges, the sociology of sex and comparative data on Polynesian kinship (1983:xiii).

Objects as scientific data

As a student of Malinowski, though influenced by Radcliffe-Brown, Firth saw a path between their opposing approaches to functionalism: the former's incorporation of 'function' as a response to biological factors; and the latter's priority of the 'functioning' of 'social structure' over individual action. In an early communication with Radcliffe-Brown he wrote: 'I should feel very pleased if an opportunity were afforded me of working under you, since, as you know, my training under Malinowski has been akin to your own methods and point of view.' (LSE Archives, Firth 7.10.4: Firth to Radcliffe-Brown, 20 January 1927). Looking back on Malinowski's work he later stated explicitly:

> The notion of social structure put forward by Radcliffe-Brown and fostered by Evans-Pritchard and Fortes in particular became part of the orthodoxy of most British social anthropologists, especially after 1937 in Oxford. In my own case, when I was working with Radcliffe-Brown as a lecturer in Sydney in 1930–31, in discussions with him and from my own field experience I had soon come to see the necessity of some formal structural concepts to provide a framework and differentiating element in the idea of a functional social system put forward by Malinowski. But whereas I saw a structural point of view as complementing the functional assumptions, other British anthropologists gave different emphases to these major concepts.
>
> (Firth 1988:17)

Firth also drew upon his training in economics, and he is acknowledged as a significant contributor to the development of economic anthropology (Frankenberg 1967). Percy Cohen noted that Firth 'has been profoundly concerned to rescue economic anthropology both from those who equated it with a study of material culture as well as from those who saw it simply as a means for documenting the hypothesis of primitive communism' (Cohen 1967:92–3). Firth placed a strong emphasis on the role of the individual within the broader social group, and particularly on the individual's choice of action rather than on the force of institutional rules (for a summary of Firth's approach according to Cohen, see 1967:93). This was a significant departure from the functionalist model, which emphasized the needs of the society over the needs of the individual. Firth emphasized the repercussions of an individual's actions to reveal how she or he was integrated into 'sets of behaviour'. In this view, the anthropologist must identify the themes of these 'sets of behaviour' as well as clarify the relationships between them (Firth 1936b:576). The identification of principles of behaviour derived from both spoken norms and individual actions (1937:77).

His principles of behaviour contrasted with Radcliffe-Brown's three 'laws' of behaviour which proposed that a society, a) must have functional consistency among its constituent parts; b) must resolve conflicts to maintain its structure; and c) be stable to ensure continuity (Harris 1968:532; Radcliffe-Brown 1952a, b). Radcliffe-Brown's 'laws' would explain social systems in a way similar to the laws of natural science. However, for Firth, such 'laws' remained simple statements rather than explanatory models of how societies operate and change.

Without endorsing Radcliffe-Brown's 'laws' modelled on natural science, Firth held that social anthropology was to be grounded in objective science, based on personal observation and the recording of scientific 'data'. He saw social anthropology as a science 'of small-scale social inter-relationships' (Firth 1937:77–8). Firth discussed issues of 'scientism' and professionalism in *We, the Tikopia* (1983:2–12), where he outlined his methodological practice (see also Firth 1939:15–22). Because 'native' statements provided only an 'index to the kind of formulation commonly produced', as opposed to the evidence of events, generalizations needed to be based on empirical facts, that is, on observed events. Firth's commitment to anthropology as a science was reflected in his early adoption of scientific terminology, apparently emphasizing the empirical nature of the methods used by social anthropologists. On occasion, he described the societies studied as 'laboratories' of change (Firth 1937:79) and as 'material' to be studied (Firth 1983:9).

Firth sought to avoid the use of cross-cultural abstraction, which distorted facts to support universal propositions, and which were subsequently metamorphosed into 'laws'. He commented on the fragile relationship between the particularist interests of the social anthropologist and the reductionist comparative generalizations of the nineteenth-century evolutionary type (Firth 1937:78). At issue were the assumptions and assertions of comparative anthropology, archaeology and material culture at that time in which:

> customs practised as part of a single institution are separated into 'strata'
> and placed in a time sequence of introduction; similarities in elements

of culture are converted into identities, and the validity of the postulates involved concerning the diffusion of ideas is blandly taken for granted

(Firth 1937:81)

But Firth acknowledged that anthropology's approach as a discipline varied significantly from the scientific method of the physical sciences (1939:15). The social anthropologist's 'material' was not subject to the investigator's control; there was no pre-existing body of statistical data to draw upon; nor did the anthropologist begin work with personal knowledge of a community and its 'commonsense' knowledge. These disadvantages, in Firth's view, did not preclude the adoption of scientific methodology in carrying out investigative fieldwork (Firth 1937, 1958).

The purpose of Firth's work on Tikopia was to establish a scientific anthropological record of Tikopia people, rather than to build upon the comments, possibly unreliable, of earlier visitors. Previous information about Tikopia included the work of Revd W.J. Durrad (1913, 1926, 1927) of the Melanesian Mission and William Halse Rivers (1906, 1914a, b, 1926). Durrad, who had lived on Tikopia for two months in 1910, gave Firth his notebooks and photographs (Firth 1983:xvii; Durrad's photographs are held in the Museum of Archaeology and Anthropology, University of Cambridge). The former contained extensive word lists and other notes on the Tikopia language, as well as data on village residences, stories of incoming settlers, descriptions of customary practices and notes on 'folklore' and material culture, including line drawings of fish-hooks, paddles and motifs appearing on tattoos, mats and house posts (LSE Archives, Firth, Durrad Notebooks 1.9.1 and 1.9.2).

Rivers visited the island for one day only in 1908, whilst researching in the Pacific for his book *The History of Melanesian Society* (1914a). His informant on Tikopia practices was John Masere, who had formerly lived on Tikopia for some twenty years. Rivers also used his own fieldwork questionnaire, in addition to Durrad's material on Tikopia. Masere was not indigenous to Tikopia but had drifted to the island with several other men while trying to make their way to Samoa (see Chapter 3). Rivers included Masere's information in his discussion of totemism and marriage classificatory systems.

Firth was concerned about Rivers' work on Tikopia because he felt it drew upon inadequate data (Firth 1983:xviii): he refuted Rivers in 'Totemism in Polynesia' stating that Rivers based his principal points on the origin of Melanesian totemism upon an erroneous understanding of 'totemism' in Tikopia (Firth 1930c:291–303). Rivers was also taken to task for 'misleading simplicity' in his use of the term 'classificatory kinship' (1930a:235).[3]

> His [Rivers'] opinion that magic is absent in Tikopia is far from the truth. For a month I could get no information on the subject but as soon as I began to work in Tikopian data became available. As will be seen from the number of texts I forward magical spells are used extensively in fishing and enter into other activities as well. I have also collected samples of [*not legible*][4] which verge on black magic, being used to bring death on people who reject lover's advances and the like.
>
> (LSE Archives, Firth 7.10.4: Firth to Radcliffe-Brown, 17 October 1928)

Firth's work in the 1930s addressed other topics of contemporary debate such as Seligman's work on dreams (Firth 1934); Robert Marett's discussion of 'covenant' as a moral basis of co-operation in society, which was expanded by Firth in his presentation of an institutionalized form of friendship in Tikopia (1936a); and the meaning of *mana* in Tikopia, in which regard he addressed the 'bulky literature' provided by Robert Henry Codrington, Robert Marett, Emile Durkheim, Edward Handy, Edward Tregear and Arthur Hocart (Firth 1940:484).

---

3   'As far as social organization goes the account of Rivers is broadly speaking correct – at least where he is dealing with the kinship system which is of the classificatory types with a very wide application of the commoner terms, as [indistinct] for brother, sister, father etc. As any brief account which I would write would be more or less of the same kind I have enclosed no separate description for the present. Information on the relations of mother's brother and sister's son – one of the fundamental points in Tikopian social organization is contained in the notes on funeral observances. In respect of local organization Rivers has hardly been so well served by his informants; many names of places on his map are incorrect and there are many definite clan and settlement affiliations.' (LSE Archives, Firth 7.10.4: Firth to Radcliffe-Brown, 17 October 1928).

4   The word written here is not legible, but the next sentence refers to the 'translation of these texts'.

Firth on material culture and economics

Firth published on Tikopia from 1930 to 1998. In his early work he viewed material culture and technology as separate domains of study to social anthropology, and adhered to the contemporary approach to artefact description which did not consider symbolic associations.

He published six works directly concerned with objects, the first in 1947, eighteen years after the completion of his fieldwork. The first article focused on the manufacture and use of barkcloth, and provided 'comparative' material for the broader Polynesian area. In this article, Firth was critical of the inadequacy of much of the information used in contemporary comparative anthropology and was particularly concerned to provide a 'systematic account' of the 'technical process' (1947:69). While focusing on the technical account, Firth commented that the cloth was 'rougher' than most Polynesian cloth, that it 'lacked elaborate decoration' and had no origin myth associated with it, excepting that barkcloth making was associated with the 'ultimate ancestress' who was found on the island beating cloth when Tikopia first settled there (1947:70).

In *Primitive Polynesian Economy*, first published in 1939, Firth experimented with Western economic concepts (Firth 1965), subordinating the symbolic interpretations of objects demonstrated by Tikopia people. Objects were treated as property (Firth expanded his discussion on individual ownership of property to include group ownership, see 1965:277) required for exchange, rather than focusing on the social implications or the symbolic significance of the objects themselves.

So for example, Firth described barkcloth as 'one of the most important of consumer's goods in the Tikopia economy' (1947:71). He discussed their equivalent value in terms of European trade goods and described the economic setting of barkcloth production in terms of the ownership and growth of trees; the division of labour; and the manner in which the cloth was distributed and used (barkcloth bundles were incorporated into important gifts to the gods and orange barkcloth was dedicated to the most important gods in the Tikopia pantheon). He noted that women were valued as barkcloth makers because their cloth was used for ceremonial purposes (Firth 1947:71) but made little comment on women's economic status. He reflected on this issue later:

I am able to say very little about the distribution of knowledge among
women, certain women are credited with special skill in crafts and can
explain the technical details better than others. On the whole women in
Tikopia know very much less about the ritual side of institutions than do
men. But they have some definite ritual functions to perform.

(Firth 1965:105)

He later again noted his lack of 'access to the more intimate aspects of
women's lives' (1978; 1990:242; and 1975 for a reflection on the discipline).

The 1947 article was followed by a descriptive piece on body ornaments
as items of traditional manufacture used in adornment and trade (Firth
1951). In a study of ritual adzes published in 1959, he concentrated on the
'social relations of technology in a Polynesian culture' (1959a:149, discussed
in more detail in Chapter 4 below). 'Tikopia wood working ornaments'
(1960b) discussed the absence of an art aesthetic in decorative designs
on wooden objects and seems to continue a thread evident early in his
fieldwork:

I have obtained a hundred or so specimens of native work: this is
rather disappointing since Tikopians seem to put all their energies into
producing and preparing food. They make nothing for instance which
is comparable with other Polynesian art in the field of wood carving.
Wooden head-rests alone show any great diversity of style. Some of the
small plaited mats, ornamented in red, are also of interest, but little else
is of really fine workmanship.

(LSE Archives, Firth 7.10.4: Firth to Radcliffe-Brown, 17 October 1928)

'Tikopia string figures' (1970b) was published ten years later, and not
until 'Tikopia art and society' (1973b) did Firth concentrate on the Tikopia
aesthetic sense, but the article is more interesting for what it reveals about
the transfer of chiefly *mana* (power) to physical objects such as headrests
than what it reveals about their visual form. A much broader paper on 'Art
and anthropology' was published much later (1992) as a mature reflection
on the role of art in the cultural patterning of human experience. The social
role of objects received much more attention in *Rank and Religion* (1970a).

Firth published data most directly related to making an artefact
collection in 'Exchange rates in a culture contact situation' (appendix III
of *Primitive Polynesian Economy*, 1965:377–80). In accordance with his

interest in an economic model of Tikopia material culture, his starting point was the 'nascent money market' of his first encounter with the Tikopia.

> The economy of Tikopia, non-monetary as it was in 1929, and with its people not even comprehending how money might be used, had depended to a very significant degree for about a century upon vessels from the outside world for iron tools and fish hooks, as well as some tobacco and cloth. Even earlier the people had sporadic economic relations with those of other islands, whereby commodities of external origin were obtained by barter or by reciprocal gifts.
>
> (Firth 1965:19)

Firth's experience acquiring objects from the Tikopia formed the basis of his discussion of rates of exchange in a pre-market economy. Firth said that he assumed the role of monopolist as the sole supplier of the goods transacted. But in focusing on the exchange of economic values, I suggest that he did not account for the social and political relationships entailed in his transactions with Tikopia (discussed in more detail in Chapters 4 and 5).

The 1965 appendix is of interest because it includes information about the way in which Firth acquired approximately one quarter of the collection. From the appendix and lists accompanying the collection (Firth 1928; Wedgewood 1930) it is clear that Firth 'sold', gave or exchanged the following types of European items while on Tikopia: fish-hooks, clay pipes, calico (individual pieces coloured blue, white and red), cotton prints, cotton belts, iron blades from smoothing planes, tobacco, razors, strings of beads, axes, tomahawks, sheath knives and knives of various sizes (see Appendix 1 for objects 'purchased' by Firth). In some cases Firth's beads were exchanged for coconut-shell beads (*somo faka*), Firth noting that they were of equal value (Firth 1951:130). He gave seven adzes as gifts, as especially valuable items, to the chiefs and other men of rank for 'religious' and 'traditional information'. He also used a supply of cotton prints as ritual offerings to canoe and temple deities while other European-made items were used to acquire 'specimens of the native craft' (Firth 1965:377). Firth identified 184 items as 'purchases'. This represents 29 per cent of the total collection of 641 objects. Over a quarter of the collection was made in the first three months of fieldwork, with events such as 'bartering' evenings providing special opportunities to acquire 'specimens'. Firth said that large numbers of items changed hands on two 'big nights' (21 and 22 September), when he purchased 23 and 20 items respectively (Firth 1928 and pers. comm. 14 November 1994). It follows that the greater part of the collection, 71 per cent, if not 'purchased', must have been made within indigenous exchange arrangements.

Firth's training as an economist is apparent in his analysis of these exchanges in terms of supply and demand. In summary, he suggested that in Tikopia there was no concept of comparative value mediated by a common denominator, but rather a 'rough scale of comparative utility of things' (Firth 1965:277). For example, clamshell adzes were more valuable than net gauges, which were more valuable than sinnet beaters. Firth suggested that his presence gave the Tikopia people opportunities to increase their wealth, negotiate their 'sale' price and discuss their wants and the quality of items, as well as to come back and complain if they were unhappy. Firth saw his position as having been a benevolent monopolist 'controlling a limited supply of goods ... of great utility'. Firth's 'wants', the 'specimens', were evaluated by him in terms of the quality of workmanship, while the Tikopia people, he suggested, wanted the most they could get: 'The Tikopia hazarded a request which he hoped I might be gullible or polite enough to fulfill' (Firth 1965:379–80). After a time, standard rates developed, although these appear not to have been openly discussed or agreed upon by Firth and Tikopia people. Some categories of items were never exchanged for others. For example, while clubs, pandanus mats and bonito hooks were offered in return for calico, beads and knives, they were never traded for fish-hooks. Firth recognised an indigenous scale of importance which dictated the exchangeability of the objects (Firth 1965:379–80).

While Firth stated that he dictated the initial rates of exchange, 'Tikopia etiquette' regarding gift and counter-gift affected the final outcome (Firth 1965:379). He discovered the 'price' below which Tikopia people would not enter into exchanges, which was independent of the cost he had incurred in acquiring and bringing the items to Tikopia. Firth regarded this as 'showing the operation of the forces of supply and demand in a situation of barter presented in the setting up of a novel market, with elements of monopoly present' (1965:380).

Firth's initial interpretations assumed an innate drive for goods based on market forces, rather than an indigenous pattern of demand. Yet, when Firth's supplies for barter were running low, the scarcity of his goods did not cause an increase in their price nor did he note that his goods were re-circulated amongst the Tikopia in satisfaction of their drive to possess such goods. Most of the objects exchanged with Firth appear to have been kept for 'productive and consumptive' use: they did not enter 'elaborate native exchanges' but were retained by the families who had acquired them (1965:380). Firth used the cotton cloth that he brought for ritual offerings and as gifts.

> My own return gifts—since I received *maro*[5] as a titular mother's
> brother—were made with calico, a fact which caused some people to
> say laughingly that all the *kano a paito* [relatives of both sides] fought in
> order to 'lift' my present. Calico to the Tikopia is equivalent of *mami*, the
> bark-cloth sheet or blanket, and is greatly appreciated.

> (Firth 1983:424, see Figure 13)

If Tikopia were eager to engage in exchange it was because it advantaged them to do so (Firth 1965:87), they were not 'driven' to engage in exchange (Appadurai 1986:29). Many years later Judith MacDonald (1991) observed that the Tikopia, with more experience of contact with European administrations, had a very conservative attitude towards the acquisition of European items. This attitude also was noted by Eric Larson (1966) for Tikopia settled away from the home island.

Firth's attempt to determine precise values for the objects he purchased, and to define those objects as 'goods and services' within the Tikopia economy, ignored the values attributed to objects by Tikopia people, as described by him in his account of traditional life (Firth 1965:377–80, discussed below). These values concerned social relations with the ancestral spirits and with living relatives. Firth's interpretations, based on concepts drawn from economics, underestimated the power of Tikopia people to determine the outcome of their exchanges with him, despite his own position as 'benevolent monopolist'. After all, Tikopia 'etiquette' won out over exchange rates. Perhaps he recognized the limitations of his analysis in consigning it to an appendix:

---

5   *Maro* has two definitions: 1) a piece of barkcloth used as a man's waistcloth; 2) a ceremonial gift consisting of barkcloth and mats.

Figure 13   'Bearing off the Gifts. The girls are taking these heavy baskets of cooked food, topped with maro of bark-cloth, as presents to the maternal kinfolk of the boy' (Firth 1983:225. Photo: Firth, courtesy London School of Economics).

> a description of the arts and crafts of a people and their concrete
> methods of producing, exchanging, and consuming goods has too often
> served as a substitute for an analysis of the organization of production,
> exchange, distribution, and consumption. [...] Too often when one
> requires the principles which govern the production of bread one is
> given a description of a stone implement.
>
> (Firth 1939:11)

Firth's insistence on studying economic systems was a rejection of the still extant ethnological approach to technology as evidence for social evolution. Instead of focusing on the artefacts themselves he analysed relations between individuals, such as collective rights in property, the distribution of these rights and their effect on production. In *Primitive Polynesian Economy* (1939) he expanded the definition of economic terms such as 'wants', 'resources' and 'maximization' to include considerations such as status, religion and ritual as social imperatives on individual and group behaviour. In this context objects were framed variously as satisfying basic wants and providing capital for processes of production. For example:

> bark-cloth, pandanus mats, coconut sinnet cord in Tikopia are not
> only meant for ordinary consumption; they are employed in many
> kinds of exchanges, including payment for productive labour [...] Their
> accumulation is thus a part of capital formation.
>
> (Firth 1965:24)

Firth examined concepts such as labour supply, resource ownership and use and the technical methods of production to illustrate that, without major redefinition, these terms were inadequate to describe the complexity of economic organization in Tikopia. This was contrary to popular contemporary assumptions that because of the absence of a recognizable market economy such societies were simple and lacked economic organization. Having proposed that Tikopia wants were dictated by bodily needs and the effects of environment and culture, Firth wanted to show how the distribution of goods between the different users represented 'a complex scheme of social relationships'. Objects, as well as food, were incorporated into these complex social relationships:

Food is not merely an object of satisfying appetite, or of providing
hospitality; it is a means of expressing obligations to kinsfolk and chiefs,
of paying for a variety of services, and of making religious offerings.
Bark-cloth and mats are not required simply for personal wear or for
bedding, but are transferred in satisfaction of mortuary and other
obligations while even fishing lines, wooden bowls, and other technical
instruments serve similar ends.

(Firth 1965:33)

Many of the object types in the collection were discussed by Firth in
Primitive Polynesian Economy and, while he labelled them on the one hand
as technological objects, he simultaneously illustrated how, depending
on the circumstance of their use, they were more than just items of
technology. In so doing he approached an interpretation of objects as
things having ideational properties; however, he did not pursue this line.
In Firth's view, the social anthropologist had to distinguish theoretically
between the economic role of an object and the knowledge pertaining to
its manufacture and use, even though this distinction was not made by the
people themselves. This resulted in minimal description of the symbolic
attributes of objects.

This segregation of objects and ideas led to a recurring inconsistency
between what Firth said about the study of objects, and his description
of the use of objects. In his descriptions of Tikopia 'ritual' and 'economy',
objects could not be ignored because people incorporated them into
their daily lives, but in his interpretation of social organization, Firth
marginalized objects because they did not seem to have significant social
functions. His disinclination to pursue the symbolic meanings of objects
was connected both to his continued reservations about contemporary
material culture studies, the realm of technology and ethnology, and to his
emphasis on observable fact; that is, on what people do rather than what
they say (although he did move to redress this in *Rank and Religion* 1970a;
see Chapter 4 below).

Early anthropological analysis ignored history in the description
of societies (Thomas 1989b). But Firth's original research application,
submitted to Radcliffe-Brown in 1927 for fieldwork on Rennell Island, listed
the following as anticipated 'results of scientific value': 'Contributions to
social and economic anthropology, and to the study of the inter-relations

between the Melanesian and Polynesian races; data bearing on the problems of *culture contact* [my emphasis] between native peoples and the Europeans.' (LSE Archives, Firth 7.10.4: 'Application for Grant to the Australian National Research Council').

Nonetheless, Firth's work in 1928 became the point from which the study of 'traditional' Tikopia culture began and Tikopia, together with its neighbour Anuta, was viewed as 'of considerable importance in the study of Polynesian culture' (Firth 1930b:117). Firth did not consider that the limited and spasmodic contact between Tikopia and Europeans before his arrival was significant enough to compromise the Tikopia's status as 'the most primitive of Polynesians' (Firth 1983:31), even though he described the consequence of the exchange of objects with outsiders as a 'technological revolution' (Firth 1959b:34; see also 1965:379 and 1983:31, 35 for importation and acculturation). Firth's scientific approach would not allow him to ignore the previous contact history, but he managed to downplay its impact.

> For nearly a century and a half they have been subjected to various influences of the 'civilizing' order, and these have left their mark. But the changes effected by the introduction of these foreign cultural elements, though seemingly fairly considerable, when viewed in total have really done very little to disturb the fundamental social structure of the people [...] the Tikopia, secure in their isolation, have been able to transform what they have received, rather than compelled to mould their own culture to it.
>
> (Firth 1983:31)

Jeremy Coote (1987) has noted that Firth, adhering to the functionalist method, 'analyzed out' factors which did not fit the assumptions underlying the concept of 'social structure' and tempered the possibility of historical interactions being interpreted in any way as significant. In the same vein, Annette Weiner noted of Malinowski, that his 'functionalist theories obscured the subtleties and the significance of symbolic action. His interest was in the cause and effect of certain actions and activities rather than in the cultural meanings that Trobrianders give to the things and people around them.' (Weiner 1988:8).

Firth was caught within the restrictions of the functionalist theoretical model that presumed societies to be self-contained, self-sufficient, self-maintaining and static, and as a consequence he neglected the indigenous meanings of Tikopia artefacts and the significance in Tikopia terms of their interactions with visitors, including himself. Firth sought to establish his own authoritative voice and assert his own inheritance from the British school of anthropology; to rectify perceived inaccuracies in the reports of earlier visitors to Tikopia; and to contribute to the body of scientific knowledge concerning diverse cultures. For Firth, the objects he collected represented scientific ethnographic facts about Tikopia life,[6] a necessary aspect of his research (the Australian National Research Council required research grant holders to make ethnographic collections), but the collection was not of central interest to him. Even so, it provides evidence not only of 'technology', but also for a new analysis of the way artefacts mediated relationships on Tikopia in 1928–9.

---

6   Firth (1930b:106) noted that he made a material culture collection and that rather than obtaining detailed accounts about how objects were made, his 'attention was concentrated more on the economic than on the technological side of industry'.

CHAPTER 3

Interaction between Tikopia and Europeans, 1606 to 1928

This chapter examines some of the interactions between visitors and Tikopia people before Firth arrived in 1928. Recent trends in the interpretation of history in anthropological accounts (Humphrey and Hugh-Jones 1992; O'Hanlon and Welsh 2000; Schildkrout and Keim 1998; Thomas 1991, 2010) have opened up studies of 'contact' to the recognition of active interaction and participation by indigenous peoples with new arrivals: this approach interrogates assumptions of one-way impacts of the colonizer on the colonized, the dominant on the subordinant, the centre on the periphery.

It is important to note too that the Tikopia had a history of exchange relationships with other islanders. Patrick Kirch, concerned to counter anthropology's view of island societies as closed and self-sufficient, noted that Firth, in his ethnographies, did refer to historical interactions with Europeans (Firth 1959b:31–45, 1961) and, further, that 'the archaeological and ethnographic signals of external contact in Tikopia are not only abundant, but prove to be key in understanding and interpreting the prehistoric sequence' (Kirch 1986:34; also Clark 2003).

Tikopia oral accounts state that the land was pulled up out of the sea. The two progenitors of the first family of the island's gods (*atua*) were found sitting on the island, the man plaiting sinnet, the woman making a mat. A second strand of their origin narrative identifies the arrival of the ancestors or ancestral gods of Kafika, one of the four clans on the island, and a third describes the arrival in a canoe of the ancestors of the peoples of the lowlands of Tikopia from Luaniua, Ontong Java. Other immigrants from islands such as Pukapuka, Luaniua, Tonga, Valua (Vanua Lava in the Banks Islands), Samoa, Rotuma, Uvea and Anuta were subsequently

Figure 14   An expeditionary party from Jules S.C. Dumont d'Urville's voyage on the Astrolabe approach Tikopia in 1828. 'Vue de l'ile Tikopia', by Jacques Arago (1790–1855), hand coloured lithograph, 20 × 34 cm, plate 172 of Voyage de la corvette l'Astrolabe, Atlas Historique. U1881 Rex Nan Kivell Collection NK 3340 (image courtesy of the National Library of Australia).

absorbed into Tikopia ancestry (Firth 1930b:116–17). Firth expands on indigenous narratives of origin in *History and Traditions of Tikopia* (1961).

Notwithstanding extensive regional connections, Tikopia does not figure large in the European history of Solomon Islands. Judith Bennett's (1987) account of explorers and travellers, whalers, traders, missionaries and government officials rarely touches upon Tikopia. Early European explorers had little direct impact on the Solomon Islands in general, most recording sightings only, and the islands were considered to have little to offer in terms of resources. However, the colonization of Australia and New Zealand changed this. Between 1790 and 1820 Solomon Islands became a shortcut for ships on their way from Port Jackson to the East. Among these, East India Company ships carried convicts to Australia, and American merchant ships carried supplies.

Towards the end of this period whaling ships re-located from depleted Atlantic waters to the Pacific. Whaling reached a peak in the 1840s and 1850s before dropping drastically and ceasing in 1887. During this period a number of regular ports of call were established at which ships restocked with food and water, and ships' crews traded with the local inhabitants and indulged in sexual liaisons with local women. Popular ports included those on Simbo and Mono (in western Solomons), Sikaiana (off Malaita Island), Sikaiana (an atoll to the north of Malaita), Santa Ana and Santa Catalina, (both islands off Makira island) and Makira Harbour on Makira Island. While Tikopia was beyond the immediate sphere of these activities, the islanders were in contact with both European and non-European visitors through the dealings of whalers, traders and missionaries.

By the time of Firth's visit in 1928, many Tikopia men were eager to travel overseas and some tried to stow away on visiting vessels:

> This keenness to visit other lands and make a closer acquaintance in particular with the works of the white man is animated by a definite object. They want to become possessed of knowledge and property from which they can reap an advantage on their return – in social prestige as tellers of breathless adventure which can be made to absorb the public interest in long hours of conversation; in the possession of prized tools and ornaments; in the acquisition of influence by acting as interpreters when a vessel calls; or even by making profit as teachers of what they imagine to be the white man's language.
>
> (Firth 1983:18–19)

Tikopia and regional exchanges

While Firth encountered objects originating from Kiribati on Tikopia (Firth 1970a:118), the Tikopia also had long-standing exchange networks with their closest neighbours. There were three significant inter-island exchange networks with the neighbouring islands in which objects, people and information circulated (Kirch 1986). These involved the Tikopia sailing in plank-built canoes to Anuta, Vanikoro and the Banks Islands in the north of Vanuatu.

Each Tikopia lineage (*tauranga*) had ancestral kinship ties or bonds of friendship with a corresponding lineage in Anuta (Firth 1954:98, cited in Kirch 1986:35) and these relationships are still maintained (Feinberg 1981). As part of the *tauranga* relationship, the Tikopia received cord made of coconut fibre, coconut water bottles, digging sticks, canoes and special fishing nets from their partners. Anutan women made *kie*, decorated

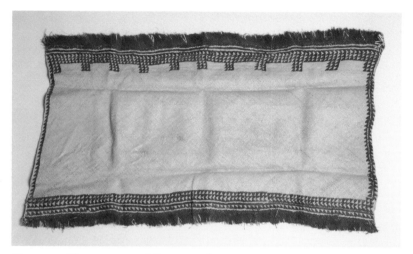

Figure 15   Kie, waist mat. 'These are of Anutan type but many are now made by Anutan women married to husbands in Tikopia. These mats are plaited from fine pandanus fibre and some examples are ornamented with an overlaid stitch from the inner bark of a tree, dyed red. They are worn in dancing, especially by men of rank.' (Wedgewood 1920:47). Firth no. 80.7. AM registration no. E84146, 100 × 55 cm (photo: Bonshek 2013)

ceremonial waist-mats of pandanus fibre, for their Tikopia partners. *Kie* were generally worn by high-ranking men for dancing (Wedgewood 1930:47). The Anuta received barkcloth from Tikopia. During Firth's fieldwork many Anuta women were married to Tikopia and living there, where they continued to make *kie*. Firth collected seven *kie*[1] (Figure 15) and a spear (*tokotoko*) from Anuta.[2] Kirch notes that neither of the islands lacked the resources to make the items they exchanged with one another (Kirch 1986:35).

Based upon Firth's records, oral tradition places the beginning of contact between Tikopia and Anuta twelve generations before Firth's arrival. Kirch noted that Firth referred to more than twenty voyages to and from Anuta recounted by Tikopia. He believed that the figure of twelve

---

1   Firth nos. 80.1 to 80.7. *Kie* – woven pandanus fibre, red pattern dyed with the inner bark of a tree (Appendix 2).

2   Firth nos. 16.1 to 16.13; (16.9 and 16.13 from Anuta). *Tokotoko* – made from casuarina wood (Appendix 2).

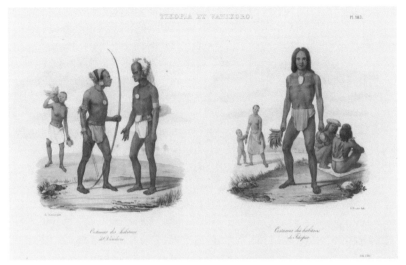

Figure 16   'Tikopia et Vanikoro. Costumes des habitans de Vanikoro; Costumes des habitans de Tikopia' (Tikopa and Vanikoro. Dress of the inhabitants of Vanikoro; Dress of the inhabitants of Tikopia). The people of Vanikoro traded their bows and arrows to Tikopia. Hand coloured lithograph, Antoine Maurin (1793–1860), 15.6 × 38.5 cm, plate 185 of Voyage de la corvette l'Astrolabe, Atlas Historique. U1894. Rex Nan Kivell Collection NK 3340. (Image courtesy of the National Library of Australia).

generations 'may be fairly close to historical reality' as evident in the archaeological record (Kirch 1986:34–5). While objects moved around, so too must have information. As with the Tikopia, the Anuta also travelled and had contact with Europeans. News of these trips must surely have travelled between the two islands. Feinberg (1981) records that the people of Anuta told how their forebears lied to the crew of a government ship about their role in the deaths of visiting Europeans, implicating the Tikopia to avoid reprisals.

The Tikopia also exchanged mats and barkcloth with the people of Vanikoro, who provided pearl-shell ornaments, cowrie-shell necklaces, and bows and arrows (Dillon 1829b:170; see Figure 16). Seven of the sixty arrows (*ngasau*) collected by Firth are from Vanikoro.[3] It is possible that

---

3   Firth no. 29.1 (Vanikoro type); 29.2 and 29.3 mainly Tikopia type (total 260 arrows, Appendix 2).

the Tikopia also acquired pigs from Vanikoro, although Firth disputed this (1959b:37n2). The Vanikoro network was maintained through seasonal voyages, planned so as to take advantage of prevailing weather conditions (Bayly 1885:153). It appears that the Tikopia went to Vanikoro and back, but that Vanikoro people did not travel to Tikopia (in contrast with the relationship with Anutans in which both parties travelled, Firth 1959b:32–3; Kirch 1986:36).

While there seems to have been no Tikopia memory of people travelling to Vanua Lava in the Banks Islands in the twenty to thirty years prior to Firth's arrival, that is from 1890, the Tikopia did recount earlier voyages. Furthermore, Vanua Lava, known as Varuka or Valua in Tikopia, is considered the mythic home of the ancestor of the Tafua chiefly line (Firth 1961:71). In 1977 the chief of Tafua, the Ariki Tafua, told Kirch that he held ancestral rights to land in Vanua Lava and that Tikopia and the Banks Islands share the place name Ravenga. When stationed in the Banks Islands between 1863 and 1887, missionary Robert Henry Codrington witnessed the arrival of eleven Tikopia canoes.

> The men said they had come to see the islands and were hospitably received ... Shortly before this a canoe from Tikopia had been driven by the wind to Mota [an island to the east of Vanua Lava], and the men in her most kindly treated, and the same thing had happened before and has happened since.
>
> (Codrington 1969:6n1)

Analysis of volcanic glass found on Tikopia suggests that contact between Tikopia and Vanuatu was much stronger than memory in Firth's time implies:

> Sometime during the late Tuakamali [AD1200 to 1800] and Historic Phases, the long-standing exchange link with northern Vanuatu weakened to the point where, by Firth's visit in 1928–29, it was largely an aspect of 'memory-culture'. It is tempting to suggest that the arrival of Europeans on the scene, and the availability of steel tools after the early 1800s (from whalers, traders, and so on), played a critical role in this by obviating the Tikopian need for volcanic glass.
>
> (Kirch 1986:41; see also Kirch and Yen 1982)

Figure 17   'Vue de la plage de Tikopia' (View of the beach at Tikopia). Hand-coloured lithograph by Jacques Arago (1790–1855), 22.1 × 35 cm, plate 173 of Voyage de la corvette l'Astrolabe, Atlas Historique. U1882 Rex Nan Kivell Collection NK 3340 (image courtesy of the National Library of Australia).

Further glimpses into their past relationships are in evidence through genetic studies which indicate a close link between Tikopia and several Banks Islands populations (Kirch 1986:36).

Visits from Europeans

Tikopia was first sighted and written into European history on 22 April 1606 by the Spanish explorer and zealot, Fernandes de Queirós (Jack-Hinton 1969). The initiative for communication came from the Tikopia who approached Queirós' ship: two Tikopia men 'gave a mantle of fine palm leaves and notice of other lands and bade farewell with great signs of regret' (Queirós 1904:233, cited in Firth 1959b:31). James Burney's *Chronological History of Voyages in the South Seas* noted the presentation to Queirós' sailing master, Torres of a barkcloth 4 yards in length and 'three palms wide' (Burney 1967:293) and described as 'like fine linen'. This was perhaps a *maro* loincloth, as used in ceremonial exchanges. According to Charles Fox, Queirós and his men had kidnapped four men at Taumako, of

Figure 18   'Tikopia: 1, 2 Naturels de Tikopia; 3 Tafoua Chef de Tikopia; 4 Bréatafou son fils; 5 Martin Bushart, matelot, né à Stettin en Prusse' (Tikopia: 1, 2 indigenes of Tikopia; 3 Tafuoa chief of Tikopia; 4 Bréatafou his son; 5 Martin Bushart, seaman born in Stettin, Prussia'. Hand coloured lithograph, Jacques Francois Gauderique Llanta (1807–64), 33 × 27 cm, plate 177 of Voyage de la corvette l'Astrolabe, Atlas Historique. U1886. Rex Nan Kivell Collection NK 3340 (image courtesy of the National Library of Australia).

whom two escaped overboard off Tikopia. (One of the remaining captives, who was in fact from Sikaiana and had been living on Taumako, was subsequently taken to Mexico, where he died, Fox 1967:5).

However, while Solomon Islands more generally was visited with increasing frequency by Europeans, Tikopia remained obscure to view in the written records until the late eighteenth century. For instance, according to John Mackay, a labour recruiter for the Queensland plantations, Tikopia had been visited in 1791 by HMS *Pandora* searching for the mutineers of the *Bounty*. While Mackay stated that Tikopia was 'frequently touched by the East India Company's ships on voyages from Calcutta to Fiji', and with the exception of American whaling ships the island was not visited frequently 'of late' (Mackay 1887:82 and Dillon 1829b:101), Firth could find no record of these voyages in the East India Company's records. Nor did Firth find reference in the ship's log of the *Barwell* landing at Tikopia in 1798, when the crew was supposedly approached by Tikopia 'brandishing weapons' (Firth 1959b:32, citing Dillon).

Reports about Tikopia became more substantive in the nineteenth century when Tikopia seemingly showed no reserve in dealing with visitors, and in travelling with them to other islands. Peter Dillon (1829a, b), third mate to Captain Robson on the trading boat *The Hunter*, recorded Tikopia men boarding the ship in 1813 and taking metal objects such as iron from the forge, as well as frying-pans and knives. At this time a Prussian sailor, Martin Bushart (Figure 18), and his pregnant wife from Fiji, were set down on Tikopia (Dillon 1829a:28) along with an Indian sailor named Joe. (Both George Bayly (1885) and Dillon referred to him as 'Lascar Joe', from the brig *Hibernia*.) The two men requested permission to remain on Tikopia after friendly relationships were established with the islanders through the purchase of yams and 'cocoa-nut mats' (Bayly 1885:22–3; Dillon 1829a:25, 28–30).

Dillon returned to Tikopia in May 1826, with George Bayly as his third mate (Richards 2005:1; Stratham and Erickson 1998:12) and met up again with Joe and with Bushart, the latter 'tattooed and clothed like the natives'. Bushart recounted the visit of an English whaling ship which he had worked on while it cruised in the area for about a month in 1825 (Bayly 1885:149, 152). He claimed that in the intervening twelve years and eight months he had been made a chief, and had married three women, as befitted a chief (Bayly 1885:151). He had learnt to speak Tikopia and considered himself fluent after two years (Dillon 1829a:33). Joe talked with Dillon in a mixture of Bengali, English, Fijian and Tikopia (Dillon 1829a:32). Firth suggested that Bushart's acquired status was consistent with the manner in which Tikopia would have customarily welcomed a stranger (Firth 1960a:10).

Bushart made a number of observations on Tikopia customs and practices,[4] and recounted how the Tikopia believed the first European ship to arrive at their islands was an evil spirit come to destroy them (Bayly 1885:171), an interpretation common to other early European visits to Solomon Islands (Bennett 1987:22). Dillon and Bayly also heard about previous European visitors to Tikopia. On Tikopia, they also saw French-made glassware and various metal and ceramic objects, which they were told had been brought from Vanikoro on a trading voyage between the two islands. Dillon was convinced that the objects were from the wreck of La Pérouse's ships, which had disappeared in 1778. He left Tikopia for Vanikoro in September 1826 (see also Clarke 2003).

Once again, the mobility of the islanders is striking. As well as Bushart, Dillon took several Tikopia men with him, although one, named Rathea, left Dillon's party at Ndende, the largest island of the Santa Cruz group, but he did not survive the return trip to Tikopia (Dillon 1829a:35). After visiting Vanikoro, Bushart was set down at the Bay of Islands, in New Zealand, but he found his way back to Tikopia, according to Bayly, to escape his life of 'dissolution' (Bayly 1885:210; Dumont d'Urville 1987:198). It seems that Bushart became integrated into Tikopia life, perhaps becoming a valuable asset to the Tikopia people.

Two years later, in 1828, Jules S.C. Dumont d'Urville sailed the *Astrolabe* (1987:197) to Tikopia to verify Dillon's account of 1826. The Tikopia initiated the first approach, paddling out in three canoes with five to six people in each. Bushart and Dumont d'Urville talked while the Tikopia men traded coconuts and fish on board ship. Bushart confirmed Dillon's account of the search for La Pérouse and added that after some quarrels he had accompanied Dillon to Vanikoro with several Tikopia as guides and interpreters. During this meeting two Englishmen, named Hambilton and Williams, sought passage with Dumont d'Urville on the *Astrolabe*. They had abandoned the ship *Harriet* (possibly the one Bushart worked on nine months before) and wanted to leave Tikopia.

---

4   Bushart's comments on Tikopia social life refer to the hierarchy of the chief, the proportion of men to women on the island, religious beliefs and prohibitions on childbirth and food (Bayly 1885:170–1).

Figure 19 'Les chefs de Tikopia recevant les officiers de l'Astrolabe'. Hand coloured lithograph, Victor-Jean Adam (1801–66), 26 × 42.2 cm, plate 174 of Voyage de la corvette l'Astrolabe, Atlas Historique. U1883. Rex Nan Kivell Collection NK 3340 (image: courtesy of the National Library of Australia).

Dumont d'Urville was impressed by the extent of regional knowledge possessed by the Tikopia. In addition to recording the names and locations of islands around Tikopia he sent a team of naturalists, Messieurs Gaimard, Lesson and Sainson, to survey the island and its residents, and to interview Bushart. They reported that they had been taken to one of the meeting houses on the island and offered 'refreshments' (1987:198, 199; Figure 19).

On the second day of their visit, Bushart failed to board the *Astrolabe* and instead three Tikopia chiefs brought food out to the ship. The chiefs told Dumont d'Urville that Bushart was sick. Hambilton and Williams, the two English sailors, explained this message as an indication that Bushart's 'direct chief', the second chief of Tikopia, did not want him to leave Tikopia as he did not want to lose Bushart's weapons and goods (Dumont d'Urville 1987:201). Dumont d'Urville countered by taking the three Tikopia chiefs hostage. He threatened to hold them until Bushart came aboard. The other Tikopia, some 48 to 75 men, returned to the island bearing Dumont d'Urville's message and by 1 o'clock Bushart arrived with

Figure 20   '*A native of the Island of Tucopea*.' *Watercolour [1827?], Augustus Earle (1793–1838), 24.8 × 22.2 cm. Rex Nan Kivell Collection NK12/90 (image courtesy of the National Library of Australia).*

his new companion, a woman from New Zealand, and announced that he was going to stay on Tikopia, and not accompany Dumont d'Urville to Vanikoro. The chiefs were released and Dumont d'Urville then left with five Tikopia men to navigate the way to Vanikoro. However, one of these men, Brini-Warrou, turned out to be from Uvea, two days from Tongatapu. He and three companions had spent thirty days at sea and had been blown to Tikopia. The five men who sailed with the *Astrolabe* never made it back from Vanikoro. Although confident that they would be assisted by their 'compatriots' living there, they turned back for Tikopia in the wrong season and were lost at sea (Dumont d'Urville 1987:202–4, 265).

According to Bennett, about half a dozen Polynesians from Tikopia and Sikaiana shipped aboard passing ships as whalers' crew and passengers every year from the late 1820s (1987:39). In 1828 Captain Lewis of the *Alfred* employed four Tikopia men as crew, one of whom he recognized from a previous trip (Anon. 1828). At least one Tikopia man went to Sydney and was later returned by Captain Lewis on the *Wolf* (Anon. 1839; Bennett 1987:39). Daniel Munn reports that several Tikopia settled with the Ngati Manu people in north New Zealand around 1828 (cited in MacDonald 1991:99); and also in New Zealand, Augustus Earle described the enthusiastic dancing style of the Tikopia men he met (Figure 20):

> ...when I began to play before the Tucopeans, the effect it had instantly upon them was ludicrous to the extreme. They sprang up and began dancing furiously; at the same time so waving their heads about as to keep their long hair extended at its fullest length: as I played faster, they quickened their pace. A lively Scotch reel seemed to render them nearly frantic; and when I ceased playing, they threw themselves down on the floor quite exhausted, and unable to articulate a word. I have observed (quite generally) that savages are not much affected by music; but these two Tucopeans were excited to a most extraordinary degree.
>
> (Earle 1832:206–7)

The European impact on Tikopia

Captain Bourne Russell of the whaling ship *Lady Rowena*, recorded on 17 March 1832 that he was told by a Tikopia who could speak some English that he should cease giving 'trinkets' to the islanders. Russell suspected that this was because the chiefs and 'the king' thought the people were getting too much (Russell 1830, cited in Treadaway 2007:9). While Russell speculated about the possible impact of the distribution of what might be perceived locally as 'prestige' items to those other than the chiefs, a definite and unforeseen consequence of such visits was the spread of disease.

After Dumont d'Urville's visit in 1828, sickness, vomiting and pain in the bowels killed three 'kings' in succession and in total 115 people died (Bennett 1987:38). Firth estimates that this represented one fifth of the population. Shortly after this tragedy, the people of Tikopia refused to let the crew of the ship *Bayonnaise* land (Firth 1959b:34). Joe, the Indian sailor who accompanied Bushart to Tikopia in 1813, left for France with the intention of lodging a claim for compensation for the losses suffered by the islanders (Dumont d'Urville 1987:265; Firth 1959b:34; Rosenman 1992:98), but he subsequently abandoned this plan in Mauritius.

Incidents of violence were recorded after this time. The *Sydney Gazette* reported that on Sunday 23 December 1838, after the chief and second officers of a ship (probably the *Achilles*, Firth 1959b:35) had landed on Tikopia to trade, a canoe approached the ship and hailed the ship's crew in good English and offered food for trade. Following this seemingly friendly exchange, the next morning, two boats went ashore to look for the men who had landed the previous day but who had not yet returned to the ship:

> ...on their approach they were received with a fire of musketry, that resembled the file fire regiment all along the beach ... natives parading to and fro in the clothes of (as we suppose) our murdered shipmates.
>
> (Anon. 1839)

According to this report twelve people were killed.[5]

Tikopia's reputation for violence lived on. In March 1875, on a trip to return plantation labourers to their homes in the Western Pacific, Mackay visited Tikopia and fired at several canoes approaching the ship (Mackay 1887:82–3). He subsequently discovered that 'barter, not warfare was their intention, each canoe containing some yams, taro, and fish for that purpose'. Mackay spoke to one of the islanders, Sam, in Fijian and they exchanged calico for barkcloth. (Firth was told that Sam was the great-grandson of one of the chiefs, the Ariki Taumako.) It is possible that Mackay may have recruited Tikopia men for the Queensland plantations during his visit in 1875 (Firth 1959b:35–7).

In 1928 Tikopia told Firth of their memories of these encounters. According to Firth, Tikopia differentiated between visits made by whaling ships (*vaka fai sinu tafora*) and labour recruiters (*vaka tari tangata*). The Tikopia named Lee and Cook as whaling captains, although Firth suggested

---

5   A second incident (or perhaps the same incident) was reported in 1839. 'Because of their continued contact with Europeans, the Tikopia in 1838 were using muskets to defend themselves.' (*Sydney Gazette* and *NSW Advertiser*, 'Ship News', 22 January 1839, cited in Bennett 1987:43).

that the latter was a confusion with Captain Cook (Firth 1959b:36). Particular individuals were remembered for their travels overseas. Fareatai went overseas three times, finally returning to Tikopia where he became 'grey', retiring to Anuta where he died. Firth estimated that Fareatai must have enlisted with a whaling ship under the command of 'Captain Van' in about 1845. Fareatai had brought back three guns, an adze, European beads and other items. Tikopia recalled that a group of men enlisted with a whaling ship in about 1850, and around 1870 Captain Martin recruited twenty to thirty men, including the chiefs of Kafika and Tafua, as well as Anutans, to work in Fiji.

Mission activity in Tikopia began when Fr. Gilbert Roudaire of the Marist Mission targeted Tikopia after unsuccessful attempts to convert the populations of New Caledonia, Wallis and Samoa. Roudaire heard of Tikopia while visiting Sydney in 1849. On the 12 December 1851 he and Fr. Jean-Baptiste Anliard arrived at the island (Laracy 1969:105–8). The following morning a number of canoes, each with five or six men, came out to meet the newcomers. Roudaire spoke to them in Wallis language and eventually got them to board the *Arche d'alliance*. Their reluctance to board could be explained by earlier experiences of violence and deaths from disease. While an armed party accompanied the missionaries to the island, the captain held twenty-five Tikopia on board as hostages. Two hours later the shore party returned and reported that Roudaire and his companions had been made welcome and that two chiefs had agreed to provide accommodation, food and protection for the missionaries.

Six months later, on 29 June 1852, Fr. Michel Anliard left New Caledonia on board the *Etoile du Matin* intending to rendezvous with Roudaire and his brother (Jean-Baptiste). The *Etoile du Matin* was not sighted again. In February 1853 a search party was organized by the Marist procurator in Sydney, who sent Fr. Xavier Montrouzier on board the charter ship the *Chieftain* to find the *Etoile du Matin*. The *Chieftain* arrived at Tikopia on 27 February 1853. By coincidence, one of the *Chieftain's* crew was a Tikopia man. On arrival, Montrouzier and the Tikopia sailor went ashore, where they were told that the missionaries had left the island. Back on board the *Chieftain*, Montrouzier then received further news that the priests had left two months previously and that the *Etoile du Matin* had not arrived at Tikopia. Montrouzier concluded that Roudaire and Anliard had become ill and left the island on a passing ship, and the *Etoile du Matin* had not reached Tikopia and was instead been lost at sea.

However, the priests did not appear in Sydney and their fate remained a mystery (Laracy 1969) until 150 years later, when an account of their deaths emerged. Ken Tufunga, a Taumako clansman, made enquiries about the missionaries on behalf of the Catholic Archbishop of Honiara, who was planning a celebration of the 150th anniversary of the missionaries' disappearance. He was told that the priests had been killed by the Taumako clan and that the chief had ordered this to be kept secret, probably to avoid reprisals. The missionaries were buried, but the site was later destroyed by a cyclone.[6]

In September 1857, Bishop Selwyn of the Melanesian Mission was the first Anglican missionary to visit Tikopia and Anuta (Firth 1959b:37–41; Selwyn 1857). The Bishop was surprised that both the Anuta and Tikopia spoke some English and that some had already travelled off the island on passing whaling or trading ships, and he complained of the 'corrupt' influence the visitors had had on the islanders. Selwyn explained that he wanted to take some children from Tikopia to learn about Christianity, but this was not received well.

> [I]t was amusing to see the way in which the women caught up their little ones, and to watch the wondering looks of the people, unable to comprehend why it should be thought with us more satisfactory to take away 2 or 3 children to be clothed and fed and taught, than to invest a certain number of axes in the purchase of pigs and coconuts.
>
> (Selwyn 1857)

Four years later, Bishop Patterson visited and noted that the inhabitants were 'dangerous fellows to deal with': several muskets were seen in the principal chief's house (Firth 1959b:37). The mission vessel visited Tikopia twice again on its run through the islands in 1888, picking up Tikopia who had been blown off course on a voyage to Anuta (three canoes had arrived at the Banks Islands while a fourth was lost at sea, Firth 1959b:38). Having

---

6   This account was provided to me by Julian Treadaway (pers comm. June 2011; 2007:27–9). Tufunga suggests that Firth did not hear of the event because he relied more heavily on Kafika and Tafua informants, whereas it was the Taumako clan that supposedly instigated the killings. The account told to Tufunga was corroborated by a similar account told to a VSA, David Alexander, in 1970 (source Hugh Laracy in communication with Julian Treadaway).

brought twenty-two Tikopia home, the missionaries were well received, but the people stood firm and still refused to allow them to take any children away, nor would they permit mission teachers to stay on the island for fear of disease (Firth 1959b:39).

When Bishop Patterson fell ill, mission visits to the islands ceased for some time (Firth 1959b:39). By 1901, two Motolava teachers named Denmet and Zacchaeus were resident on the island, but they were removed when they became ill (Firth 1970a:306). In 1907 the mission placed Ellison Turgatok on the island, and in 1911 he married a Tikopia woman named Mere (Firth 1959b:40). By 1908 there were five teachers and by 1909 two schools were established with 200 attendees (Firth 1970a:306). In the same year, relationships between the Melanesian Mission and the Tikopia improved significantly, when the mission undertook to secure the return of four men who had been kidnapped by a ship travelling from Vanuatu. The four chiefs expressed their thanks by allowing two boys to attend the mission station in Norfolk Island (Firth 1959b:39; Selwyn 1857). In 1910 Revd Durrad[7] resided on the island for two months, attended by a Maori companion named Kaini Poata, but with tragic results, as Durrad wrote:

> Among the many occasions I can recall of severe illness following the ship's visit none stands out so prominently in my memory as an epidemic of pneumonia that raged on Ticopia [sic] when I was put down there on one occasion for a few weeks while the 'Southern Cross' cruised among the Solomons. What should have been one of the happiest of experiences was converted into one of the most tragic. The message of the Gospel was stultified by the terrible sufferings of the people. Forty persons, most of them in the prime of life and many of them fathers and mothers of large families of children, were struck down in death. Others, though very ill, survived, but were reduced to the condition of living skeletons.
>
> (Durrad 1922:6)

Durrad also noted that Tikopia had told him that 'they get ill every time the S.X. [*Southern Cross*] comes here and they look upon the Mission

---

7   The Museum of Archaeology and Anthropology, University of Cambridge, holds forty-eight objects from Tikopia collected by Revd Durrad.

as a bringer of death & sickness ... They say they have never died in such numbers before' (Firth 1959b:40).

From 1911 Ellison Turgatok and two Tikopia assistants ran the mission. By 1916, four Tikopia boys attended school at Vureas on Vanua Lava in the Banks Islands. The first mass conversion on Tikopia occurred in 1923, when the Ariki Tafua adopted Christianity, taking the residents of Faea with him (Firth 1970a:308). The first church on Tikopia, St Mary's, was built in 1928 and three Tikopia teachers were placed on Anuta (Firth 1970a:307). By 1929, half of the population of Tikopia was ostensibly Christian (Firth 1983:4).

In a practical sense it can be said that the Anglican Church facilitated Firth's arrival at Tikopia. Firth arrived on the *Southern Cross* (Figure 12) as a guest of the Bishop of Melanesia, who was conducting a tour of the synod. Firth joined the boat at Tulagi, and the party arrived in Tikopia (towards the end of its tour) at 10 a.m. on Monday 23 May 1928. According to the diary of Revd Richard Godfrey, a member of the 'Synod Trip', the Bishop of Melanesia 'paved the way' for Firth to enter Tikopia (Godfrey 1928). The Mission had established four 'Central Schools' in Melanesia (The Melanesian Mission 1926): one of these, St Patrick's, was located at Sanlang in the Banks Islands. Godfrey had taught at this school and a number of his former students were living on Tikopia. He recorded that they were 'very helpful as go betweens & one has been able to smooth things for Firth' (Godfrey 1928). Firth and Godfrey made a tour of some of the villages and in Ravenga Firth presented his gifts (a tomahawk, a whetstone, a clay pipe and two sticks of tobacco each) to the Tikopia chiefs.

The anthropologist William Halse Rivers[8] preceded Firth in Tikopia, arriving on the *Southern Cross* in 1908 but staying for only one day (Rivers 1914a). On board the *Southern Cross*, Rivers met John Masere, who provided him with information about Tikopia. Masere had lived on Tikopia after drifting there with several other men – John Patita and Moses Tongana from Uvea or Wallis Island, and four men from Tonga – who had set out together for Samoa. Masere lived on Tikopia for twenty years, before being banished from the island (Rivers 1914a:303–3). While Rivers (and Durrad) were concerned about the accuracy of the information provided by Masere, Rivers recorded his account, believing that it might

---

8   The Museum of Archaeology and Anthropology, University of Cambridge, holds three objects from Tikopia collected by W.H. Rivers.

have some historical interest in the future (Rivers 1914a:301). A similarly short visit was made four years later by Felix Speiser[9] (Firth 1959b:40), who is perhaps best known for his documentation of the material culture and customs of Vanuatu (Speiser 1990).

Unlike anthropologists, the British authorities generally displayed little interest in Tikopia. HMS *Ringdove* visited in September and November 1894, and in June 1898, during a visit by HMS *Mohawk*, Tikopia was declared a British protectorate. Occasional visits were made by Australian ships, including HMS *Melbourne* and HMS *Adelaide*, while Solomon Islands administrators visited irregularly until the outbreak of the Second World War (Firth 1959b:41–2).

Interactions between Tikopia and visitors reflect complicated relationships. The few visitors, including Anutans and drifters from other islands such as Rotuma, Uvea and Tonga, often stayed for some time. Men from Germany and India took up semi-permanent residence with wives from Fiji and New Zealand. European drifters or deserters stayed until they could leave on the next ship.

That some visitors became long-term residents demonstrates the willingness of Tikopia to incorporate strangers, whether they spoke related Polynesian languages or learned Tikopian, and to share cultural and geographical knowledge with them. Compared to some other parts of the Pacific, European visits were few and their impact of conflict and disease relatively slight, though there was ample opportunity for the movement of people and the exchange of objects and ideas, a two-way process in which the Tikopia took an active part. It is against this background, a history of transactions between Tikopia and visitors, that Firth made his collection.

---

9   See Speiser (1913:287–91).

CHAPTER 4

Objects as sacred

Mediating the spirits in Tikopia

A number of the objects in the collection are described as *fakatino*, embodiments of the gods of Tikopia. These include sacred adzes, spears, a conch-shell trumpet and a neck ornament. These objects are identified later in the chapter, but first I examine the Tikopia spirit world as described by Firth, to provide a background with which to assess the significance of the presence of *fakatino* in the collection.

To do so, I use the data in Firth's ethnographies in an attempt to discern the agency of such objects in their broader social context, that is, beyond economic uses. I suggest that an examination of the customary circulation of these objects, as documented by Firth, might reveal how certain objects came to be moved out of the Tikopia context into Firth's collection in a culturally appropriate manner; or to put it another way, whether this transfer could have happened, because Firth had been drawn into, and absorbed into, Tikopia social practice. This is a theoretical, or perhaps speculative, interpretation, but one which is nonetheless a valuable exercise in thinking about how the objects may have been collected.

This approach draws upon Arjun Appadurai's (1986) conception of the 'social life of things' and Igor Kopytoff's (1986) 'biography' of an object, both of which focus upon the path along which objects are circulated. The view of objects as more than the sum of their visible parts follows upon the tradition of Mauss's 'spirit of the gift' (1990), in which the transfer of objects incorporates super-material attributes that require symbolic and collective commitment from the people making and transacting them. John Liep's (1990) discussion of developments in the interpretation of gift exchange, and the conceptions of ranked gifts (Campbell 1983) and inalienable objects (Weiner 1985) have also influenced my approach to an examination of the objects transferred into Firth's collection and the social relationships which might have mediated these transfers.

In drawing upon the descriptions provided by Firth, I have tried to remove Firth's analytical interpretation and discern the broader significance of the objects in Tikopia society. However, Firth modified his interpretation of objects, not unsurprisingly given the period over which he was writing, and his later works, especially *Rank and Religion* (Firth 1970a) are important in my examination of the use of objects to mediate between people and the gods of Tikopia.

Gods and spirits

Firth described the Tikopia pantheon as comprising a hierarchy of named and ranked gods (*atua*) who inhabited an invisible, immaterial sphere known as *i a nga atua*. This sphere mirrored the human world, with invisible counterparts of the physical landscape (Firth 1970a). Each of the four chiefs (*ariki*) was the primary representative of the god of that clan and was responsible for its invocation. Each chief was associated with one of the four principal food crops on the island, these being yam (*kafika*), taro (*taumako*), coconut (*tafua*) and breadfruit (*fangerere*) (Firth 1930c:293), and was responsible for ritual activity to ensure the supply of the crop, as well as the abundance of fish and general well-being (Firth 1930b, 1967a:27). Together they contributed to a cycle of ritual activities, the 'Work of the Gods', said to have been established by the principal gods (Firth 1930b:61).[1]

The four chiefs were hierarchically ranked in ritual duties. Elders (*pure matua*), the heads of commoner kin groups, possessed considerable ritual knowledge and had a special relationship with the chief of their clan. To explain this relationship, Firth drew an analogy between the relationship of *ariki* and *pure matua* and that of a European king and his aristocrats. While both positions mediated with the gods, the chief of the clan was senior to the elders, and the Ariki Kafika, the chief of the Kafika clan, was paramount amongst the chiefs (Firth 1965:188). Chiefs and commoners had similar access to garden land and orchards through their relatives in

---

1   'This was a translation of the their word *fekau*, and I remember the old chief saying to me in essence, 'It really *is* work, you know, all this ritual stuff.'"(Firth, in Parkin 1988:329).

all lines, but commoners were excluded from shrines (*marae*)[2] and other ritual sites (Firth 1965:57–8).

Atua were spirits of the dead (both humans and non-humans) who resided in *i a nga atua*. They were invisible, as was *i a nga atua* itself, which incorporated its own geographical and social landscape. Moving between the world of the living and *i a nga atua* were the spirits of living humans known as *ora* or *mauri*. Firth translated these words as 'soul' (Firth 1970a:64–5) but also as 'mind' or 'consciousness' (Firth 1970a:64–5n.1). *Atua* could take any shape (1970a:67) and become immanent in objects.

Firth's account of the Tikopia spirit world (1970a:68–98) presented a number of divisions, or categories. The first of these were unnamed, non-personalized wild spirits of the sea, woods, orchards and the mountain, who were responsible for accidental or unusual events and bad luck. The second group included named spirits of the dead, the larger proportion of the spirit world, who conducted the spirit (*ora*) from the body to ensure its successful transition to a god (*atua*). The third group comprised specific ancestors who had held religious functions when alive, and they were invoked during ritual activity. They represented the genealogical apex from which contemporary lineages were reckoned, previous generations being undifferentiated. *Tupua* formed the fourth group: named senior spirits who had never been human, or at least whose 'humanity was regarded as an incidental phase in their spirit existence'. They were the most powerful gods, distinguishable from ancestors by their superior powers and pre-eminent position in the *kava* ritual. The Atua i Kafika was an exception; as the foremost of all the gods he held elevated ancestor status. Lastly, there were lesser spirits, often of modern origin, originating with human acts, generally the work of spirit mediums (Firth 1970a:69).

Material and ephemeral signs of the spirits

Spirits could be invoked through rituals to gain their support and sometimes they dealt directly with people, as in spirit mediumship, or in very dangerous sexual encounters (Firth 1970a:99–100). Powerful spirits were *vave* (swift/speedy, see also Firth with Tuki 1985:598). In the human

---

2 'There are, however, limitations to these land rights. Certain portions of land, those surrounding temples and the *marae*, the open spaces on which important public religious rites take place, are reserved from cultivation.' (Firth 1965:58).

world someone who had physical strength was described as *makeke*; someone who was powerful might be *vave* (swift); a person who could project their personality aggressively was *toa;* a person with *manu* held mystical control over physical forces. Spirits who were *vave* combined all these elements. While invisible, they were thought to have human form, and they attended some of the ceremonies undertaken for them (1970a:98). 'Spirits who were *vave* were represented as being able to rush around the heavens, in a state of furious activity, and able to perform gigantic tasks, including the production of thunder.' (Firth 1970a:107). The major gods were endowed with *vave* from the very beginning, but other spirits could acquire it. A leaf decoration tucked into the belt at the back was the symbol of the spirit wearer having *vave* (Firth 1970a:107–8).[3] Such spirits were powerful forces in human life, enmeshed in society on the human plane and organized through descent.

The ability of the gods to make themselves manifest in objects has particular relevance for some items in Firth's collection. Certain objects, plants and animals were 'standard identificatory signs of particular named spirits involved in the major religious system' (1970a:113). These included features of the landscape, such as rocks, trees and cave shelters, as well as items used more frequently in ritual activity (1970a:113). These visible signs of the presence of spirits included *fakatino, fakaata* and *fakamailonga*.

A *fakatino* was an embodiment of a god: a 'permanent concrete symbol of the supernatural being, a definite individual object of known locale' (Firth 1930c:303) such as a stone, club, conch shell or building. Such objects, which were decorated and revered, were often the 'idols' or 'images' of missionary concern (Firth 1930d:396).

Embodiments had great religious significance because the god 'was corporately represented by the object in question' (Firth 1970a:117). For example, the moon was perceived to be the body of the god Semoana; the constellation Pleiades was the Female Deity; certain other stars represented the Atua i Taumako; while rainbows, waterspouts and the foam of the sea were the embodiments of other gods. Most embodiments were manufactured, including house posts and rafters, as well as objects kept in temples. In Motuapi, the house of the Ariki Tafua, in 1929:

---

3   'It was this leaf ornament which was conceived to represent the speed endowment of the spirit – a kind of "outboard motor" set at his back, enabling him to move swiftly through the skies.' (Firth 1970a:108).

there were various objects hung up: a dart, a paddle, a double ended
spear, a club, all associated with the Atua i Tafua; a Gilbert islands sword
with shark's teeth brought by an immigrant in a canoe about 1870 and
dedicated to the god Tufaretai; a club from a traditional Tongan canoe,
named Safoka after the Tongan chief and dedicated to the god Tuna; and
another spear associated with the ancestor Pu Tafua Lasi and carried
to the turmeric ritual. All these objects were described as belonging to
the various gods, some as signs (*fakamailonga*) of them, others as their
embodiments (*fakatino*). They were treated as sacred heirlooms, and
some were given ritual use. In a time of disorder after a fight, I was told,
the club of the Atua i Tafua might be taken down and 'announced' to the
god to get his help to restore order. Accordingly, such objects tended to
be treated with great respect. Pa Rangimaseke of Tavi, a friend of mine,
refused to let me have a spear which was in his house. He said it was the
fakatino of a sea god Pu i te Moana who was man-eating. 'I am afraid for
myself and my children.'

(Firth 1970a:118)[4]

In the temple of Resiake, embodiments were ceremonially redecorated
during the 're-carpeting of the temples'. The objects (four spears, one arrow
and two clubs) had their old decorations removed; then the objects were
washed in the lake and returned to the temple, where, accompanied by
invocations to the appropriate gods, they were reclothed with vegetation
and strips of barkcloth (Firth 1967a:207–9).

Temple buildings (or their parts) and canoe sheds were also
embodiments of the gods. For example, offerings of orange barkcloth were
made to the main post of the Ariki Kafika's canoe shed (Firth 1967a:106–7).
This post, representing the two major gods Tafika and Karisi, jointly known

---

4   Firth collected sixteen spears (*tokotoko*) (Firth nos. 16.1 to 16.16, see Appendix
     2): 16.6 was acquired from Pa Tavi, ritual elder of Kafika clan. It is described
     as 'an embodiment (*fakatino*) of a sea deity Pu i te moana, belonging to Paito
     i Tavi. [It h]as been carved with steel tools, succeeding an earlier specimen,
     when the latter decayed.' (Wedgewood 1930:18). A second (16.12) is described
     as a 'religious emblem, embodiment (*fakatino*) of Pu Te One roa, a sea deity
     from Paito Niuwaru of Kafika' (Wedgewood 1930:18). Paito Niuwaru was an
     important man of rank (Firth 1967b:111).

as Pu ma,[5] was decorated with *Cycas* leaves bound with barkcloth strips. A mat in front of the post represented the resting place of another god. The canoe shed of each chief had its own female god who was in charge of the floor, which men were forbidden to sit on for fear of copulating with her, a very dangerous act.

In 1952, during Firth's second visit, embodiments still held power. But by 1966 the gods were believed to have 'withdrawn' and most of the spears and clubs which formerly embodied them had been sold to European visitors (Firth 1970a:119).

Gods also appeared to humans as *fakaata*, animate manifestations in the form of animals and plants. There were also *fakamailonga* or signs, such as barkcloth streamers (*noa*) which indicated the presence of a god, or the proximity of ritual activity. These were often plants identified with a particular god by leaf pattern, stem or colour. These were used to adorn objects considered to be embodiments. Plants were used to mediate ritual pronouncements to gods.

Firth's analysis

In his description of embodiments (*fakatino*), Firth recorded some ambiguity as to whether the god was actually present in a particular object (Firth 1970a:118). In 1939 he wrote that, in 1929, a cut in a sacred canoe was smeared with turmeric as an ornament. However in 1970 he changed his interpretation considerably, recalling that he had been told that the canoe was the body of a god, hence the turmeric would have celebrated recovery from the injury:

> I overlooked a statement by the Ariki Kafika that the turmeric was put
> on the canoe since the body of the god (i.e. the hull) had been cut. This
> aligned the decoration with the rite of smearing turmeric on a person
> to celebrate his recovery from danger or illness. The decoration of
> the canoe was then a symbolic act of celebration of restoring, not just
> ornament.
>
> (Firth 1970a:119n.1)

---

5   'The bark-cloth spread out there is spread out to Pu ma – Pu ma are two,
     Tafika and Karisi.' (Firth 1967a:106).

Firth's change of interpretation, the application of restorative substances to heal the body of the canoe rather than of ornament, is a significant one, because it permits an understanding of the canoe as more than a marine vessel, and the substance applied to it as more than ornament. Firth comes to acknowledge the canoe as associated with the *atua*, and the turmeric smeared onto it as a substance with the power to affect the body of the *atua*. However, Firth remains ambiguous in his interpretation of the *fakatino* as an object which is the physical manifestation of the *atua* as opposed to an emblem of the *atua*. For example, in *Work of the Gods* (1967a), *fakatino* is translated by Firth as both 'embodiment' and 'emblem'. In discussing a number of weapons housed at the temple Resiake he says:

> It is not held that the object reveals the actual shape of the god; he is spoken of and treated as if he were anthropomorphic. Sometimes it serves as a vehicle of expression for him if he should wish to appear to human eyes in concrete form, but more often it is held that the god does not dwell in it or actually appear in it in person. Thus of one such weapon, the club of Rakiteua, it was observed 'It is termed the embodiment (*fakatino*) of the god, but he does not enter into it'. (*Tino* means body). A clear distinction is always drawn between the material and the spiritual entity: these objects are not called *atua* themselves; they are known to be only representatives of *atua*. In every case by reason of their supernatural associations they are *tapu*, and must be handled with considerable caution and only at the appropriate times.
>
> (Firth 1967a:207)

Firth identified other signs of the gods which were not recognized by Tikopia themselves. He suggested that *noforanga*, stone slabs set on the temple meeting place (*marae*), generally indicated a sitting or dwelling place of the gods. Firth also recorded the spirit medium as a dwelling place (*vaka atua*) and suggested that the relationship between *noforanga* and *vaka atua* paralleled that between embodiment (*fakatino*) and manifestation (*fakaata*), discussing this in detail in *Rank and Religion* (1970a:120ff.).

Firth's conclusions were that embodiments (*fakatino*) 'provided a set of concrete things which could be operated upon on critical ritual occasions' and which also provided a map for 'navigation in ritual behaviour', and that *noforanga* acted as mnemonics 'serving to remind generation after generation of what had to be done' (Firth 1970a:126). A parallel can be drawn with the use of *malangan* funerary carvings in New Ireland (Küchler 1987), which provide the locus of generational memory, a cognitive map of the place and origin of a particular group of people within their natural and spiritual environment. In Tikopia, *noforanga* stones on the meeting place indicated the seating patterns for those involved in the ritual, but this mnemonic use could equally apply to the other embodiments. Such items were not simply symbolic of the qualities typifying the gods but also had a 'proprietary' role, indicating control and power. They were thus embedded in a network of social relationships and the visual form of the objects, the quality of workmanship and materials, were not important (Firth 1970a:127). The lack of interest in a visual aesthetic is contrary to the emphasis placed upon the object in a Western aesthetic that prioritizes the object's form. More important in Tikopia is the embeddedness of objects in their social context.

Objects as material aids for communication with the gods

While the gods and spirits could appear anywhere at any time, communication from people to gods required material aids. The kava ceremony formed the basis of most interaction, and generally included offerings of barkcloth to the gods or ancestors; recital of formulae using the stem of the kava plant as a medium; and invocations to the gods to ensure good fish catches, food crops, turmeric-processing, calm weather, the eradication of disease and the general welfare of the land. Invocations were followed by offerings of kava, food and betel-nut to the gods (Firth 1967a:38). Within this pattern there was great variation, as illustrated in Firth's (1967a) detailed account. Special types of food were included, the exchange of food being important in the maintenance of social relationships (Firth 1967a:53, 1973a), and very 'weighty' rituals used special food bowls (*raurau kumete*).[6] Smell and cleanliness were important in the presence of the gods: both men and women wore their new, clean barkcloth and made sure that new clean mats were used. Turmeric, the most highly valued item on Tikopia, 'the scent of the gods', was also used as a mark of their presence, having also the red and orange colour that was pleasing to them (Firth

---

6   During the rite of the 'Hot Food' in the 'Work of the Yam', the Ariki Kafika's offering of sacred food was made in such a bowl, which Firth describes as 'sacred property' of the chief (Firth 1967a:154).

1967a:416). 'But if the perfume and the oil are not applied, then he will act disgustingly towards the Ariki.' (Firth 1967a:150). Maybe for Tikopia, visual aesthetics were not as important as the aesthetics of smell.[7]

Mana was a quality attributed to chiefs (Firth 1967b) in their ability to mediate with gods and ensure the welfare of the island and its people: in Firth's terms, the 'efficacy' of the chief in maintaining the quality of life for the people on the island. For the Tikopia there was no strict division between technical and ritual knowledge (Firth 1965:105). While chiefs generally possessed esoteric knowledge, commoners could also acquire this, but only chiefs possessed *mana*. This quality, focused on the head, was transferred to any objects they touched, making them *tapu*, sacred. Objects associated with the chiefs, including sacred adzes, sacred canoes and, more broadly, nets and headrests, were all repositories of the chief's *mana*.

Sacred adzes (*toki tapu*) made of clam-shell were important symbols of chiefly status and *mana*, and Firth collected two of them (see Figure 21).[8] According to the Ariki Kafika, chiefs were given the right to use sacred adzes by the gods, and the most important ones originated with Pu ma (Tafaki and Karisi), the principal gods of the Kafika clan (Firth 1967a:60).

---

7   Treadaway (2007:20) notes that dancing remains popular in Tikopia and that smell is as important as attire when people prepare for dancing. Turmeric is mixed with coconut oil and rubbed on the arms, legs and face, and flowers and scented leaves are used to adorn the body.

8   Firth collected seven stone adzes heads (Firth nos. 86.1–86.7) and five shell adzes (85.1 to 85.4 and 67.1). The adze registered with the Australian Museum no. E64070 could be either 85.3 or 67.1 of Firth's collection. This item, along with nine other adzes, made of either clam-shell or black stone, was registered into the Australian Museum collections on 8 July 1969, transferred from the University of Sydney. The nine adzes are positively identified as being from Firth's 1928 collection, but two adzes, including E64070, have deteriorated labels, making identification of individual Firth numbers difficult. However, given the description of the *toki tapu* given by Firth (1959a) regarding size and cross-section, I am confident that E64070 is one of these. A second hafted adze (Firth no. 85.4, AM no. E84886) is listed in Firth's List as a *toki tapu* (Wedgewood 1930:50). However, this item does not fit the description given by Firth (1959a) so is not included in this discussion. Made from the hinge of the giant clam, *Tridacna maxima*, the word *toki* refers to both the adze and the shell it is made of (Firth with Tuki 1985:534).

Figure 21   Shell Adze (toki). This adze might be Firth no. 85.3, a sacred adze, but is too small in length for a principal adze, and may be a supporter, or protector (pipi) (Firth 1959a:149, 1967a:58). It was transferred from the University of Sydney, Department of Anthropology to the Australian Museum and registered into the collection on 9 July 1969. AM registration no. E64070, 11 cm long; 2.6 cm high; 3 cm wide. (Photo: Paul Ovenden, Australian Museum).

According to Pa Vainunu they were made by the female god, Pakora, and given to the Atua i Kafika, 'supreme culture-hero of Kafika, and the principal deity of Tikopia as a whole' (Firth 1967a:60). The sacred adzes were then distributed by the various chiefs of Kafika, two being given to the Taumako family line, two to Pu Tafuaroa of Tafua, one to Fakaarofatia, the progenitor of the Fangarere clan, and one remaining with Kafika (Firth 1959a:150).[9] Another blade was said to have originated in Tonga and arrived with the ancestor of the Taumako clan, Te Atafu, on the canoe Tukupaisia (Firth 1967a:59).

Sacred adzes were of two types: principal adzes (*matua toki*), which were large clam-shell blades measuring from 20 to 30.4 cm long and approximately 5 cm thick; and *pipi*, also made of clam-shell but smaller (Firth 1959a:149). The *pipi* were the 'supporters' (Firth 1959a:149) or 'protectors'

---

9   Firth recounts other stories associated with the *toki tapu* in *Work of the Gods* (1967a:60–5).

(Firth 1967a:58) of the principal adzes. Ordinary adzes (*toki*) for general use were also clam-shell blades of 7.5 to 10 cm long (Firth 1959a:149). The sacred adzes were kept on a special shelf in the prime temple of each chief and were handled only by him on ceremonial occasions, never to be seen by women and children, and their very existence was not divulged to casual observers. Because of the sanctity of these blades, any activity involving their use was accompanied with considerable ritual (Firth 1967a:57).

> These sacred adzes are regarded as property to be carefully guarded. Pa Vainunu said that one is never handed over to another chief. 'It is not given, because should it be given, the chief and his clan (the donors) will die'. Its speech is the 'life of the clan'.
>
> (Firth 1967a:61)

Some canoes (*vaka tapu*) were also considered sacred, and were controlled by chiefs, ritual elders and the heads of the most important kin groups (Firth 1967a:55), who could draw upon both the physical and social resources needed to make them. The canoe belonged to the deities to whom the canoe was dedicated by a chief, these being gods or ancestral spirits of one of the four clans. The person initiating the building of a sacred canoe had primary rights of usage and allocation of usage, but the Ariki Kafika, as the primary chief of Tikopia, ultimately controlled access to all the canoes on the island, no matter who initiated their construction or participated in building work. Sacred canoes were ceremonially reconsecrated by the appropriate *ariki* (Firth 1965:117).

The effects of *mana* might be reflected in all objects considered valuable, such as houses, land, bonito hooks and fishing equipment. So, for example, because of the association between the chief and the gods, the large fishing net (*mata kupenga*) of a chief was subject to ceremonial care the first time it was taken out of the house to be used. A mat was placed in the doorway as a mark of respect 'just as such a mat is laid down for a person of rank to sit upon, or coco-nut fronds for a sacred canoe to rest upon' (Firth 1965:175). The net was considered foremost amongst all nets and the success of other nets was reliant upon it: if a man caught a large number of fish in his net, he had to take part of his catch to his chief to acknowledge him. The chief would recite words over the net to ensure its continued success (Firth 1965:176). Experts who held ritual knowledge for fishing were also subject to the power of the chief through the chiefly *mana* of the net.

The gods resided in specific parts of sacred objects. In canoes they occupied the side away from the outrigger, from which the nets were thrown and into which the fish came: this was the high-status side of the canoe. The gods had to be ritually removed from the vessel should any work need to be carried out on it, using barkcloth to carry them away, in a ceremony known as 'lifting down the gods' (*fakauviuvi o nga atua*) (Firth 1965:119–21; see also barkcloth referred to as a seat for the gods, Firth 1965:226).

Similar distinctions applied to dwelling houses (*te patio*), which were divided into men's and women's, and sacred and profane spaces (Firth 1983:78). Entrance points into the house were also subject to restrictions. Women, children and casual visitors used the entrances on the *tuaumu*, oven side, while the head of the household used entrances at the ends of the dwelling. Depending on the age of the house and the rank of the family living in it, the supporting posts of the structure may have been subject to restrictions also. Generally, women did not lean against the house posts as these were used as backrests by the senior men of the household or respected guests: hierarchical precedence governed the use of the posts as well as the household space (Firth 1983:80–1).

> In an abstract schematic way one may think of Tikopia as a circle of land bounded by the wastes of the ocean, and just within the land edge a circle of houses, end to end, their profane sides backed by cook-houses and leading inwards to the orchards whence food comes, their sacred sides opening out on to the canoe-yards, also sacred, and leading down to the beach whence the vessels set out for fish. It is safe to say that no Tikopia thinks of the situation in this diagrammatic way, but there is a consistency of this kind about the general arrangement.
>
> (Firth 1983:80)

Kirch (1996) suggests that Firth did not continue the house analogy far enough, and that the very island itself represented a house, with the mountain peak of Reani representing the central post. MacDonald (1991:136ff) extended the discussion, suggesting natural and architectural features, including the pathways across the land, held social identifications. She described geographical space as gendered, and hierarchical within gender: women's social space incorporated the reef, the sea shore, the lake and the paths on the island. Men were associated with the sacred, which geographically incorporated the deep sea, and had free access across the island, with no restriction to the established paths. Married women operated in a narrower sphere than men or unmarried women, and in addition to prescriptions on dress, hairstyle and activities, they were constantly chaperoned as they moved around the island. MacDonald outlines a complex set of relationships between women of different statuses. Indigenous views of spatial organization were also asserted in church. In 1966, menstruating women were not permitted to enter the church,[10] and women sat towards the back: by 1980, the women had moved to the left, while men sat on the right side. This was congruent with the spatial division of the house (MacDonald 1991:84–5).

Firth (1967a:198–9) documented different types of restrictions on spatial orientation and access to sacred buildings. Firstly, there were actual dwellings, with floor-mats covering the graves of noted ancestors and one or more of the house posts dedicated to the gods of the clan. Secondly, there were structures which had become too sacred to live in because of the burial of the ancestors there: these were visited for religious rites and were termed 'sacred houses' (*fare tapu*). Thirdly, the oven houses of *fare tapu* were also sacred because these were the ovens of the gods. The thatched roofing and ancestral grave-mats inside were renewed in the special 'recarpeting' ceremony (1967a:198–254).

Each clan also had its own temples, the most important of which were analogous to the primary sacred canoes (*taumauri*) and originated in historical and mythical events. Firth (1967a:199) describes the temples of Kafika, Resiake and Taumako, and the former temple of the Tafua, as being of 'outstanding size'. The central post represented the body of the primary god, while other posts and various parts of the structure embodied other deities, including some from other clans with which there were historical relationships. For example, during the ceremonial cycle of the temple of Resiake, a mat was tied around the central post and it was 'washed' or 'cleansed' with water and rubbed with aromatic leaves, as were the bodies of people involved in ceremonial activity, enhancing the relationship between

---

10   Menstruating women had to stay away from men in case their blood, which was considered *toto pariki* (bad blood), came into contact with them. As God was considered male, menstruating women had to stay away from church: blood was not to be brought into contact with or in proximity to the mats placed there or with Christ (MacDonald 1991:84–5).

the chief and the god (Firth 1967a:209–11). After the post was washed the mat tie was cut so that it fell to the ground, adding to a heap of mats around the base of the post left from previous ceremonies, and the decoration of the other parts of the structure proceeded, reflecting the manner in which people decorated themselves for dancing (Firth 1967a:212).

If a new chief was elected, the first sacred canoe that he built was known as the 'renewal of the adze hafts' (*singa kau toki*), as the sacred adze of the chief was rehafted in the process. The hafting used on the 'most prized working tools' (Firth 1959a:151) was of criss-cross design (*sumu*), in contrast to plain binding (*rii*). The criss-cross binding was also used to attach the ridgepole of a house to the central posts, and the lineage of Avakofe were acknowledged experts in this work.

When new lashing was put on, the adze was brought into a canoe yard, and the canoe it was associated with was brought out while the work was undertaken. The construction of a chief's second sacred canoe was accompanied by the rehafting of the supporting blades (*pipi*), and was known as 'sacred building' (*tangu tapu*). If a third sacred canoe was built, any of the sacred adzes which needed rehafting were mended. The sharpening of the sacred adze blades was also a ritual act, involving cleansing and a libation of coconut water.

The relationship between sacred canoes and adzes included an association between the sea and adze deities, which in some cases were personifications of sea creatures, such as eels (Firth 1967a:62). The adze of Taumako was associated with the eel god and was therefore very dangerous (Firth 1967a:63). The sacred adze was fundamental to canoe rites and the efficacy of fishing. The relationship was poetically expressed in kava rites associated with fishing expeditions (Firth 1967a:75):

> Bite, thy adze
> On the head of the fish,
> To come to thy starboard side.

In this invocation the deity travels in the canoe and strikes a fish with his adze, for the fishermen to hook it. The motion of the adze leaves gashes on the head of the fish (Firth 1967a:74–5). Other associations include large nets (*mata kupenga*), made for setting in the lake or dragging on the reef, which were analogous to canoes, being called 'the canoe of the shore' (waters) (*te vaka o nga uta*). 'People may say of a house where a net is being made, "the house there is building a canoe". In this connection "a new canoe" means a new net; "an old canoe" indicates an old net' (Firth 1965:174–5).

Grave-mats (*inaki*) placed on the floor to indicate the 'mat of the ancestor' (Firth 1967a:204–6) also had multiple associations. They were made by women and replaced as part of the recarpeting and rethatching of the temples each season.[11] The replacement of mats and thatch was described by the Tikopia as an equivalent exchange for payment (*tauvi*), in this case for land. The richer a man was in land, the more grave-mats he had to provide in the temples, acknowledging the provision of food from the gardens and orchards by former generations.

> The real significance of the *inaki* lies not in its value as floor-covering but as a mark of attention to an ancestor by virtue of which he is induced to continue his favourable interest in family lands. Should the renewal of a mat be omitted and it rot in the house then the ghostly owner may become annoyed and blight the crops.
>
> (1967a:204)

Old mats – *punefu*, the term for a type of funeral gift (Firth 1967a:206) – were removed from the temple as a part of the recarpeting ritual and burnt, for to reuse them would have been disrespectful. Whoever used the family land assumed responsibility for renewing the mats during the Work of the Gods. Thus 'if a family splits up and agrees to divide its lands the head of the elder branch may say to his junior: "But come you then and renew the mat of our ancestor, and I will have a breathing space". (Firth 1967a:206).

The re-carpeting of the temple site at Somosomo of Kafika employed canoe imagery. The temple itself had been washed away by a tidal wave in 1918, but the site was still used and re-carpeted. In laying the mats, the site was divided into 'port' (*ama*) and 'starboard' (*katea*, the outrigger side),

---

11   Firth describes two exceptions (1967a:384).

instead of using the terms for left and right (Firth 1967a:385–90).[12] The plaiting of the mats for Somosomo was carried out as a sacred task, the women sitting in the high-status 'port' side of the temple facing Uta, and with neither men nor women allowed to speak to the other.

Firth's ethnography describes a highly complex world where objects are used as material aids, not only in communicating with the gods but also in manifesting connections with them that were materialized in household and temple spaces, canoes and canoes yards, as well as in the tools and techniques needed to construct these. Both the internal plan of architectural spaces, their structural elements (posts, doorways) and the objects contained within them (mats, sacred objects) manifested the *mana* of the chiefs and demonstrated their good relationship with their gods.

New objects, innovation and renewal

Firth recorded several examples of Tikopia adopting imported materials and objects: even Firth's toothbrush, for instance, 'supplied a new medium for the making of earrings' (Firth 1983:38). However, from the Tikopia point of view, perhaps the use of new materials in place of old was itself irrelevant to the significance of the artefacts. As will become apparent, the enduring identity of some objects over time was of more concern than the continuity of their material composition. For example, to ensure the effectiveness of fishing nets they might be dedicated to ancestral spirits (Firth 1965:98). To maintain the relationship between a net and an ancestor, old nets were frequently repaired, rather than replaced, floats and sinkers were reused: and so a net maintained its connection to an ancestor despite the fact that the materials used to fix it were new.

> I was told by a kinsman of the Ariki Taumako that the net of this chief was the only one on Ravenga of any antiquity. 'Indeed it is an ancient

---

12 'No reason for the application of these terms to the Marae was given, save that they were first introduced by the Atua i Kafika who attached them also to his turmeric-making. As one stands in Somosomo and faces towards Uta, Katea and Ama correspond with right and left, and it is possible that the idea expressed is of this kind. Whatever be the origin of the figurative sense of these terms here, however, it is certain that their use gives a much greater esoteric significance to the spatial division than the mere "right" and "left" would do, for which the Tikopia have ordinary words.' (Firth 1967a:389).

thing.' It was 'the same net' as was made by the chief's grandfather and
great-grandfather. It was explained that as one part got into bad repair
it was replaced but that the net as a whole was never cast aside. The net
of the Ariki Kafika, however, was begun afresh by him; the original net
of this family was rejected by him on his father's death. Here is to be
seen the convention of continuity which operates for nets as for canoes,
houses, sacred spears and other Tikopia material things – a convention
bound up with the ritual affiliations of these objects.

(Firth 1965:99–100)

Likewise, the sacred canoe of the Porima house was said to be the
direct descendent of the vessel which brought the ancestors of Kafika
to Tikopia from Rotuma. The sacred canoe of the house of Maneve was
acquired in the spirit world from the god, i te Uruao, by Rakaitonga, the
ancestor of Taumako (Firth 1967a:98). Maintenance of the object ensured
'continuity' between the god and the human world and this in turn ensured
the efficacy (*mana*) of an object (Firth 1967b).

'Sacred things' (*anea tapu*) such as the adzes important in canoe
manufacture (e.g. Firth 1967a:90–2) and the digging sticks for crop
cultivation (e.g. Firth 1967a:212) were housed in the temple. Firth describes
the sacred digging stick of Kafika as:

one of the most intensely sacred articles in the island. Through
its association with the yam, the vegetable food-stuff of primary
significance, this digging stick has become as it were the prototype of
all instruments of cultivation, the material symbol of agriculture. Like
all other objects in this particular context it is regarded as the property,
even the embodiment, of the Atua i Kafika, and therefore must be
handled with extreme care, and only by persons authorized by the Ariki
and at the appropriate time. No women, for instance, would dare to
touch it nor is it probably ever seen by them.

(Firth 1967a:181)

Like the fishing net, the digging stick was renewed when it decayed
beyond use, but the 'new' item retained the sacred association. Certain
objects and structures, irrespective of the freshness of the materials used to
repair them, carried a sense of continuing connection with previous lineages,
ancestors and gods, and formed a focus for ritual and other activities (Firth

1967a:199–200). Temples embodied the relationship of the Tikopia to the gods, housing as sacred objects the implements essential to ensure successful canoe-building, fishing and agriculture. Other objects, possessions of the gods, heightened the sanctity of the temples.

Firth's description of how objects manifested the gods makes little reference to artistic qualities. He noted that wood carvings were decorated, but that such decoration was minimal. While a discussion of a well-carved turmeric container highlighted qualities of depth and inside finish, Firth preferred to locate possible indicators of Tikopia aesthetic sensibilities (Firth 1960b, 1992) in their use of poetry (Firth with McLean 1990). It is clear that the 'importance' of an object in terms of its spiritual potency did not lie in attributes associated with visual patterning.

The difference between sacred and secular canoes is a case in point. The sacred canoes, the *taumauri* held by chiefs, had names and were celebrated or reconsecrated every year during the first rite of the 'Ritual of the Sacred Canoes'. *Fua riki* or 'little fleet' were the subject of a second rite, the Fainga Vaka (Firth 1967a:55–7). However, ordinary canoes (*paopao*), including decommissioned sacred canoes (*tovi*), were more common, and owned by both men of rank and commoners. Nearly every independent household had or could get access to a *paopao*. All canoes were used for deep-sea fishing, but if a sacred canoe became unfit for this due to age or damage it could be retired and used for lake fishing. Regardless of their status as sacred or secular, canoes were highly valued, a *paopao* being considered an 'orchard of the commoners' (Firth 1965:117). The sanctity of particular canoes lay in their association with chiefs and gods, not in their material properties alone, nor through the 'artistic skill' revealed in their manufacture.

Firth's acquisition of the sacred

How then, given the social contexts of sacred objects, their association with the gods and the relationship between the human and spirit world that they mediated, did Firth acquire such objects? Firth collected two sacred adzes, highly valued ritual items associated with canoe-building which were usually stored on a special shelf in the temples along with the sacred digging stick and other 'sacred things' or 'embodiments' of gods. He also acquired

Figure 22   'Sacred whale tooth necklet, kasoa – tapu specimen, unique. From Mapusanga house, property of former Ariki Kafika – ?[sic] brought from Fiji' (Wedgewood 1930:38). Firth no. 64.01. AM registration no. E92060, 25.5 cm diameter (photo: Bonshek 2013).

two sacred spears (see footnote 21), a necklet[13] (Figure 22) and a shell trumpet.[14] The necklet and trumpet were from Mapusanga house of Kafika clan, not listed by Firth as a principal temple (1967a:199), but an important house: the trumpet was sounded in the 'Freeing of the Land' ceremony of the Work of the Gods (1967a:255–62) through which the island was formally made free from ritual work (Firth with McLean 1990:19).

Sacred objects were kept in sacred places with limited access, including temples, canoe houses and canoe house yards. The sacred adzes should have remained in the temple, of which successive chiefs assumed the role of keeper (along with that of medium between the gods, the ancestors and the people for whom he was responsible). Rather than the adzes being

---

13   Necklet (*kasoa*), Firth no. 64.1 (see Appendix 2) from Mapusanga house, and the property of the former Ariki Kafika. The item was possibly brought from Fiji (Wedgewood 1930:38).

14   *Pu tapu*, Firth no. 63.1 (see Appendix 2, not in AM collection). Obtained from Pa Tarairaki, it is described as a 'tapu specimen, unique' from Mapusanga house. It was 'cleaned annually and blown' (Wedgewood 1930:38).

passed between individuals, people moved around the adzes and their gods (Firth 1967a:62).

So how can the acquisition of such objects described by Firth as associated with the gods be understood? Were they really embodiments (*fakatino*) when Firth acquired them? It seems likely that by the time of Firth's first visit, Tikopia attitudes to such objects were changing as their new relationship with Christianity developed.

Prior to Firth's arrival in 1928, half of the island's population had embraced the introduced religion. While the Ariki Tafua had adopted the new god without forswearing the old, the abandonment of his ritual work must have had repercussions on the religious system that Firth described in 1928 as traditional. For example, during Firth's 1928–9 fieldwork not all of the four chiefs participated in the ritual he described as the most important ritual event in Tikopia, a proclamation of moral order: but this did not prevent him from giving an evocative account of its full recital.

> Of the many ritual formulae [...] none can have been more striking than
> that formerly recited as a public address or proclamation at Rarokoka.
> Not only was it picturesque in setting – the glade in the forest, the rising
> sun, the expectant silent crowd, and the towering figure of the chief of
> Tafua rolling out the phrases – but the speech itself was remarkable for
> its dignity and rhythm and for the moral code which it promulgated
> [...] it was not of frequent, irregular occurrence as occasion required,
> but a specific unique event, occurring once only in the year on the day
> fixed by the sequence of ceremonies in the seasonal cycle. Again, it had
> not the character of a personal extempore speech on some affair of the
> moment; both matter and phraseology were prescribed by tradition.
> Moreover, it had strong religious associations, and the chief who spoke
> was deemed to be the mouthpiece of the gods. In other words the
> sanction of the *fono* [public address[15]] in Rarokoka was not simply social
> and political, exercised through the authority of presiding chiefs, but
> was intensely religious as well, receiving its validity from its superhuman
> origin. It is essential to understand this in order to realize the force of
> the impression produced on the audience by this recital.
>
> (Firth 1967a:263–4)

---

15   'Make a public address; hold a public assembly for discussion (in long standing
     Tikopia tradition, continued into mod. times.' (Firth with Tuki 1985:129).

Firth's use of the past conditional tense does not disguise the fact that he never attended this particular ceremony, but neither does he emphasise that it had been dropped from the ritual cycle ten years previously, when the main participant, the Ariki Tafua, converted to Christianity. Similarly, the 'Dance to Quell the Wind', a rite which had also involved the Ariki Tafua, was modified so that it could still take place, with the people of sa Fangerere substituted for those of sa Tafua (Firth 1967a:305). Firth presented the rituals as he believed they would have been and indulged in reconstruction, despite his own opposition to historical speculation. He did have informants who had actually taken part in these events, but his presentation of their accounts undermines his claims to a scientific approach. The account of Rarokoka was recounted to Firth by the Ariki Tafua, who was indeed the appropriate person to hold such knowledge, but omitting the new religious allegiance of the chief involved does distance the ethnography from it historical context.

The removal of a sacred adze from the 'traditional' context described by Firth is a most significant indicator of changes occurring in Tikopia. One (Firth no. 67.1) was given to Firth secretly by Pa Tekaumata, a spirit medium (Firth 1970a:67), brother of the elder of Ngatotui, of Taumako clan (Firth 1967a:58n.1). The adze had been used in canoe ceremonies and by Firth's account was extremely sacred (Wedgewood 1930:39). It had been buried with others at the time the Ariki Tafua adopted Christianity, and was dug up from the house of Ngatotiu and given to Firth. The burial of the adzes 'nearly resulted in a fight through the anger of the other chiefs' (Firth 1967a:58), indicating that some were unhappy that Tafua had taken up Christianity. Giving one of the buried adzes to Firth clearly reflected the increasing influence of Christianity. Besides, the Christian chief the Ariki Tafua had already demystified the origin of the blades, explaining that they had been made by men who dived for the shell (Firth 1967a:59–60). That Firth could acquire the adze is a reflection of the adjustment of Tikopia society to Christianity. There are discrepancies between the 'traditional' way of life theorized in his early writings and his own descriptions of ceremonies. Hence the initiation ceremony of Munakina which, instead of lasting four days, was reduced to three after discussion between the chiefs and elders was initiated by the Christian mission teacher (Firth 1983:412–13).

Firth's acquisition of these and other embodiments illustrate that for at least some Tikopia, such objects had in some way changed. They either no longer contained the gods, in which case they had already moved out of the sphere of restricted objects, or they were felt by some to be dangerous, and therefore their removal, perhaps by burial, was advisable. Firth arrived on Tikopia during this process of change, not before it began. Indeed, much later, he commented that: 'For me the fate of paganism in Tikopia by 1929 was hardly an open question – the odds were on the continuing presence of the Mission from outside and on the local advance of Christianity.' (Firth 1970a:310).

Other objects had already changed their status. Again, in a much later publication, Firth noted that by 1928 stone-headed adzes appeared to belong to a liminal zone:

> stone blades have been regarded by the Tikopia as in the category of *toki tapu*. But their sacredness seems to have been by no means as intense as that of the major shell blades and their place in Tikopia ritual is not quite clear to me. In 1929 I was given these blades [see 86.1–86.7] as objects of great importance with some aura of *tapu*. But the fact that they could be handed over to me by chiefs indicated that they did not play an integral part in any major Tikopia ritual. (I saw none in use in any of the very many rites I attended).
>
> (Firth 1959a:154)[16]

However, Firth also documented other sacred artefacts which do not appear in the collection held at the museum. The *rarau kumete,* a ritual food container, a flat rectangular dish made of wood, is not represented in the collection. This item was used to hold food offerings to the Pu ma and was considered to be the 'special sacred property of Kafika', used during the 'Work of the Yam' (Firth 1967a:154, 233). A second type of bowl not represented in the collection is the *nafa*, described as a 'huge bowl shaped trough' (Firth 1965:227) that was used when large quantities of food were prepared: at such times a chief may lend another his *nafa* to assist in the

---

16   The British Museum holds a basalt adze head (Oc.7402) from Tikopia, acquired in 1871 from Sir Walter Calverley Trevelyan (1797-1879), Fellow of the Geological Society and the Royal Society of Edinburgh and a collector of art, antiquities, ethnographic and archaeological artefacts (British Museum online catalogue). This is the earliest object from Tikopia that I have found, but the circumstances of its collection are not known.

preparations. When considered the possessions of the *atua,* such as the Pu ma, they were sacred (Firth 1967a:292).

Firth discussed the co-existence of Christianity and Tikopia religion in *Rank and Religion* (1970a:304–32): he suggested that conversion was associated with political and kin relationships, resulting in selective omissions of elements of ritual rather than the total abandonment of Tikopia religious practices. The two religions were reconciled to some extent and conversion to Christianity by some Tikopia was pragmatic rather than doctrinal. But when the gods were 'put away', so too sacred objects were buried or given away. Firth suggests, in hindsight, that he was able to collect objects such as the sacred adzes in 1928–9 because of the peoples' conversion to Christianity (Firth 1959a:150).

While Firth was able to collect the kind of artefacts which still held power for some Tikopia, mediating relationships with the gods, the transfer to Firth of particular items betrays a growing ambivalence of some Tikopia towards the traditional religion as Christianity was adopted. Perhaps the sacred adzes were buried or given to Firth to dispose of dangerous powers. Perhaps they were disposed of because they had lost their power in Tikopia's changing society.

CHAPTER 5

Koroa (valued property)

Objects binding people

The ceremonial side of life in Tikopia is very strongly developed – and is especially associated with the consumption and exchange of food. Reciprocal presentation whether of food or other property is a characteristic feature of practically every ceremony and the intricate forms which it assumes in the more important aspects of life are well shown in the description of the system of gifts and exchange connected with death and mourning.

(Excerpt from a letter from Firth, dated 17 October 1928, written in the first months of his fieldwork on Tikopia to Radcliffe-Brown at the University of Sydney, LSE Firth 7.10.4)

Scarcely a day passes without baskets of food being carried from one village to another across the island in payment of some obligation incurred in connection with the command of a chief, the visiting of a new baby, sub-incision, a boy's first torch-light fishing, a marriage, a death, a recovery from illness or the like, and months may elapse before all the customary usages are fulfilled. Another prominent feature of the economic life is the exchange of property, in particular, rolls of kafa *(sinnet),* menga *(pandanus leaf mats) and* mami *of* fakamaru *bark cloth which mark the performance of certain ceremonies. In connection with funeral rights, indeed, as many as eight different sets of gifts may have to be made, each, of course, involving a counter-gift; on these, as on many other occasions, the principal people concerned are the mother's brothers of the chief actor, or on the other hand his sister's sons.*

(Firth 1930b:109)

While the sacred objects discussed in Chapter 4 mediated relationships between people and the gods, the objects discussed in this chapter were used to initiate, maintain and consolidate relationships between people, often in ceremonial activities. In terms of the expected movement of objects, their 'life cycle', such objects were destined to move from one person to another (or one group to another) as part of their 'social life'. They included *maro* (bundles of mats and barkcloth which constituted ceremonial gifts to people as well as to the gods), fish-hooks, coils of plaited rope made from coconut fibre, wooden bowls, paddles and wooden containers for cooking turmeric. These objects had significances in addition to their immediate uses for catching fish, propelling canoes or containing food. Such objects were recognized by Tikopia people as valued property (*koroa*). Failure to exchange these objects appropriately (to move outside or beyond the bounds of what was expected) may have had social consequences (Firth 1983:422–3).

This chapter investigates some of these types of objects, which I refer to as objects that bind people together. Details of the objects in Firth's collection are provided in the footnotes, which may be passed over by readers unconcerned with the particular items. Firth and Tuki's (1985) dictionary definitions for a selection of object types referred to in this chapter follow immediately below. This precedes a description of object types with reference to the individual objects in Firth's collection. It will become evident that there is some overlapping of meanings in some of the terms.

> *fakamarū* – Barkcloth prepared from inner cortex (bast) of tree (*rakau fakamarū* or *māmi*) in common cultivation. Waist garment for men, made of barkcloth.
>
> *fakasiki* – Insert overlaying strips, usually red material, as ornamental pattern in *kie* mat. Complete (Firth with Tuki 1985:82, 264, 266).
>
> *kafu* – Blanket; sheet (traditionally) of barkcloth.
>
> *koroa* – Goods; property; valued object; treasure. Gen. category of non-food items in contrast to *kai*, food.
>
> *māmi* – Barkcloth sheet used for bedding, woman's skirt, and formal gift; contrasted in rectangular shape with long narrow *fakamarū* of man's girdle, also used for formal presentation but of lesser value.
>
> *maro*[a] – Waistcloth, traditionally of barkcloth, used normally of male girdle round waist, passed through legs, with large flap hanging down in front.

maro[b] – Formal item of presentation or reciprocity in exchange, consisting of one or more pieces of barkcloth (*fakamarū* or *mami* according to context) and/or pandanus mat(s) [*menga*] (with modern addition of substitute of calico or other machine-woven cloth).

Traditional offering to gods and ancestors, commonly associated with kava rite.

maro[c] – Roll; bolt of cloth (perhaps cognate with *maro*[a]; held that analogy with pile of barkcloth for ritual presentation).

marotafi – Barkcloth dyed (*maro tafi*) an orange colour with turmeric, worn especially by men on formal traditional occasions as status symbol, but not completely restricted to this. In traditional ritual used especially as symbol of Atua i Kafika.

mēnga – Sleeping mat plaited from pandanus leaf strips; used also as a major ritual present e.g. at funeral, marriage etc. exchanges.

Collective term for marriage gifts from bride's kin to groom's kin, including barkcloth, but with *matua mēnga* [large mats, "principal mats] as major item.

mēnga fakasikimero – *Mēnga* decorated with a coloured band on one or two edges.

mero – the colour red (Firth with Tuki 1985:82, 264, 266).

pa atu – Bonito lure, hook, usually of clam shell shank, turtle shell barb, 'whisker' of hibiscus fibre [...] Shell shank alone (*raurau pa*) often worn traditionally by men as neck ornament. With barb attached (*pa tu manga*) usually an ornament only of men of rank [...] Note: bonito hook with barb traditionally a property of great value, a prime compensatory gift [...] bonito hook and sinnet cord are equivalent to a canoe; the bonito hook with standing barb and the sinnet cord, great are their value, the property of chiefs alone. (1985:324)

pa tu manga – See *pa atu*.

rāroa – Woman's skirt, traditionally of barkcloth sheet.

raurau pa – See *pa atu*.

Objects as ceremonial offerings

Maro were gifts to gods on ritual occasions and also a symbol of the female gods (Wedgewood 1930:42). A *maro*[1] comprised square barkcloth sheets (*mami*)[2] and plaited pandanus mats (*menga*),[3] both items made by women and folded in special ways (Firth 1983:418; Wedgewood 1930:49). Individual barkcloth sheets were worn as clothing by men (*fakamaru*)[4] and women

---

1   Firth collected three ceremonial bundles (*maro*), 82.1–3. Item 82.1 was used
     as an offering to the canoe 'gods' and included *mami* (barkcloth squares)
     and *marotafi* (barkcloth dyed with turmeric). It was given to Firth by Pa
     Nukurenga. Bundle 82.2 consisted of seven *fakamaru* (men's waist cloths) and
     one *marotafi* (barkcloth dyed with turmeric). One of the *fakamaru* is now held
     at the Macleay Museum, University of Sydney (86.3). Bundle 82.3 consisted of
     five *fakamaru* (see Appendix 2, Wedgewood List 1930:49).

2   Barkcloth was made from the inner bark of the tree, *Antiaris toxicaria* (Firth
     with Tuki 1985:222). Firth collected 21 *mami*, individual barkcloth squares,
     acquired in five bundles containing 4 items (73.2–6) and 1 single item (73.1, see
     Appendix 2). It is not possible to match up the individual cloths in the collection
     with the cloth bundles listed in Firth's specimen list (Firth 1928): the individual
     components of the each bundle have been split up and the individual *mami*
     numbered separately. However, Firth's specimen list (see Appendices 1 and 3)
     records that he received four pieces as gifts from: Rakeitino, Pa Tekaumata,
     Ellison Turgatok ('a g[oo]d specimen' Firth specimen list no. 28), Pa Raro Akau.
     One *mami* was from Pa Motuangi, but it is not stated whether this was a gift
     or part of an exchange. One other was exchanged with Pa Nuku nefu for five
     fish-hooks and two pipes.

3   Firth collected twenty-nine *menga*, 75.1–29, some plain and some decorated.
     'Mats of pandanus, used primarily for sleeping on, but also as a main article
     of ceremonial exchange. Normally decorated with a simple coloured band
     along either edge, then termed *menga fakasikimero*.' (Wedgewood 1930:44;
     see Appendix 2). Firth's specimen list lists woven pandanus mats (*menga*),
     turmeric dyed barkcloths (*marotafi*), and men's barkcloth waist garments
     (*fakamaru*) as purchased from the Ariki Tafua for three pieces of calico and
     one pocket knife.

4   There are three bundles of *fakamaru* in the collection (72.1–3), which when
     given on ceremonial occasions are 'folded in special ways and termed *maro*'
     (see footnote 32 and Appendix 2; Wedgewood 1930:41).

(*raroa*)[5] and were also used as blankets (*kafu*)[6] (Wedgewood 1930:42; Firth also refers to blankets as *mami*, 1965:294). All are distinguished by their size and shape, and the appropriate cloth was given to a male or female god. Significant high-ranking gods were given turmeric-dyed cloth (*marotafi*).[7] *Maro* were given at funerals, marriages and initiations (see Figure 13)as well as for payment of 'specialist services' such as the composition of songs (Firth 1965:294; Firth with McLean 1990:68; Firth with Tuki 1985:264).

Generosity was displayed by the number of *maro* presented: the quality of individual items and combinations of mats and barkcloth might vary (Firth 1983:416ff.). A return gift was usually made (termed *te fakapenu* or *te penu*). During the presentation of *maro* as part of a boy's initiation ceremony, mats were announced with the name of the woman giving them, while barkcloth were announced with the name of the man giving them (Firth 1983:410–11). Mats were ranked in importance, from *menga*, a plain mat,[8] followed by *menga fakasikimero*,[9] decorated with a red border, to *taka furinga*, which were larger in size and used at funerals as well as initiations

---

5   *Raroa* are listed with *mami* in Wedgewood's list (73), see Appendix 2.

6   *Kafu* are listed with *mami* in Wedgewood's list (73), see Appendix 2.

7   There are two *marotafi* in the collection, 83.1 and 2, see Appendix 2.

8   Firth collected seven undecorated *menga*, see Firth no. 75 in Appendix 2. No. 75.9 (not in AM collection) was a 'very large example, made by Nau Porima, presented to paito i Nukufuti as gift to *tuatina* (mother's brother) on incision of the eldest son in Porima' (Wedgewood 1930:44–5). Five *menga* are also listed as 'purchased' from Pa Avakofe, the Ariki Tafua, Pa Rat and Kasumata. One was given as a gift from Ellison Turgatok (see Appendices 1 and 3).

9   Firth collected twenty-two *menga fakasikimero*, 75.1–4; 75.7–8; 75.10–17; 75.19–21; 75.23–4; 75.26–8. These mats were usually decorated with a coloured band along either edge of the mat (Wedgewood 1930:44). The word *mero* is the term for red, the colour of the edging (Firth with Tuki 1985:266), while *fakasiki* has two meanings: first, 'to insert overlaying strips, usu [*sic*] red material, as ornamental pattern in *kie* mat [the *kie* is a mat which is worn, and not used in exchange]. *Fakasiki mero* – red border strips' as well as 'Complete ... *Fakasiki te raranga a nga atua* – put the final decoration on the plaiting/ complete the plaiting of the gods i.e. complete the ritual cycle' (Firth with Tuki 1985:82). Firth no. 75.10 was used as a bed mat at incision ceremony; 75.11 was presented by Pa Fenuatara; 75.13 was used as a sleeping mat (see Appendix 2).

(Firth collected two, see Firth 1983:416–17).[10] Principal mats (*matoa menga*) and pillows (*urunga*, see below) were presented at marriages (Firth 1983:460–1). The former are not represented in Firth's collection.

Maro were indispensable items of exchange and Firth left Tikopia with three bundles: one of them given to him at a young boy's initiation and two, which had also been used in ceremonial exchange, acquired from prominent Christians, the Ariki Tafua[11] and Ellison Turgatok, the Melanesian Mission teacher.[12]

Firth says nothing about the significance of mat-making for women's roles in Tikopia, but the status of fine mats elsewhere in Polynesia suggests that he may have overlooked their importance. He does comment on the status of women as follows: 'Since there is mutual deference between husband and wife, marriage by explicit social custom means freedom not servitude for [a woman].' (Firth 1983:434, 1978). As the exchange of mats played an important part in relationships between households, we may suppose that mat-making contributed to maintaining the status of married women in Tikopia.

Other objects that formed part of formalized exchanges included wooden bowls (*kumete*, Figure 23), sinnet rope (*kafa*), paddles (*foe*) and

---

10   Firth received two *taka furinga* before he left Tikopia. They were presented to him by the households of the Ariki Kafika and Fenuafuti; these houses had received them at the initiation ceremony of a boy of the Porima family, in return for their services as cooks. They were made by Nau Porima (Firth 1983:417). These mats may possibly be identified as Firth nos. 75.9 and 75.10 (Wedgewood 1930:44, see Appendix 2).

11   According to Firth's specimen list (1928) he purchased one bundle of ten items (including *menga, marotafi* and *fakamaru*) from the Ariki Tafua on 4 November 1928 for three lengths of white calico and one pocket knife.

12   Given to Firth by Ellison on 13 August 1928, at the *punga umu* 'firing of the ovens' of a boy's initiation (Firth 1928, 1983:394). Firth noted the rite served the role of 'social integration' (Firth with Tuki 1985:365).

bonito hooks (*pa tu manga*). Wooden bowls (*kumete*)[13] in addition to being used for daily household tasks (preparing and presenting food, coconut cream, mud, lime and turmeric, see Wedgewood 1930:1) were exchanged at marriages and deaths, and were presented as 'placating gifts' (*te malai*). For example, if a woman had been snatched from her father's family for marriage, the next day the family of the 'abductor' presented a wooden bowl and sinnet cord to the senior man of the woman's family. If the woman was from a chiefly family a bonito hook with a turtle-shell barb (*pa tu manga*, Figure 24) was also sent, sometimes with a paddle. The presenters had to crawl to the woman's family in a show of humility.

---

13 Firth collected eighteen bowls 1.1–18. Eleven of these were 'purchased' from named individuals. See Firth's Specimen List (Appendix 1): from Pa Nukuomanu, in exchange for one piece of white calico; another exchanged for eleven fish-hooks; Firth number 1.18 from Paito Faranga noa in exchange for twelve fish-hooks; one from Pa Rangitisa, in exchange for five fish-hooks and two pipes; one from Rangi rikoi, in exchange for one piece of white calico; Firth no. 1.15 from Pa Niu kapu, a bowl and staff (*tokotoko*), in exchange for one axe; the bowl was noted as 'good, old named after maker Pu rangi Tisa'. Firth no. 1.10, a bowl for *roroi*, from Pa Rangi furi, in exchange for one plane iron. Firth no. 1.9, a new bowl for *roroi*, also from Pa Rangi furi, in exchange for one plane iron; from Ariki Mata in exchange for one piece of red calico and six fish-hooks; and from Titus in exchange for one piece of red calico and three fish-hooks. One was acquired in exchange for fifteen fish-hooks (Firth 1928).

Of the eighteen bowls collected by Firth twelve (67 per cent) or possibly thirteen (72 per cent) were purchased by him. The following bowls were indicated as 'from' the listed donors, and I have interpreted this as a gift: Firth no. 1.1 from Paito I Oliki, carved with steel tools by Ariki Kafika several generations ago and given from Kafika clan to Taumako as part of *malai* marriage gift for a woman from the Taumako clan, only two examples made (Wedgewood 1930:1–2). Firth no. 1.2 from Pa Rangimaseke (Wedgewood 1930:1–2). Firth no. 1.7 from Pu Resiake (Wedgewood 1930:1–2). Firth no. 1.11 from Ariki Tafua, old specimen Pu Resiake (could be purchase no. 115 or even 131, more likely the former, which is listed as 'good' and 'old' – Wedgewood 1930:1–2). Firth no. 1.12, turmeric- making bowl, from Pa Paiu. Firth no. 1.16 from Pa Mukava (Firth 1928; Wedgewood 1930:1–2). The remaining two bowls are not identified with a donor or purchaser (see Appendix 2).

Figure 23 'Kumete for making turmeric; ordinary small, from Pa Mūkave'
(Wedgewood 1930:2). Firth no. 1.16. AM registration no. E84297, 54 cm long, 13 cm
high, 6 cm at widest point (photo: Paul Ovenden, Australian Museum).

In acquiring bowls for the collection, Firth drew upon the resources of
a number of important and high-ranking men.[14] The gift of a bowl made
or possessed by a chief would have imbued the item with a greater status,
stemming from the transfer of *mana* from the chief to the bowl. A bowl
such as Firth no. 1.1 (AM reg. no. E84300), made by the Ariki Kafika several
generations ago and given to Firth by the house of Paito i Oliki, would have
been a significant gift. Bowls were prized possessions, which might be
destroyed at a man's death if the deceased had no canoes (Firth 1965:346).

Sinnet rope (*kafa*) of soaked, beaten and plaited coconut fibre
(Wedgewood 1930:24) was made by men and used by them in house-

---

14   These included Pa Nukuomanu of Kafika clan; Pa Rangifuri, one of Firth's
bond friends and a son of the Ariki Tafua; from the Taumako clan, Pa Rangitsa
was an important man of rank; as was Pa Rangirikoi, a ritual elder of Taumako
and a very old, much-respected man who had travelled to 'the lands of the
white man'. Pa Rangimaseke of Kafika clan was heir to the elder, Pa Tavi, one of
the ritually privileged of the Kafika clan who was among the party to the 'Work
of Somosomo' (Firth 1965:284, 1967a:385, 393, 1967c:110, 1983:62).

building and to make fishing nets and lines.[15] Ordinary rope was made of a three-ply twist; a stronger, more rounded rope was produced with four ply (termed *matai kafa*). One coil of sinnet between three to six metres long could take up to five to six weeks to make and around six coils were kept to hand for ceremonial exchange (Firth 1965:252). Sinnet, made by an expert for shark-fishing lines and nooses (*maia noa mango*),[16] was especially valuable and generally kept only by chiefly families (Firth 1965:252). A finer quality sinnet was also used for men's belts (*tautu*),[17] and in former times these had been worn during warfare. If a man caught a shark with new sinnet which had been given to him, he was obliged to take the shark to the maker of the sinnet (unless he preferred to give it to a chief, see Chapter 4). 'Such a gift is called a *sunusunu o a kafa*; it is a kind of celebration of the efficacy of the tackle in doing its work.' (Firth 1965:283). The efficacy of the sinnet was credited to its maker.

Generally coils of sinnet were given as return gifts (*fakapenu*), although Firth noted that 'nowadays' fish-hooks or a pipe were also used (Firth 1965:373, 1983:424). While Tikopia told Firth that there was some choice as to whether a return gift was required, Firth noted that a failure to give the *fakapenu* would have resulted in a loss of reputation (Firth 1983:422–3). When exchanged one for another 'coils of sinnet are carefully

---

15   Firth collected fourteen examples of *kafa*: two are noted as being of poor quality, 33.9 and 33.10. Another two items were collected to illustrate the manufacturing technique (33.13) and the raw material the rope was made out of, *rau rino* (AM no. E84678). The former was probably given to Firth by Clement (Firth 1928: no. 18), who also gave Firth a coil of sinnet (Firth 1928: no. 17). The latter was from Pa Motuangi (Wedgewood 1930:24). In addition, another coil was given to Firth by Ellison Turgatok, the mission teacher from the Banks Islands, along with two paddles as a gift at his son's *punga umu*, 'kindling of ovens'. Other types of rope were also made using hibiscus fibre, *matai fau* and the inner bark of a plant called *suka* (*Gnetum gnemon*) which was called *matai kari suka* (Firth with Tuki 1985:249).

16   Firth collected three shark nooses: nos. 40.1–3 (see Appendix 2; Wedgewood 1930:26).

17   Firth collected six *tautu*: 40.4–9 (see Appendix 2). Only one donor is named, Pa Ranigfuri, Firth no. 40.9: this is probably item no. 228 on the purchase list (Appendix 3), a belt given to Firth in exchange for fifteen fish-hooks (Firth 1928).

Figure 24   Pa tu manga. Fish-hook necklace, with tortoiseshell barb, from the Ariki Kafika. Firth no. 44.5, 9.5 cm long, 1.7 cm wide. AM registration no. E59459-5 (photo: Paul Ovenden, Australian Museum).

matched. The recipient of one goes to his house, takes down his bundle, and selects from it that coil which is most nearly the same to the one he has received' (Firth 1965:252). Sinnet, along with a bowl, was given to Firth by Pa Rangifuri, the eldest son and heir to the Ariki Tafua who had led the mass conversion of the Tafua clan to Christianity before Firth's arrival.

Bonito-fishing hooks, *pa atu* and *pa tu manga*, were considered significant: both were composite hooks (comprising separate shank and barb) used for fishing and also in ceremonial presentations. Ordinarily the *pa atu* was made entirely of pearl-shell while the *pa tu manga* had a barb

made from turtle-shell or whalebone with a pearl-shell shank.[18] Firth's
purchase information (Firth 1928, no. 102) notes that the *pa atu* was *koroa
ariki*, meaning 'property of the chiefs or appropriate for presentation to
chiefs' (Firth and Tuki 1985:194; see Figure 24).[19] *Pa tu manga* were gifts
given to chiefs to appease offenses against them (Firth 1952a; Wedgewood
1930) and thus were placed outside of general circulation. *Pa tu manga*
were hung on the ear lobe of their dead owner and buried with him. They
retained their close association with the chiefs even if given to someone
else:

> If a commoner has a good tree for a canoe growing on his land [...] and
> a chief desires it, the man may be unwilling to part with it. But if the
> chief presents him with a bonito-hook his objection vanishes. I was told
> that he will hold the hook among his treasures, but he will not term it
> his; it is held as 'the property of the chief'. When the time comes that he
> goes to 'the hearings of the chiefs', an important ceremony such as the
> death of the chief and the succession of his heir, he takes the bonito-
> hook and presents it to the new ruler. It is not handed over to another
> commoner.
>
> (Firth 1965:338–9)

In what Firth terms 'exceptional circumstances' a person could obtain
a canoe with the presentation of a *pa tu manga* and a coil of shark line,
which confirms their high status, as primary use rights of canoes normally
lay with chiefs, high-ranking people or elders (Firth 1965:339).

---

18   Firth's collection list (Wedgewood 1930:29) does not distinguish *pa atu* from
     pa tu manga by name. However, of the thirteen *pa atu* Firth collected, five
     have turtle-shell barbs and can be understood to be *pa tu manga* and therefore
     highly valuable. A further five are stated to have 'bone' barbs. The shank itself
     is referred to as *pa* and was usually made of clam shell, with a lure made of
     hibiscus fibre (Firth 1928; Firth with Tuki 1985:324; Wedgewood 1930:29–30).
     Firth collected 13 *pa atu* nos. 44.1–13. No. 44.1 was acquired from Pa Rarovi,
     an elder of Kafika; 44.4 from the Ariki Fangarere and which shows the 'correct
     lashing'; 44.5 from the Ariki Kafika; 44.9 from Pa Motuata of Taumako clan
     (see Appendix 2 and Wedgewood 1930:29–30).

19   Firth collection no. 44.13.

Both the Ariki Kafika, the foremost chief of Tikopia, and the Ariki Fangarere, the fourth-ranked chief, gave *pa tu manga* to Firth. He acquired another from Pa Rarovi, the highest-ranking of the Ariki Kafika's principal elders, who had to carry the 'sacred things' during the ritual of the sacred canoes (Firth 1967a:67). The implication is that they accorded Firth high status. Other *pa atu* were given to Firth by Pa Porima, a ritual elder of Kafika clan (Firth 1983:176–7); by Pa Vainunu, an important 'brother' of Ariki Kafika; and by Pae Sao, a good friend of Pa Porima, a man of high status and a knowledgeable informant of Firth's (Firth 1983:41).

The 'diplomatic' associations of the bonito hook were reflected in the presentation of a *pa tu manga* to Queen Elizabeth II in 1966: this was an acknowledgement of her status through *arofa*, a 'material token, gift, of sympathy, loyalty; expression of obligation' after a dispute between the Tikopia chiefs and the British Solomon Islands government (Feinberg 1981:69; Firth 1969:364).

Lastly, paddles (*foe*), used for sailing in open seas, were also used as ceremonial gifts (Wedgewood 1930:13), for instance at a boy's initiation ceremony (Firth 1983:380ff.).[20] Two of the paddles in the Firth collection were acquired from Pa Pangisi, the mission teacher from the Banks Island (also known as Ellison Turgatok).

The social fields in which such artefacts moved reflected the high value attributed to them. The objects themselves were not regarded as equivalent to one another, as Firth found when he pressed his informant Pa Rangifuri to make a comparative statement on the value of specific items (Firth 1965:338). Pa Rangifuri, the eldest son of the Christian Ariki Tafua, employed the terms *mafa*, 'weighty', and *mama*, 'light', in discussing the comparative sanctity of ritual formulae, types of ceremonial activity and the names of gods. Objects too were 'light' or 'weighty'. 'Weighty' objects included bonito hooks, sinnet cord used for catching sharks, bowls and

---

20   Firth collected four paddles, 11.1–4. Two of these (11.1 and 11.3) were given to Firth and had been used as a gift on the incision of a boy named John Munakina, the son of Pa Pangisi, the Motlav teacher on Tikopia who had married a 'well-connected' woman of Taumako clan (Firth 1983:47, 393). The paddles were a gift to the boy's mother's brother. A second pair of paddles (probably 11.2 and 11.3), were made by Philip Seramata, who was known as Pa Maneva upon his marriage, and were a gift to Firth from Ellison Turgatok (Wedgewood 1930:13; Appendix 2).

spears; 'light' ones included arrows, bows and pandanus mats. Quoting his informant, Pa Rangifuri, Firth stated:

> The mat and the bonito-hook are not equivalent; they are not exchangeable. The mat is somewhat heavy (*mamafa*), but the bonito-hook, it is alone, in the forefront. And the sinnet for the shark-hook is next to the bonito-hook, while next to it is the mat. The mat and the sinnet (of ordinary type) are reciprocally equivalent.
>
> (Firth 1965:338).

'Weighty' and 'light' were ritual values, associated with the chiefs and gods.

Tauarofa: objects as heirlooms

Certain objects were worn or stored as material connections with the dead. If not buried with the deceased, a man's sinnet cord, bonito-hook necklaces, betel mortars and headrests might become family heirlooms (*tauarofa*). Other objects, such as mats, sinnet cord, barkcloth, paddles, bowls, fish-hooks and tobacco might have been distributed through ritual payments to the deceased's mother's family and other mourners: some objects went to his daughters in other households and their children.

In commenting on his own expectations concerning his inheritance from his father, Pa Fenuatara said: 'the person himself will be dead, but he is as one living constantly in the presence of his sons through his property that is in the possession of them and their children' (Firth 1983:168). Thus 'heirloom' objects were understood to maintain connections between people and their deceased relatives.

The personal nature of this connection is seen in the treatment of headrests after the owner's death. While women slept on soft barkcloth pillows, men used wooden headrests (*urunga*)[21] that took two forms: 'chiefly' headrests, generally made by expert craftsmen and distinguished by the projecting 'wings' that lay to either side (Figure 8); and 'non-chiefly' headrests which took a variety of shapes (for example, see Firth 1960b; Figures 10 and 25). Firth also suggested that there was a relationship between the number of feet on headrests, coconut-grating stools (*rakau saro niu*)[22] and kava bowls (*tau kava*),[23] as well as between their heights from the ground, which might be linked to ritual and social status (Firth 1973b:40–1).

Firth commented that the Tikopia invested objects such as headrests 'with strong symbolic value' (Firth 1973b:31).

> But principally [the headrest] has a peculiar association with its owner's personality since it pillows his head, the most important part of the body, which it is forbidden to a man's children to touch. Though not taboo, the headrest of a householder ordinarily is handled by others with discretion, as a piece of his private property. As a consequence of this, a man's headrest tends to be one of the items of his property most

---

21   Firth collected thirty-eight headrests, 4.1–38. They were made of a hardwood, *fetau, Calophyllum inophyllum*, as well as softwoods such as breadfruit, *afatea, Plumeria poumuri* (Firth 1973b:33). *Urunga* associated with an individual's name are: Firth nos. 4.1, Pae Sao's first piece of woodwork; 4.2, given to Firth by Pa Ngatitiu; 4.3, given to him by Pa Niukapu; 4.4, given by Pa Maniva; 4.5, made by Pa Fangatau in about 1890; 4.6, given by Paito i Veterei; 4.7, made by Pa Rangifuri; 4.8, made by Pa Avakofe and mended by Pa Motuata; 4.10 and 4.19, given by Mairunga; 4.12 and 4.16, given by Pa Fenua tara; 4.17, from Paito Tanimua; 4.18, from Pa Vae Toka; 4.20, given by Pa Taunga; 4.22, from Paito Fetauta; 4.25, from Pa Fenua fara; 4.26, acquired from Ti Forau; 4.27, from Rongo Taono; 4.29, from Pa Fare ata; 4.30, from the Samoan family; 4.31, made by the father of Pu rangi rikoi (who was 'about' seventy years old); 4.32, from Pa Niu Kaso; 4.34, from Kavarauniu; 4.37, from Paito Fetauta; 4.38, from Pa te Kaumata (Wedgewood 1930:5–7; Appendix 2).

22   Firth collected three *rakau saro niu*, nos. 5.1–3 (Wedgewood 1930:8, see Appendix 2).

23   Firth collected three *kava* bowls; nos. 2.1–3. 2.1 was obtained from Pae Sao, *Pure* of Ariki Tafua and had been 'in his family for generations'; 2.3 was from Pa Niu Kapu (Wedgewood 1930:3, Appendix 2).

Figure 25 Headrests, used for sleeping and resting. Left: Firth no. 4.31 'old specimen cut by father of Pu rangi rikoi, (the latter being about seventy years old)' (Wedgewood 1928:6). AM Registration no. E84029, 25 cm at widest point, 14.5 cm high. Right: Firth no. 4.12, 'common type; with bulbous stand, given by Pa Fenua tara, cross on foot purely decorative he is not a Christian' (Wedgewood 1928:5). AM registration no. E84024, 18 cm high, 20 cm wide (photo: Paul Ovenden, Australian Museum).

> commonly buried with him. A headrest is the death property of this land and when a man dies, he is pillowed upon it. After a man has slept constantly upon it, when he is put into the ground, his head laid upon it, then he is wrapped up and buried.
>
> (Firth 1973b:36)

Arguments could ensue about who would inherit a headrest if it was not buried with the owner (Firth 1973b:36). But sometimes

> after a man's death his son or daughter may decide to have his wooden headrest as a neck ornament. It is slung round the neck and worn on the back – much as a tooth is ordinarily kept as a relic. It is usually the woman who does this. When she dies she may direct that the headrest shall be buried with her, in order that her father may see that it comes with her on her arrival into the spirit world.
>
> (Firth 1983:167–8)

While Firth was on Tikopia the men of the Avakofe lineage had a special reputation for their woodworking, which extended to the manufacture of wooden bowls and canoe building (Firth 1973b:29).[24] Some objects therefore carried the history not only of the owner, but also of the maker. Major items such as canoes and bowls 'can have their maker identified not only by those who commissioned the work, but also by other people at large' (ibid.). Further, '[t]he construction of such important objects is a matter of social interest and consequently the maker is borne in memory' (ibid.). Sinnet belts, clubs, spears and body ornaments also held specific histories, which were known. Firth called these 'items of named personal authorship.'[25] Such objects were not given away lightly (Firth 1983:167–8).

Betel-nut mortars could also become heirlooms or be buried with their owners (ibid.). Other objects in Firth's collection which might be treated as heirlooms were flasks (*umu renga*) used for cooking and storing turmeric (see Figure 26).[26] Like the bowls and headrests, they were also given titles (Firth 1967a:445). Turmeric was used as an aromatic dye: it was given in ceremonial exchanges; on ritual occasions it was smeared on objects and on the body; it was called the property of the chiefs and was buried with them at death. Processing turmeric was part of the Work of the Gods and so was concealed from ordinary people. In addition to the wooden flasks, the processing of turmeric required graters[27] and needles (*sau*)[28]

---

24 Firth no. 4.8 was made by Pa Avakofe (Wedgewood 1930:5).

25 Songs and string figures also fell into this category.

26 These containers, also referred to as *taonga* (Wedgewood 1930:9), usually had a notched design on them. According to Firth 'workmanship of these varies considerably and specimens are valued by the natives according to the volume and finish of their interior. Certain men are noted craftsmen in making these cylinders.' (Wedgewood 1930:9). Firth collected seven; 7.2, 7.3 and 7.5 are listed as noteworthy in quality. Four of the *renga* were from Tafua men: 7.1 from Paito i Marangaone; 7.5 from Pa Nukufuri; 7.6 from Pa Mesara; and 7.7 from the Ariki Tafua (Wedgewood 1930:9; Appendix 2).

27 Firth collected three turmeric graters, 21.1–3: 21.1 was from Paito i Fetu; 21.3 had belonged to the family of the Ariki Tafua for 'several generations' and had new lashings put on, and was given to Firth by Pa Rangifuri (Wedgewood 1930:20; Appendix 2).

28 Firth collected one *sau*, 62.1, an 'old specimen' made from whale bone (Wedgewood 1930:38; Appendix 2).

Figure 26 Cylinder for cooking turmeric (umu renga) or storage (taonga). 'Fine specimen, both in finish and design. It carries renga as the natives say' (Wedgewood 1930:9). Firth no. 7.3. AM registration no. E84797, 28 cm high; 12.5 cm diameter (photo: Paul Ovenden, Australian Museum).

to sew bags[29] used to hold and filter the turmeric (Firth 1967a:417–64; Wedgewood 1930:26). As well as equipment Firth also collected samples of turmeric (*renga*).[30]

---

29 Firth collected three *kaka*, 77.1 to 77.4. 77.3 was from the Ariki Tafua (Wedgewood 1930:46; Appendix 2).

30 Firth collected four samples of *renga*, 38.1 to 38.4. These were acquired from the Ariki Tafua, Firth no. 38.1; Pa Korokoro, 38.2; Pae Sao 38.3; and from the Ariki Tafua, 38.4 which was described as a 'large specimen, generally reserved for chiefs' (Wedgewood 1930:26; Appendix 2).

Figure 27   'Hair circlet, fau, worn by women, made of hair of male relatives, esp[ecially] husband, brother or father. Cherished as an heirloom (tauarofa).' (Wedgewood 1928:25). Firth no. 34.01. AM registration no. E.84697, 21.5 cm diameter (photo: Bonshek 2013).

Clam-shell bead necklaces (*rei*), which were also noted as rare, were heirlooms particularly associated with chiefs, although they were no longer made at the time of Firth's fieldwork in 1928–9 (Firth 1951:131). Firth received several as gifts from the Ariki Taumako and other men of rank (ibid.).[31] Hair too was a strong memento of those who had died: the hair of a deceased father, husband or brother might be woven into a headband (*fau*)[32] and worn by a bereaved woman as a cherished heirloom (Figure 27, E84697; in Figure 6 the widow Mane wears a *fau* – she also placed her husband's headrest in front of her when I suggested taking her photograph).

Firth's principal informants were from chiefly families and/or were elders, but among them he singled out his particular friendship with Pa

---

31   Firth collected six groups of *rei*, 53.1–6. One of these, Firth no. 53.1 was obtained from the Ariki Taumako; 53.2 was obtained from Pa Nukura; 53.4 was from Pa Siamano (Wedgewood 1930:35; Appendix 2).

32   Firth collected one, 34.1 (Wedgewood 1930:25; Appendix 2).

Figure 28 'A *Tikopia Aristocrat. Pa Fenuatara, heir to the chieftainship of Kafika, and an exceptionally intelligent man. He is here in dance array, with loose hair and fringed cordyline leaf and seaweed circlets at neck and brow'. (Firth 1983: facing title page, image held in the London School of Economics, courtesy of Hugh Firth).*

Figure 29 'A *token of filial sentiment. Pa Rangifuri wearing a tooth of his father,*
the Ariki Tafua.' (Firth 1983:256, image held in the London School of Economics,
courtesy of Hugh Firth).

Fenuatara (Figure 28), the eldest son of the Ariki Kafika. They entered into a formalized 'bond friendship' requiring mutual aid and assistance in all manner of things from the exchange of objects to support in dealings with other people (Firth 1936a). 'Our relationship followed a well-known Tikopia pattern that a man of rank should receive a visitor from abroad and bind him to himself in ties of friendship.' (Firth 1960a:10). This allowed Pa Fenuatara to benefit from any gifts the stranger brought with him, from prestige due to the novelty of the visitor and to access to knowledge from outside Tikopia. Over the period of Firth's fieldwork, Pa Fenuatara became a key informant.

> Scientifically and professionally, in general, I was much indebted to him for a great mass of information about Tikopia culture and many special insights into Tikopia custom [he was] prominent in general economic life [...] under the aegis of his father, the Ariki Kafika, he acted as senior executive in the affairs of the Kafika lineage, and as a leader in the affairs of his clan.
>
> (Firth 1960a:3–4)

Firth also had a bond friendship with Pa Rangifuri of Tafua (Figure 29), but he describes this as having a greater formality to it than his relationship with Pa Fenuatara. These and other friendships must have played a part in the acquisition of his collection, through exchanges similar to those in which objects changed hands among the Tikopia themselves. A list of all the people Firth named as giving or selling objects to him is given in Appendix 3.

Objects that bind and include

Many items in Firth's collection are associated with formal exchange activities.[33] Objects such as bowls, paddles, sinnet rope, barkcloth and mats, including *maro*, all circulated between groups of people. The fish-hooks moved between high-ranking men and only occasionally left this circle. The gift of these objects to Firth was consistent with their local use, to initiate, maintain and further relationships and repay services rendered, thus formally incorporating Firth into Tikopia society. As Firth (1983:8–9;

---

33 Other objects in the collection not discussed in this chapter are listed in Appendix 2.

Institut für den Wissenschaftichen Film 1993) tells us, he did not merely observe the activities he recorded, but participated in them (after an initial period of exclusion). This, I suggest, is how he acquired most of the objects now in the collection.

These objects that bind people together are different to those described as 'embodiments' (*fakatino*) in Chapter 4, above. The sacred adzes, weapons and other objects representing the gods were kept in temples and were not to be circulated: these objects were cared for by successive generations of chiefs whose status they legitimized. Giving them away reflected a departure of some significance from pre-Christian religious practices.

Both Christian and non-Christian donors are represented in the collection. The objects described as embodiments were possibly being disposed of because of changing circumstances in Tikopia, but such gifts, exchanges or purchases were not unprecedented in transactions with Europeans.[34] In making the collection, Firth was inadvertently documenting change in the indigenous religion as a result of the impact of Christianity, but the collection also illustrates how Firth, arriving as a stranger, was incorporated into Tikopia life.

In January 1996, when I showed Moses Lonsdale Firth's collection in the Australian Museum storerooms, he was surprised at the size of the collection and intrigued as to how Firth had transported it from the island to Sydney. He was perhaps most surprised that the collection included what he described as 'disposable' material, such as fire-tongs and baskets. Lonsdale agreed that carved wooden objects would not have been easily given away, because of the significance relating to their use, as well as the labour required to replace them. He suggested that such items as turmeric flasks, chiefly headrests, paddles, clubs, mortars and pestles would only have been given to someone of comparable social standing.

An understanding of Firth's acquisition of the collection as one which involved the agency of Tikopia has implications for an interpretation of ethnographic collections held in museums that see them as the 'cultural property' of others that must have been forcibly removed. The latter assumption accords priority to the idea that all objects associated with indigenous peoples, if not removed from their context of origin illegally,

---

34   Appendix 4 lists objects from Tikopia collected before 1928 and now held in
     public collections.

have been removed immorally. While the repatriation or return of ethnographic collections is often associated with cases of illegal or immoral acquisition (O'Keefe and Prott 2011; Prott 2009; Prott and Specht 1989), the close examination of the circumstances surrounding the acquisition of this particular collection clearly reveals a more complex history of interaction, which includes the agency of the community of origin.

As other studies have shown for regions as distant and different from Tikopia as the Congo (Schildkrout and Keim 1998), histories of artefact collecting can help to illuminate colonial relationships, revealing transactions which cannot easily be summarized simply as theft, extortion, purchase or gift. Regardless of the terms used to describe the acquisition from the perspective of the collector, those collected from would have viewed the transactions in their own terms, according to their own understandings of the relationship between objects and people. In the case of Firth's collection, I suggest that the manner of acquisition was appropriate and reflected the nature of the relationships in which he was engaged within Tikopia society. The acquisition process was enacted through the exchange of gifts of various kinds according to the social values dominant at that time and in that place: Firth's collection reflects the relationships in which he became enmeshed. What this collection and its presence in a museum signify to Tikopia people today, constitutes a separate question that awaits thorough investigation.

CHAPTER 6

Tikopia collected

The social life of a museum collection

Letter from Firth to Peter Lawrence and James Fox, Australian National University, dated 4 January 1979:

I am writing to you in connection with a proposal to transfer to the Honiara Museum a collection of Solomon Islands artefacts formerly held by your department and now in the custody of the Institute of Anatomy.

In 1929 after a field expedition in the Solomons I deposited my collection of ethnographical objects in the Department of Anthropology of the University of Sydney, for teaching purposes, and they were used by me in 1930–1932 when I was first lecturer, then acting-professor, in the department. When I left for London in 1932 I assumed that the collection would remain in the department, but as time went on and the interests of the department changed, the collection was transferred to Canberra, and came to rest in the Institute of Anatomy. I had thought that there it might be of teaching use to the Australian National University, in common with a similar collection made by James Spillius and myself much later and deposited in the Institute of Anatomy in 1953. The collections however have turned out to be of only marginal value to the anthropologists in ANU. On the other hand, the Solomons now have a national museum in Honiara, and with the attainment of independence there is a very strong move to have Solomons material abroad returned to the islands. The Museum is rapidly becoming a centre of intense cultural significance to the Solomon Islands people themselves, as a repository of the art and craft work of their forebears. It now houses much material of great scientific and historical importance.

It would be most appropriate then for this collection of ethnographical objects, acquired first half a century ago, and supplemented by the more recent addition, to be housed in the Honiara Museum. I myself wish this to be so, very strongly. I understand that this view is shared by the Federal Ministry of Home Affairs, which has overall jurisdiction over museums in this country. It may be that your department and University may be thought to have some right, or at least some residual interest, in the collection. I gather that a letter has gone from Home Affairs to your Vice-Chancellor asking that your University waive any such right or interest, and will raise no objection to the transfer of the material to Honiara. I hope that you too will share the view that the material should return to the Solomons, and that you will use such good offices as may be needed to help the proposal along,

Yours sincerely,

Raymond Firth(LSE Archives 1.9.15: Firth Specimens)

Letter from Firth to Anna Craven, National Museum of Solomon Islands, 19 November 1978, regarding his selection of objects for the Solomon Islands museum:

Don't expect too much [...]; I was making an ethnographic collection, not a fine art collection. There are no sculptures but a lot of fibre skirts.

(LSE Archives 1.9.15: Firth Specimens)

In Chapters 3, 4 and 5, I investigated the cultural context of Firth's collecting: how Firth interpreted the artefacts from the perspective of the discipline of anthropology at the time of collection; and through an interpretation of Firth's ethnographies, how such objects might have mediated relationships among the Tikopia, with their gods and also with Firth. In Chapter 6, I turn from a deliberation upon the context of collecting – the specifics of the meaning or significance of objects at the time of their acquisition – and look to the events which saw the physical relocation of Firth's collection from one institution to another within Australia. From an institutional perspective, these events reflect the transformation of this collection, by the mid-1970s, into 'cultural heritage'.

This chapter has two parts which examine, firstly, the relocation of the collection from Sydney to Canberra in 1957 to become a part of Australia's 'National Ethnographic Collection' and, secondly, the request for the repatriation of the collection to the National Museum of Solomon Islands, which was followed instead by the return of the collection to Sydney in 1989, where it continues to be held as the 'cultural heritage' of Solomon Islands. Firth was involved in a number of discussions about the collection during these transfers.

In Chapter 7, I continue to focus upon the collection as 'cultural heritage', but draw upon Firth's accounts, supplemented by those of later anthropologists Eric Larson and Judith MacDonald, concerning the ways in which Tikopia people conceived of a 'treasure place' on Tikopia for the preservation of selected 'sacred things'.

The concluding chapter reviews how Firth's work and his ethnographic collection have come to hold varying and contingent significances: specifically, for the way Tikopia might regard their past and think about their cultural heritage; and, more broadly, for the ways in which museums, on the national and international stage, are implicated in the transformation of collections into 'heritage'.

The Tikopia collection as part of the Australian national estate?

The Anthropology Department at the University of Sydney was the first home of the 1928–9 Firth collection. While the School was established in 1926, as early as 1928, storage of the university's collections had become a problem. Radcliffe-Brown, Chair of the Department, wrote to A.J. Gibson of the Royal Society to inform him that he had raised this matter with the Prime Minister, Mr Bruce, as well as the Minister for Home and Territories, Mr Marr. Radcliffe-Brown had suggested that there should be a National Museum of Ethnography in Canberra, to which these collections, which he referred to as the Australian National Research Council Collections, could be added. The Australian National Research Council was consulted because it had funded the research and stipulated the making of ethnographic collections: the establishment of a national museum would ensure proper storage for the collections it had funded (Radcliffe-Brown 1928; also Stone 1960 and 1968). In the following December, Radcliffe-Brown received a positive reply from the Australian National Research Council, which supported a proposal for a national collection and a suitable home (Gibson 1928).

As a part of the larger collections at the University of Sydney, the 1928–9 Firth collection appeared to have acquired national significance.

In February 1929, Radcliffe-Brown was informed that the Executive Committee of the Australian National Research Council had discussed the concept of developing a Commonwealth Museum. The Council felt that the issue should be adopted as a matter of policy, and that immediate action should be taken to set up an anthropology section (Gibson 1929a). A series of letters in April 1929 indicate that the matter was raised at the Department of Home Affairs (Gibson 1929b) and that funding was sought for the preservation and storage of the collection of photographs and glass-plate negatives being built up by University of Sydney researchers (Radcliffe-Brown 1929).

However, Leonie Oakes (1988), who collated correspondence relating to the University of Sydney collections for the Australian Museum, has suggested that Radcliffe-Brown lacked interest in the collections and sought their relocation, proposing to G.B. Cook, Private Secretary of the Prime Minister, that the coal store at the Powerhouse in Canberra could be an alternative storage location (Tigger Wise, cited in Oakes 1988:6). Perhaps Radcliffe-Brown's stance reflected his research interests, which lay within the social anthropology of the time, in which aspects of social behaviour, the identification of social institutions, social structure and social organization took precedence over material culture (Radcliffe-Brown 1952a, b, c; see also Stocking 1984, 1985).

Radcliffe-Brown's successor, Professor A.P. Elkin was, however, interested in the collections and in museums: he became a Trustee of the Australian Museum in October 1946, and later President of the Board of Trustees in 1962. In contrast to Radcliffe-Brown, Elkin supported maintaining the collections at the University of Sydney and wanted to build a small museum or a 'fixed research laboratory', however he lacked the funding to achieve this (Oakes 1988:7). After Elkin's retirement in 1957, his successor Professor Barnes, moved the collections to the Institute of Anatomy in Canberra on a permanent loan.[1] Barnes intended that it should join the 'National Ethnographic Collection' (Oakes 1988:2), held there since 1931, when the building was home to the National Museum of Australian Zoology (Stone 1968).[2] However, according to E.H. Hipsley (1959), Medical

---

1   However, a few pieces made their way to the Macleay Museum at the University of Sydney and to the Australian Museum, Sydney (Oakes 1988:7, 13–14).

2   This building is now home to the National Film and Sound Archive, Canberra.

Officer at the Institute of Anatomy, Barnes had wanted to move the University of Sydney collections because he urgently needed office space, and so had drawn attention to the fact that they had never been put on display, catalogued or used for research. The 'National Ethnographic Collection' comprised a number of collections which had been presented to or purchased by the government over preceding years and which had been held in various parts of the country.[3] Storage at the Institute of Anatomy was considered to be temporary until a national museum was erected (Stone 1968). The transfer of the collections from the University of Sydney was not accompanied by any documentation (there appears to be no paperwork outlining the loan conditions associated with the relocation via a 'permanent loan') – an omission not without repercussions.

In 1959, Hipsley wrote to the Deputy Crown Solicitor concerning the status of the University of Sydney collections because the new Head of the Anthropology School at the University of Sydney, Professor Geddes, had expressed interest in having them returned to the University. Concerned about relocation costs (the Sydney-to-Canberra move had cost £400), Hipsley sought clarification about who owned the material. However, despite Geddes' request, the University of Sydney collections remained in the Institute of Anatomy basement for another twenty-three years.

In 1989, the Pacific Islands component of the collection was moved back to Sydney, but this time to the Australian Museum. The transfer followed extensive deliberations over the legal title to all the ethnographic collections housed in the basement of the former Institute of Anatomy, and took place in parallel with the development of the National Museum of Australia's acquisition strategy regarding ethnographic objects. When the museum decided to focus it attentions on indigenous Australian materials, collection items originating from Pacific Islands were dispersed where legally possible.

Thus, all of the Pacific Islands collections that had been held at the Institute of Anatomy at that time were reassessed for their suitability to remain in the 'National Ethnographic Collection' (this included not only the Firth collection of 1928, but also his 1956 collection made while he

---

3   For example, the 'Official Papuan Collection', comprising collections acquired by Australian Administrators and officers in New Guinea. This collection is now housed at the National Museum of Australia (Schaffarczyk 2008) and has been the subject of doctoral research by Anna Edmondson (2013).

was employed at the Australian National University). The legal status of these collections remained in question until February 1989, when the National Museum of Australia (NMA) received notification from the Attorney General's Office that, as the legal situation was unclear, the possessor could dispose of the unwanted components of the collection. The collections made by University of Sydney researchers who had worked in the Pacific region (including Firth's 1928–9 collection) could be disposed of by the university, which decided to transfer ownership to the Australian Museum, Sydney. The Australian National University took back the Firth-Spillius material (1956 collection) and other collections acquired by their departmental researchers and visitors. The 'Official Papuan Collection' was moved to alternate storage in the NMA, where it remains.[4]

On receipt of the Pacific component of the University of Sydney collections (which included objects from Papua New Guinea and Vanuatu in addition to Solomon Islands), the Australian Museum advised the National Museum of Solomon Islands that the collection was now in its ownership and possession. The possibility of repatriating the Solomon Islands collection was discussed at a meeting held at the Australian Museum on 6 May 1988, attended by Jim Specht, Head of the Anthropology Division; Lissant Bolton, Pacific Collection Manager; and Lawrence Foana'ota, Director of the National Museum of Solomon Islands (Specht and Bolton 1988).[5] However, while the Tikopia collection had been subject to a repatriation request by the National Museum of Solomon Islands in the 1970s (see below), circumstances had changed since then: Foana'ota stated that his institution lacked appropriate storage space to receive large quantities of material from Australia at that time and also lacked trained staff to care for the collections.

Furthermore, Foana'ota was also concerned that the Solomon Islands was not a signatory to the UNESCO Convention on the Means of Prohibiting and Preventing the Illicit Import, Export and Transfer of Ownership of Cultural Property of 1970, and felt that there was a need for reciprocal relationships between Melanesian countries concerning illegally

---

4   This collection has been under consideration for repatriation to Papua New Guinea (Craig 1996).

5   Grace Molisa and Godwin Ligo, representing the Vanuatu Cultural Centre, and Soroi Eoe, Director of the National Museum and Art Gallery of Papua New Guinea, were also present.

exported items. He added that the National Museum of Solomon Islands was working towards national legislation to protect cultural property,[6] particularly with regard to combating the black market.[7] Interestingly, Foana'ota also added that it was important to consider the wishes of the collectors in the disposal of their collections (University of Sydney file, Anthropology Division, Australian Museum 1988).

During the sixty years between its acquisition in Tikopia and its transfer to the Australian Museum in Sydney, Firth's 1928–9 collection had been valued in different ways in different contexts: as an important teaching collection; as an important national collection; but also, perhaps, as an impediment to the efficient use of space. When the NMA established its focus on Australian social history and indigenous Australia, the National Ethnographic Collection was divided into Australian and non-Australian regions, effectively demoting the significance of Firth's collection and all the collections made by the University of Sydney researchers who had worked in the Pacific: these collections ceased to be of 'national importance'.

Yet the transfer to, and acceptance of, the Pacific Islands material by the Australian Museum in Sydney, signalled an interpretation of the collection as having both ethnographic and cultural heritage significance – if not national significance (Bolton 1985). While the Solomon Islands National Museum was not in a position to accept the Solomon Islands component of the Sydney University Collection in 1989, that museum had expressed great interest in the Firth collection in the years leading up to independence, and had enlisted the assistance of Firth and others in an attempt to have Firth's collection repatriated. Indeed, Firth's interest in his

---

6   Under the Local Government Act, 1981, provincial governments were given greater responsibility to legislate in cultural affairs. As a result of this, Guadalcanal Province and Western Province, two of the seven provincial governments, established cultural centres for the purposes of protecting cultural heritage and promoting traditional knowledge. However, while these centres were established, their functioning at a practical level had been impaired by similar issues: lack of funding, and lack of real power to prevent developments in the area of logging and forestry (Riley 1991; Roe and Totu 1991; Totu and Roe 1991).

7   Many of these issues remain for many Pacific Island museums, and have formed the basis for cultural heritage workshops in subsequent years (see, Eoe and Swadling 1991; Foana`ota 1991, 1994; Lindstrom and White 1994b).

collection as the cultural heritage of contemporary Tikopia people led him, at the behest of Anna Craven, Curator at the Solomon Islands Museum, to become an advocate for the repatriation of his collection.

Repatriation request for Firth's 1928–9 collection

In the 1960s a number of colonial officials of the British administration and two Solomon Islanders formed the Honiara Museum Association to build a museum to house the various collections scattered throughout government buildings. They obtained funds from the Gulbenkian Foundation and the first gallery opened in 1969. Annual contributions from local councils as well as local and international donations provided further financial support. In 1972, the Honiara Museum became the Solomon Islands National Museum and Cultural Centre, under central government control. Its aims were to collect cultural materials and information, carry out research, disseminate information through exhibitions and educational programmes, and to entertain the general public. The collections were mainly ethnographic and archaeological, but also included artefacts of colonial history, relics of the Second World War, and natural history and geological specimens (Foana'ota 1994:96, 2007).

A curator from Britain, Anna Craven, commenced work at the Solomon Islands Museum in 1973. Very shortly afterwards she approached Australian museums holding Solomon Islands collections to request their repatriation. She also approached Firth directly to enlist his aid in the return of his Tikopia collection, then held in the basement of the Institute of Anatomy (but administered by the NMA). Firth was supportive and wrote to the NMA as follows:

> there is an increasing interest in the Solomons in objects of 'custom', i.e. the traditional cultures, and the museum has plans for storage and extension. Since the Museum has very few Tikopia specimens, and since my collections have duplicates, it seems appropriate that some duplicates should go to the Solomon Islands Museum, not founded when the Tikopia collections were made.
> (Firth, 16 March 1973, NMA, University of Sydney file, Anthropology Division, Australian Museum 1988).

And some eight months later, he wrote again, renewing his request that part of the collection be returned to Solomon Islands.

Though I used to think that such a collection should not be divided,
I think the situation now has altered, and the needs of the people of
the region should be very seriously considered; they have a right to be
educated in their cultural heritage.
(Firth to Mrs Keith, NMA, 3 December 1973, University of Sydney file,
Anthropology Division, Australian Museum 1988)

From Craven's point of view, there was so little material held in
Solomon Islands that Firth's identification of 'duplicates' was irrelevant.
She wrote to the NMA:

I am inclined to say that, since we would like so much, that it is perhaps
better for you to say what you are willing to let us have. Although many
items seem to be duplicates according to the description, of course they
are probably not ... Please work under the assumption that we have next
to nothing, and what we have is insignificant. We want all we can get.
(Craven to Keith, NMA, 14 January 1974, University of Sydney file,
Anthropology Division, Australian Museum 1988)

Craven challenged the concept of 'duplicate', anticipating a 1978
UNESCO debate on the status of ethnographic collections as cultural
heritage (Edwards and Stewart 1980). Despite her efforts, by 1977 no
material had been returned to Solomon Islands, and again she wrote 'We
are being very patient! But it is a bit discouraging to seem to move no
further getting things back – especially since the interest in such things in
the Solomons has increased enormously since I first came here in 1973.'[8]

In 1978 Firth wrote again to the Public Affairs and Cultural Relations
Division of the Department of Foreign Affairs, stating that in earlier
times the Solomon Islands had no museum where these objects could be
preserved, but:

The cultural situation has now radically altered. For some years now the
Solomon Islands has had a Museum, which under a vigorous Curator
has been developing rapidly and most effectively. In particular now
that the Solomon Islands have attained Independence, the Museum is

---

8   Craven to Keith, NMA, 19 January 1977, University of Sydney file, Anthropology
      Division, Australian Museum 1988.

becoming the centre of intense cultural interest to the Solomon Islands
people themselves, as a repository, indeed a treasure-house, of the
art and craft work of their forebears. It now houses much material of
great scientific importance and historical interest [...] It would be most
appropriate then, for these early Solomon Islands collections, or for a
substantial proportion of them, to be housed in the Museum in Honiara
as part of the Solomons national heritage which people have access to as
part of their modern cultural experience.
(Firth to Wilson, 5 October 1978, NMA, University of Sydney file,
Anthropology Division, Australian Museum 1988)

In January 1979 Firth raised the possibility of repatriating his second
collection, made in conjunction with James Spillius in 1956 under the
auspices of the Australian National University. Spillius requested that
twelve items be reserved for him and asked Mrs Keith of the NMA to pick
out the 'most elaborately carved'.[9] Both Firth and Spillius further asked that
some objects remain in Canberra at the Australian National University,
for display and teaching purposes.[10] After all this, conservators assessed
the collection and preparations were begun for the return of 980 objects
(Preiss 1980). The return was approved by the Department of Home
Affairs[11] although by April of that year, changes to the proposed return
had been made.

 While there appear to be good arguments for the retention of
 duplicated items and we would not anticipate the Solomon Islands
 objecting to this request, we consider that, in the spirit of the UNESCO
 Director-General's call for the restitution of cultural property, the
 National Museum of Honiara should be given a description of all items
 in the collection and their agreement sought to the retention in Australia
 of those items which Professor Firth and Dr Spillius would like to

---

9   Spillius to Fox, NMA, 17 July 1979, University of Sydney file, Anthropology
     Division, Australian Museum 1988.
10   Firth and Spillius to Fox, 6 July 1979, NMA, University of Sydney file,
     Anthropology Division, Australian Museum 1988.
11   Letter from Ryan, Department of Home Affairs to Moyle, Department of
     Health, 26 March 1980, NMA, University of Sydney file, Anthropology
     Division, Australian Museum 1988.

keep as teaching aids and as personal mementos. This will provide an opportunity for the Solomon Islands to ensure that items of the greatest cultural significance are lodged at the National Museum. We should not wish to lay ourselves open to future criticism from the Solomon Islands that important items were retained in Australia without consultation. (McPherson, UN Social and Technical Section, Foreign Affairs to Parret, Department of Health, 24 April 1980, National Museum of Australia, University of Sydney file, Anthropology Division, Australian Museum 1988)

Ostensibly, all parties involved prior to McPherson's letter to Parret on 24 April, 1980 supported the return, and importantly, funding and resources were committed to effect a return. Despite these arrangements and photography of all the items in preparation for packing, the collections were not returned. The only explanation apparent in the NMA files relates to the perceived concern that the National Museum of Solomon Islands might object to retention of objects by ANU, Firth and Spillius.

It is ironic that the failure to repatriate the Tikopia collection did not appear to rely upon any anti-repatriation orthodoxy: nowhere in the files was it argued that museums have 'salvaged' objects that otherwise would have been destroyed if not collected; that objects in museum collections form part of the world's heritage and belong to a common humanity and so enhance everyone's cultural experience and education; that the collections were acquired illegally or unethically; that repatriation compromises scholarly research, while encouraging black market activity; or that 'return' to original contexts is impossible because the conditions of the past no longer exist (Warren 1989; see also, Eyo 1994 and other discussion essays in Allen 1998; Messenger 1989).

Pro-repatriation arguments, that people have a right to own and have access to their own cultural heritage and that the removal of objects from their country of origin diminishes the cultural integrity of the objects because they are no longer in their 'true' context, appear not to have been challenged. Towards the end of communications on file, concern was expressed that not all of the collection would return. The ambiguity surrounding the events was noted by Firth, who, when I met him in 1994, asked me to confirm whether the collection had been sent to Honiara or not. Clearly for him too, the matter remained unresolved.

The obscurity surrounding legal ownership of the collection may well have been a significant obstacle from the Australian end of negotiations; though it seems concerns over appropriate consultation may have extinguished the project, seemingly outweighing the significance of returning the larger portion of the collection.

Dr Jim Specht (former Head of the Anthropology Division, Australian Museum) suggested that bureaucratic complications too may have been contributing factors to the final outcome, suggesting that the number of different departments involved may have obscured clear lines of action and responsibilities. The collection had been held at the former Institute of Anatomy, which was administered by the Department of Health; by the National Museum (which then fell under the Department of Home Affairs) and repatriation itself involved the Department of Foreign Affairs (Specht to Firth, 19 October 1978, LSE Archives 1.9.15, Firth Specimens). And then there was the passing of time: requests for the return of the Solomon Islands collection began in 1973, when Anna Craven commenced as Curator at the Solomon Islands National Museum. Six years later, in February 1979, after the nation achieved self-governing status in 1976, and then independence on 7 July 1978, she returned to the UK. It may be that the various Australian agencies remained unable to proceed without prompting from the Solomon Islands National Museum.

Evident in this brief history of the Firth collection repatriation request is the absence of direct Tikopia representation. Tikopia people, a small minority in Solomon Islands, were not directly involved in the negotiations between the National Museum of Australia and the National Museum of Solomon Islands. In this case, however, it could be argued that both Firth and the staff of the National Museum of Solomon Islands were their proxies in efforts to articulate Solomon Islands' nationhood. In May 2016, Craven reflected that the request had been concerned with 'raising consciousness in SI [*sic*] and the whole issue of making "traditional" culture (which was so under fire from missionary/church activity over the decades) worthy of respect and to be valued, especially the indigenous knowledge vis a vis the environment'. Further, despite this policy stance, museum staff had worked within a broader administrative environment which did not necessarily support cultural development (Craven, email, 18 May 2016).

But what does the absence of a Tikopia voice in the repatriation request really reflect? Does it necessarily suggest that the Tikopia were uninterested in 'heritage'? In the following chapter, I suggest that a nascent view amongst Tikopia of specific objects as 'cultural heritage' can be glimpsed in comments by Firth and later anthropologists working with them. This can also be seen in the correspondence of National Museum of Solomon Islands staff as they prepared the new national institution in the run up to independence. In this emerging view of cultural heritage, for some Tikopia, specific objects had come to materialize connections with the past and brought about awareness and reflection upon social and cultural change.

CHAPTER 7

The idea of a 'treasure place'

The development of a sense of cultural identity as an expression of difference across the Pacific has been discussed in Linnekin and Poyer (1990). Firth, Eric Larson and Judith MacDonald (see below) appear to prefigure this debate, but to what extent Firth's early presence in Tikopia can be said to have affected this is surely difficult to evaluate, and the role of Firth's ethnography must perhaps wait for a comment by Tikopia themselves. However, Firth did discuss with Tikopia the idea of a 'treasure place' and what such a place might be. This discussion occurred within a specific historical context in which one of the Tikopia chiefs was already using his temple as a storage place for pre-Christian objects, while other chiefs had chosen to dispose of many of their 'old things'. Firth's work appears to have reinforced a sense of cultural identity, a result speculated upon more recently by Julian Treadaway (2007, see below).

When Firth re-visited Tikopia with Torben Monberg in July to August 1966, the Work of the Gods had been abandoned for ten years. While many of the temples had been left to deteriorate or had become domiciles, Raniniu in Tai, the former 'control centre' of the rites of the Taumako canoe yard, was still standing and housed a number of 'sacred objects' from pre-Christian times, as well as objects gathered since the adoption of Christianity. These had been retained in it by the Ariki Taumako.

It ... held various important relics, including a broken spear used by Pu Resiake to kill Kaitu of Tafua... The Ariki Taumako took me over to see this weapon. He said 'Let's crawl over quickly, the place is taboo.' We stayed about a minute while he showed me how the deed had been done... In the house also was a wrist ornament of Matakai II, the

Ariki Taumako who voyaged frequently to Vanikoro. A couple of little
cylindrical boxes contained bonito hooks. The chief had not looked
into them – 'sacred things'; he discussed showing the hooks to me but
decided better not. Also there was an *useru*, a bundle of sage pinnule
ribs bound together and used by chiefs to beat time to the ritual dirges
known as *seru*; this was a replacement of an earlier implement.

(Firth 1967a:254).

The Ariki Taumako also invited Monberg to see the items in the
temple, but requested payment from him of four shillings (Firth 1967a:475).
Pa Ngarumea, who bore the invitation, said to Firth:

Some chiefs ... had been stupid and had given away their sacred things.
But the Ariki Taumako had gathered his together in Raniniu. When
formerly Father Stephen Talu, wishing to uproot all traces of paganism,
had tried to obtain them the chief told him to go away – he held that
this attitude was wrong and was very indignant. These objects were
things of olden time. Though people no longer believed in the efficacy
of the powers formerly attributed to them, they were memorials of the
ancestors, if only because, like the sacred shell adzes of the canoes, they
represented enormous work.

(Firth 1967a:476)

Clearly some Tikopia continued to store specific objects in dedicated
storage areas, though with an altered purpose: these objects no longer had
ritual uses but instead lived on as important objects from their history that
manifested a connection with the past.

Some (see Stanley 2007) have discussed whether such acts of storage
in indigenous contexts represent autochthonous forms of preservation.
During his 1966 visit Firth certainly discussed the idea of caring for
objects as a museum might do, but whether such acts of storage occurred
endogenously remains moot (Firth 1967a:476–8). Nonetheless Firth, Pa
Ngarumea and Pa Ngatotiu, a former ritual elder, discussed who should
be allowed to see such important objects: Firth stressed the importance
of respect towards the objects, so that they should only be shown to
responsible people. Pa Ngarumea asked Firth to make this last point
directly to the Ariki Taumako, so Firth visited him and spoke to him about
showing the objects to visitors. The chief repeated that he did not think

the objects were powerful any longer, but they were 'weighty' because 'they were things of ancient times, things of the ancestors, and as such deserved respect'. Up until that time, the general Tikopia population had not been allowed to see these objects. But his thinking now was that they were objects which should be retained for future generations (Firth 1967a:476–7). In this sense, the sacred things represented 'heritage' for future generations.

Both Firth and Monberg were taken to see the objects in the temple, which housed six sacred shell adzes, oil bottles for anointing sacred canoes, and objects already seen by Firth in 1952. One of the shell-adze blades was the Matua Toki ('principal adze'), another was Te Niapu (probably the 'adze of the seashore'). Both were termed *faingata*, adzes of great destructive force (Firth 1967a:477). The chief initially described the objects in hushed tones, but did permit the visitors to handle them and photograph them. At the end of the visit, Monberg gave the *ariki* twice the amount asked for, plus additional tobacco.

Discussion concerning what constituted a fair price revolved around a number of issues: Firth was concerned that the Tikopia chief should not give the impression that he wanted to sell the objects to visitors. Firth suggested that the term *fakapenu*, meaning 'reciprocity', might be appropriate to describe the viewing of the objects, because an alternative word discussed, *tauvi*, had connotations of sale. The 'fee' was discussed, and Firth suggested that it should be paid not as a demonstration of an equivalence of value for seeing the objects, but as a fee for the participation in the event of viewing the objects (Firth 1967a:478). Firth suggested that while the objects in the temple had ceased to be ritually important, significance now lay in their historical and cultural associations (Firth 1967a:478–9). The Ariki Taumako spoke of them as memorials and manifestations of work, and as such they should not be given away but kept safely in a respected place – a location that had once been a temple.

A sense of the enduring sanctity associated with specific objects emerged thirty-two years later, in 1980. The Ariki Kafika showed doctoral researcher Judith MacDonald the sacred adzes used by his father for the Work of the Gods (MacDonald 1991:28). A day later, he asked her not to let the late chief's brother know that she had seen them, as they were still not to be viewed by women. Evidently the objects still maintained significant associations and prohibitions in relation to gender.

The Tikopia chiefs amidst social change: the 1960s to 1981

During her fieldwork MacDonald recorded that while the subsistence lifestyle and kinship system described by Firth in 1928 had been maintained, significant changes had occurred with the adoption of Christianity. She also noted social change in terms of Tikopia's increased exposure to the outside world and the increased mobility of people moving between Tikopia and the Tikopia settlements elsewhere in Solomon Islands. She further observed that Tikopia discussed past events in terms of the maintenance of their cultural identity (1991:69–113). Their expression of difference appeared to operate at two levels: migrant Tikopia felt different to those residing on the island itself; but regardless of this, all Tikopia viewed themselves as distinctly Tikopia in relation to the broader Solomon Islands population. In fact, past interactions with Solomon Islanders had worked to emphasize the positive value of difference.

> While some of their accounts of the adoption of new religion and technologies, of their response to overpopulation and migration, and of their relationship with the wider Solomon Islands and its administration may appear as post hoc rationalisation of the inevitable, these accounts illustrate Tikopia ideas about the ways in which they coped successfully with change while maintaining the integrity of their cultural identity.
>
> (MacDonald 1991:71)

The assertion of cultural identity had been noted earlier by Eric Larson also (1977:257–60), who carried out work in the migrant settlement of Nukufero in the Russell Islands in the 1960s. Nukufero, the original name for Tikopia,[1] was established in 1956 with the assistance of the Levers plantation at Samata (Larson 1960, 1966, 1968, 1977).[2] The name of the new settlement was chosen to emphasize the link with the home island (Larson 1966:55; MacDonald 1991:105, 107). Larson also suggested that, in 1964,

---

1   '*Nukufero ma Tikopia e tau fongo tasi* - Nukufero and Tikopia are the same.' (Larson 1966:55).

2   In 1949 fifty-nine Tikopia men were taken to work for the Levers plantation at Samata in the Russell Islands. Many died of malaria and others suffered severely from homesickness (Spillius 1957a). In 1952 a second group was sent and with the assistance of Spillius the operation proceeded with greater success (MacDonald 1991:101ff).

Tikopia were aware that he, as an anthropologist, was interested in their cultural activities in a way that differed from other 'Europeans' (Larson 1966:39): he noted their reflexivity regarding Tikopia cultural practices. However, the people living on Tikopia and those living in Nukufero differed in the degree of confidence expressed about their own cultural values. Tikopia on the home island felt themselves to be Larson's social equals and were unreserved in their treatment of him. In Nukufero, he found that the residents distinguished him as an European anthropologist and were more reserved in discussing cultural practices with him (Larson 1966:40). Larson suggested that anthropological interest in Tikopia may have reinforced cultural conservatism and pride in being Tikopia: for example, Tikopia felt that Melanesians had incorporated the word 'custom' into their vernacular languages and that they had lost their culture (Larson 1966:40) by failing to maintain their traditions (Larson 1966:48, 55).[3]

MacDonald also noted: 'While the Tikopia do not appear to feel particularly threatened by the Solomon Islands majority, they nonetheless choose to emphasize their difference' through their 'technology',[4] their dancing and their behaviour in terms of spatial arrangements and dress (MacDonald 1991:115). For example, in 1991 almost all Tikopia wore a turtle-shell hook on a string hung around the neck that served to identify them as Tikopia and so distinct to other Polynesians in the Solomon Islands (such as the people of Rennell, Bellona or Sikaiana). The hook also indicated to other Tikopia that the wearer was *soa*, a friend (MacDonald 1991:116).

One of the major factors contributing to a sense of difference from the rest of Solomon Islands was the continuing power of the Tikopia chiefs in Tikopia and in the settlements, which was reflected in their ability to gainsay government policy. MacDonald (1991:92) noted disregard for national legislation (also commented on by Firth, below): for example, Tikopia complied selectively with Solomon Islands' law requiring

---

3   Tikopia commented that others used the pidgin word '*kastom*' whether they spoke pidgin or not. In contrast, the Tikopia equivalent was *faka puri*, which means 'in the way of darkness', a phrase adopted under missionary influences (MacDonald 1991:16–17).

4   In 1996 Lonsdale repeated these sentiments as part of a commentary on the photographs of objects in the collection, declaring 'these are the things that make us Tikopia'.

compulsory primary schooling for both boys and girls. On Tikopia island the two schools were mostly attended by boys.[5]

The authority of chiefs in Tikopia as observed by MacDonald during her fieldwork had been clearly seen in instances of early negotiations with Europeans. The division of the island's population through the establishment of settlements away from Tikopia (Larson 1966, 1968, 1977; Spillius 1957a, b, c) left the authority of the chiefs unquestioned: the chiefs decided who could and could not leave Tikopia for the overseas settlements. In addition, the conversion of the entire population to Christianity in 1956 served to strengthen the chiefs' status, as the rivalry between the two districts of Faea and Ravenga, which Firth documented in 1928 (1983:71–6) and which had also represented a split between the Christian and non-Christian inhabitants, softened: rather than losing the respect and rank accorded to them, the locus of chiefly power shifted from the religious to the secular sphere. The chiefs continued to symbolize unity on the island, and they became the focal point in negotiations between the central government and other islanders on three notable occasions between the 1960s and 1980 (Firth 1969:360): the Tikopia chiefs opposed the central government on issues of taxation, universal suffrage and constitutional rights.

In the 1960s all Solomon Islanders were expected to pay taxes through their local councils (Firth 1969:354–6; Larson 1966:67–70; MacDonald 1991:94–6). While the residents of Tikopia were exempted from payment because the central government had not provided any facilities on the island, with the establishment of settlements such as Nukufero in the Russell Islands migrant Tikopia were required by the government to

---

5   The reason for this dates back to 1952, when eight boys were sent to the mission schools in Paama, on Makira. All completed their education successfully and some went on to become prominent figures in Solomon Islands life (becoming bishops, customs controllers, headmasters and one Chief of Police). However, the girls fared differently: of a group sent away in the fifties, one caught polio and was sent home. Her illness was interpreted as a bad omen for girls' education, and since that time girls were not encouraged to attend school. The other girls grew up to marry non-Tikopia and were so 'lost' to the island. This was viewed unfavourably (MacDonald 1991:91). Despite the success of the boys in the 1950s group, schooling for boys was viewed as good, but not absolutely necessary (MacDonald 1991:93).

pay taxes to their local council. However, the chiefs directed the Russell Islands' Tikopia not to pay the tax. The District Commissioner responded by sending a government boat to the Russell Islands to pick up Tikopia representatives, press charges against them and take them to Honiara to settle the matter in court. They abandoned this plan when all the Tikopia resident in the Russell Islands turned up at the boat, declaring that should their representatives go to Honiara, they too must go, as all had refused to pay their taxes.

The Levers Plantation management settled the matter by paying the levies on behalf of the Tikopia workers because they did not want to lose their labour force. The Tikopia workers subsequently reimbursed the company management (Firth 1969:355). According to Larson (1966:69), the Tikopia understood the tax to be a tribute to the headman in Nukufero, who they considered did not deserve this payment, as only chiefs received such tribute. In refusing to pay the tax, the Nukufero Tikopia rejected integration and expressed their allegiance to the chiefs of Tikopia. While they were initiating new forms of organization in the way the village worked, through the establishment of a village committee with a headman (Larson 1966:62), these new structures were founded upon the authority of the chiefs in Tikopia (Larson 1966:62–7, 1977:251ff.).

However, the relationship between the home island and the settlements was beginning to generate internal tensions for some. An elderly mission teacher who had worked in the Russell Islands did voice criticism of the situation during the 1966 stand-off between the chiefs and the District Commissioner (Firth 1969:368). He commented that many Tikopia who worked away from the home island wished to stay in their new homes and did not want to return to Tikopia. Their life away from Tikopia was easier; they had access to schools and medical clinics. But people felt constrained against voicing any disagreement with the chiefs, even when they were away from the home island.

A visible representation of their difference was made at the official visit of the District Commissioner to Tikopia in 1966, to resolve the matter of unpaid taxes on Nukufero with the chiefs, and to try to persuade them to agree to making the payments. The day before the meeting the chiefs organized an assembly and directed Tikopia to wear their traditional barkcloth clothes, not European clothing, to meet with the District Commissioner. The purpose of this was to impress upon the District Commissioner the islanders' separation from the European government.

The chiefs themselves wore their sinnet belts and fine pandanus mats. Firth, who witnessed the meeting, commented on the 'vivid sense of the symbolic value of uniform traditional clothing' and the force of the Tikopia chief's statement of difference (Firth 1969:366).

The question of universal suffrage was at the centre of a second dispute with the Solomon Islands government. After independence in 1980, Tikopia became part of the Eastern Outer Islands Province for the nation's first general election. The regional administrative centre was located at Graciosa Bay, Ndende Island, in the Santa Cruz group, some 320 km to the west of Tikopia. The electoral candidates did not canvas Tikopia because it was unimportant to them. On their part, the Tikopia were unconcerned about the election because Solomon Islands affairs were regarded as separate to those of the Tikopia (MacDonald 1991:96). A government ship visited Tikopia to ensure that the people were informed about the electoral process, in which voting was compulsory. While two hundred Tikopia men were put on the roll, only sixty voted. Five voted for a Tikopia man, the rest for a Santa Cruz man who had given up land in Santa Cruz for the burial of Tikopia people who had died there. In contravention of federal law, Tikopia men did not allow Tikopia women to vote, because the election was seen to be an external matter, and therefore men's business. The women concurred (MacDonald 1991:97). The special status of the Tikopia chiefs was also noted by Murray Chapman: 'The four great chiefs of Tikopia [...] insisted that they be given "Constitutional power to recall home any Tikopian [...] causing public nuisance across the nation" [...] because that reflected poorly on all Tikopians' (Mamaloni, S.S. 1988 *Constitutional Review Committee Report*, cited in Chapman 1991:284).[6]

MacDonald (1991) noted that the chiefs had a strong sense of cultural continuity that manifested itself in antipathy on their part towards a number of introduced items of material culture, including items such as tables and chairs. Tikopia conventions concerning the body ensured that

---

6   The concern of the chiefs reflected a pan-Solomon Islands concern in relation to the acknowledgment of community over individual rights. In the Constitutional Review of 1987 rural community leaders proposed that visitors be expected to notify the acknowledged local leaders before leaving their own place and arriving at another. In this way the problem of strangers taking over the land of other people and the disrespect shown by strangers to local customs could be controlled (Chapman 1991:281–3).

no one stood higher than a chief. This adversely affected the adoption of any objects which provided the potential for lifting something above the level of the head – especially a chief's head (MacDonald 1991:89).

In the 1980s the chiefs continued to exercise control over new influences brought to Tikopia by returning migrants (MacDonald 1991:88): the senior men of Kafika smashed guitars and ukuleles because they did not want young people going off by themselves to sing foreign songs instead of joining in the *fuatanga* compositions, which were the central focus of Tikopia music making (MacDonald 1991:90; for Tikopia songs and music, see Firth with McLean 1990).

Hair length was also a matter of concern for the chiefs. Prior to the adoption of Christianity, men's hair was left to grow long and bleached with lime to produce a golden colour. In the 1980s, while young men considered following European fashion and cutting their hair short, chiefs could not cut their hair from the time of their accession.

> Strength and well being of the land were believed to be reflected in the physical well being of the *ariki* and no part of him should suffer damage which included diminution of his person through hair cutting.
>
> (MacDonald 1991:124)

Hair was significant to the chiefs, as it was under the control of the clan deity and associated with the *tapu* of the head, especially of high-ranking men (MacDonald 1991:124). The practice of incorporating hair into head circlets (*fau*) to be worn by female relatives of the deceased continued.[7] In 1980, while older men still wore their hair long, younger men were more

---

7   MacDonald noted that the closer a woman to the deceased, the shorter her hair was cut. However, the *fau* was also worn by older single women as a sign that they had given up on the idea of marriage (MacDonald 1991:125). In general, for women, short hair indicated a decorous person. MacDonald also suggested that Firth underestimated the significance of women's hair length as an indicator of social relations and the relationship of the cutter to the person being cropped (MacDonald 1991:126). She suggested that hair and sexuality were controlled at pre-pubescence and post-marriage: the act of cutting the hair was controlled by the women who have married into the patriline (MacDonald 1991:128).

hesitant to do so, being more aware of European influences (MacDonald 1991:123).

The conservative stance of the chiefs was reflected generally in the material culture of the island: people on Tikopia still wore barkcloth or a piece of material covering the knees, while children went about naked. Married women and older single women wore their barkcloth held by a red sinnet rope and a turmeric-dyed rope on special occasions. A few wore a cross on a chain or a *manga* turtle-shell hook on a string. Many women coveted bras and some wore them, despite the *ariki*'s order not to do so (because supposedly bras hid pregnancy). Nevertheless, some pre-Christian practices had been forbidden by the mission priest and tattooing had been abandoned since the cessation of the ritual production of turmeric (MacDonald 1991:130–1). Furthermore, away from Tikopia, the young people in Nukukaisi were beginning to tattoo themselves, but not using Tikopia motifs (Ishmael Tuki pers. comm. 1996), while European shorts were becoming fashionable among men (MacDonald 1991:131).

The 'weight of tradition': Tikopia in the new millennium (1980s to 2010)

Some thirty years after MacDonald's fieldwork, subsistence farming continues to be the foundation of the island's economy and its social and exchange relationships (Treadaway 2007).[8] While a few trade-stores have opened on the island, there is no sustainable cash economy: there are no cash crops on the island; salaried staff comprise 16 people (teachers, two nurses and two priests); and while marine products such as fish, crayfish, shells, trochus, bêche-de-mer and shark fins are abundant, they are not marketed. Remittances provide cash for the purchase of tobacco, sugar, salt, batteries, soap and kerosene, but when the trade-store runs out of these items people do without (ibid.:141).

Objects such as *kumete* (wooden bowls) and *kafa* (rope made of coconut fibre), along with *menga* (mats) and *mami* (bark cloth) remain important items of wealth for ceremonial exchange. The production of these objects requires intensive labour. For example, a circumcision ceremony requires 20 to 30 barkcloth, each taking one to two days to beat;

---

8   Julian Treadaway made four visits to the island of Tikopia in addition to the settlements between in 1980 and 2005 and remains in close contact with Tikopia in Honiara, where he now resides.

20 mats are also needed, made by a boy's mother and relatives (ibid.:59). At the funeral of an elderly woman, Treadaway witnessed 50 mats placed on top of the deceased prior to her being buried in them (ibid.:108). Obtaining these items outside of Tikopia can be difficult (ibid.:61) and there is also pressure to celebrate occasions in 'Western style' and include non-traditional items. For example, in some marriages sinnet is being replaced by rolls of cloth (ibid.:78). While the purchase of non-Tikopia items is more costly, the acquisition of such objects can be less onerous, especially when the extensive obligations involved in ceremonial activity are taken into account. There is then, according to Treadaway, a combination of factors converging: the competitive values which originate from urban living and the values underpinning customary practices combine to form the 'weight of tradition' as 'people try to outdo each other using cash and things bought with cash' (ibid.:85).

The devastation caused by Cyclone Zoe, which hit the island on 28 December 2002 (ibid.:183–95), wiped out the stores of wealth held by most families, as well as the resources with which to replace them. This has led to the inclusion of mass-produced objects instead of traditional objects in ceremonial exchanges. But putting aside the devastating nature of the cyclone (it remains to be documented how Tikopia respond to the event in the long term), Treadaway's description of Tikopia in the new millennium identifies a number of challenges. Faced with changing views concerning what being Tikopia might entail, Treadaway's description of contemporary Tikopia life reflects a growing rift between conservative elements, as represented by the chiefs together with their supporters, and those who support the younger generation, who are increasingly engaging, or want to engage with, non-Tikopia ways of doing things.

There have been palpable changes in the circumstances of the Tikopia since MacDonald's fieldwork (again, discounting natural disasters). MacDonald described communities who were coping with change while maintaining social and cultural integrity: she also documented highly mobile populations, moving away from and back to Tikopia, and enabled to do so by a reliable shipping service. Since that time privatization has removed regular shipping between the island and the settlements. Today, Treadaway records that the growing numbers of Tikopia born in the settlements (he largely focuses on Nukukaisi and Honiara communities) have never visited Tikopia, and are unlikely to do so because of the practical difficulties and the cost of the journey. Included in the 'cost' by

Treadaway are both the price of the boat ticket and also the gifts required to take back to the home villages (ibid.:80).[9]

While in the 1980s Tikopia in the settlements felt themselves to be firmly connected to Tikopia on the home island, today parts of the community in Nukukaisi have allied themselves with their Melanesian neighbours and hosts. The conflict concerning land ownership which broke out between Malaitan migrants living in Guadalcanal and local Guadalcanal landowners made the residents of Tikopia settlements uneasy, because they felt that they too might be subjected to hostilities at some future date (ibid.:99–100). In June 1994 two leaders of the Nukukaisi settlement on Makira performed a ceremony called *he anga'a*. They presented large quantities of shell money to two local Melanesian chiefs to mark the acceptance of the Tikopia settlers into the Makira community (ibid.:159). Tikopia participation in this exchange was aimed at securing their status within Makira: henceforth, they could legitimately say that they were 'from Makira' rather than 'from Tikopia'. But there were detractors, and the performance of *he anga'a* divided Nukukaisi.

Following the ceremony the Mapungamanu Cultural Group was formed 'to help young [Tikopia] people to learn and preserve their original culture' but also to learn aspects of Melanesian culture to facilitate the integration of young people into the Makira community (ibid.:160). The group adopted the pan-pipes, associated with Melanesian performance, as part of Tikopia cultural practice. The group has been highly successful and was selected to represent Solomon Islands in the Pacific Arts Festival in American Samoa in 2008. But Tikopia traditionalists disliked the introduction of new elements and the adaptation of existing dance forms to meet audience expectations. They felt that this promoted Tikopia for the sake of money, rather than for the sake of Tikopia culture (ibid.:162).

---

9   Treadaway cites the case of a man who deferred returning to Tikopia for a visit because of the 'weight of custom': that is, he felt that he could not afford to acquire all the gifts expected of him should he return to Tikopia. According to tradition, he should return with gifts for his relatives and the four chiefs comprising baskets of baked food, pandanus mats, betel nut and local tobacco. Today he should also include bags of rice, sugar, flour, manufactured tobacco, drums of kerosene and bottles of whisky (2007:80).

On the island other activities, such as sport (soccer, rugby[10] and volleyball) or playing Western music, have also not been well received (ibid.:152). While young people are enthusiastic about traditional songs and dances (including the *mataavaka*, and those that provide a way of marking and remembering events),[11] they also want to listen to the pop, reggae, rap and hip-hop that they are exposed to once they leave the island (youths returning home from school for the holidays bring tape recorders and ghetto blasters).

While the chiefs destroyed guitars and ukuleles in the 1980s, today they tolerate them, but have restricted their use to late in the evening after traditional forms of celebration have finished (ibid.:21). Treadaway connects the elders' dislike of Western music with alcohol consumption, which they associate in turn with an increase in fighting amongst youth. But apparently in support of cultural practices, Treadaway (ibid.:19) also noted that younger men were again beginning to wear their hair long in traditional fashion.

A further shift in social relations can be seen in the partial breakdown of the division between the two districts of Faea and Ravenga: formerly divided by religious and clan lines, the residents of Tikopia today are intermarried and the clans distributed across the island (ibid.:13). As suggested by Firth, the adoption of Christianity has served to lessen the division between the two areas, but a sense of affiliation through local residence continues some fifty years after the whole island converted.

Treadaway describes a growing rift between old and young, as more and more Tikopia leave the island and find that it is difficult to return. The island itself is home to a population of 1,300, whose youngsters are destined to leave if successful in schooling and unlikely to return until their retirement if successful in finding work. Increasingly, Tikopia living away from the island marry partners from other parts of Solomon Islands (ibid.:163–4). The high mobility of islanders recorded by MacDonald is no longer evident: while people can now use a radio-telephone for communication, especially concerning the arrival of ships, visitors must

---

10 Treadway (2007:152) notes the Tikopia chiefs were particularly worried about rugby because it could cause damage to the head.

11 The Tikopia have instituted a Gulf War dance; a dance that commemorates the cyclone of 1952; the Saraphina dance inspired by viewings of a popular film made in South Africa; and a Rambo dance (ibid.:16–17).

not only raise the fare but also have the time for the boat trip to the island and then to wait an unknown period for the return trip. If people have jobs to return to, travel to Tikopia is not a simple matter.

Tikopia entered the national political arena in the mid 1980s, when they elected their first member of parliament in the Provincial Assembly. The MP achieved some success, securing a shipping company to call in at Tikopia to pick up marine products. The result was a short term injection of $10,000 into the island's 'economy' and the opening of trade-stores, two of which began showing videos in 2000 (ibid.:145). However, the shops caused jealousy, as some felt that the benefits were accruing to individuals rather than the community and that the chiefs were not being respected. However, community-owned stores failed (ibid.:143).

To be successful, Tikopia MPs need the support of the chiefs. However, the lifestyles of Tikopia in the settlements and of those on the island are diverging: residents in the former (more than half of the total Tikopia population, ibid. :8, 119–20, 151) are more closely integrated into a cash economy, which makes the position of the chiefs ambiguous, as cash is absent from the island economy (ibid.:120). Also, because of the fear of the consequences of a chief dying when away from the island, the chiefs do not leave Tikopia. Treadaway suggests that today the settlements are now largely self-governing and that the chiefs are becoming increasingly isolated from the rest of Solomon Islands (ibid.:120).

The four chiefs continue to be respected, but some Tikopia are beginning to see them as irrelevant to their society (ibid.:114), and to acknowledge them in a formal sense rather than from conviction.[12] While the chiefs do make unpopular decisions, such as banning videos, they cannot in fact enforce any decree (ibid.:117). In pre-Christian religion, the basis of the chiefs' power had rested on ritual concerns: their leadership in ritual affairs ensured success in productive activities, such as fishing and gardening. According to Treadaway, they have become 'more consumers of other people's labour and less the initiators and performers of productive activities. However, they still give as much as they receive and do not accumulate goods or wealth.' (ibid.:117).

In Treadaway's description of contemporary Tikopia life, interactions with the world beyond the island have built expectations of a better life

---

12   For example, the chiefs sit on special seats at the front of the church and are
      the first to take communion (ibid.:112).

being available through the adoption of 'Western ways': and so people's view of their tradition has come to be devalued (Pendergrast foreshadows something similar in his discussion of the decline of interest in tattooing, 2000:14). Tikopia think of what might be achievable if only they could access jobs, money and a good education for their children. For Treadaway, this is the development of a Tikopia consciousness of concepts of equality and inequality (ibid.:147–51).

> Traditionally, Tikopians would not have thought of themselves as poor people living on a remote and isolated island, but that is the image of themselves that they are acquiring through many of their contacts with the outside – through education and the media, as well as through videos. Furthermore, videos – and to some extent the media – provide a distorted view of the outside, which most Tikopians believe is real.
>
> Tikopians always knew that they were not the only people in the world, and they had contacts with many other Pacific island communities. But they saw these as equals and did not think of their island as being any more 'remote' or 'isolated' than any other. To most of them, Tikopia was the world, or the most important part of it. They were rich people. They had an abundance of food and of natural materials for houses, clothing, canoes, mats and other items they needed for a comfortable life. Their culture was rich in that it was based on a highly complex set of relationships between people [...] they had no real concept of rich and poor.
>
> Now, however, they see a different world on the videos, and learn about this world at school and in the media; and it is a world that tells them they are marginal and poor. They have been taught to judge themselves and others only by the standard of material goods, especially those manufactured in 'developed' countries. They have been taught, and are beginning to accept, that, by these standards, they are 'poor'. So Tikopians themselves, especially the young ones, will now tell you how poor they are.
>
> (Treadaway 2007:147–8)

Like MacDonald, Treadaway encountered familiarity among the Tikopia with Firth's work, and little criticism of it. A growing number of educated Tikopia have read Firth's ethnographies and agreed with most of it 'except one history book' ibid.:171). In a conversation between Treadaway and the Ariki Taumako, the latter suggested that:

> Sir Raymond's influence was partly responsible for the resistance to
> the more extreme forms of missionary teaching, which suggest that
> traditional customs are the work of the devil, and for the integration
> of so much of Tikopian tradition into Christianity. He also suggested
> that this influence may have partly been responsible for one chief not
> accepting Christianity until 1952, over 40 years after the first chief was
> converted.
>
> (2007:173)

The Ariki Taumako attributes at least some of Tikopia's tenacity in holding on to traditional practices to Firth's work there. However, Treadaway's vision of the future for Tikopia highlights a number of challenges to the traditional values Firth had helped to preserve: the disintegration of the extended family; a shift from land ownership based on clans to ownership based on individual families, and an increasing focus upon individual accumulation through, and a desire to participate in, business, rather than an emphasis on community wealth and communal labour (ibid.:198–9). These trends are felt more strongly in the settlements, although 'Tikopia culture' is still 'very much alive and well' and:

> its strength is shown by the way it is adapting to contact with other
> cultures but retaining its identity. Culture in the settlements is not
> entirely traditional, but it is still distinctively Tikopian. If the culture is
> not to be absorbed totally by outside pressures, however, it is important
> that the roots of the culture remain in Tikopia. If these roots are severed
> the whole culture could begin to wither.
>
> (2007:199–200)

CONCLUSION

Creating cultural heritage

Anna Craven (National Museum of Solomon Islands) to Firth, 27 September 1976:

> It was a fascinating visit [to Tikopia Island], and of course far too short. However, now I know some of the people we have been writing to, and they know me – particularly Edward Faka, son of Chief no.2 and a teacher. He is a useful contact. They are very keen to get our help for traditional culture promotion – the recording of songs, stories etc. So we will be working on that.
>
> One thing I tried to find out was whether they had around any copies of your books and other publications. Do you always send back to Tikopia your books and articles as you publish them? In the Solomons we have got to the stage where we are establishing Council libraries, of course starting off in the centres but hopefully in time helping smaller communities to get their own libraries going. It would be great to think that Tikopia had a small collection of your publications for their reference.
>
> (LSE: Firth Specimens 1.9.15)

Firth to Craven (National Museum of Solomon Islands), 7 October 1976:

> I think there may be a few [books] on Tikopia. I gave a copy of We the Tikopia to Pa Rangiao, son of Ellison the priest, and himself a teacher, and I have an idea there were others. I have given several of my books and papers to Ishmael Tuki [co author of Tikopia–English Dictionary] at various times. I have not sent books etc. back to Tikopia as a rule

because until quite recently no-one there could read them; what I have sent, and I suspect what they are usually most interested in, are pictures of people. Apart from the question of use – which is up to them – there has been that of preservation; you know how quickly books and papers deteriorate in that climate. This is why I sent as full a collection of my books and papers as I could to the Library at Honiara some years ago, so that they could be available for consultation as the years go by, since hopefully the Library has adequate conservation measures.

The idea of Tikopia having a small collection of my books etc for reference appeals to me of course. But who would take care of them and safeguard them from decay? And to put them in a Council Library would be reasonable, if only the Tikopia would join the Council!! Anyway, I'll tentatively put aside a few copies in the event of a serious proposition for a local Library developing in which the Tikopia will have a direct interest.

Now for other things.

I have had prepared about 35 half-plate portraits of Tikopia – a few women but mostly men – from 1929 and 1952; they include the old Ariki Kafika, Pa Fenuatara, the old Ariki Tafua and the then Pa Rangifuri (Edward's great-grandfather and grandfather) and other notables, as well as some younger men whom now I can't identify. I did have the idea of sending them back to Tikopia – I had them done for that purpose – but have hesitated, first on the score of preservation, and secondly because quite serious quarrels might arise about who should have them, which I could not handle from a distance. I have thought of sending them to one man as distributor... But now an idea has struck me. Why should they not go to the Museum at Honiara, where (presumably) they could be taken care of and be available to all Tikopia who pass through and wish to see their forebears and relatives, instead of being tucked away in boxes.

(LSE Firth Specimens 1.9.15)

Although unable to maintain regular contact with Tikopia with ease, by the 1970s Firth, already ahead of the contemporary wave, was engaged in the return of information to 'communities of origin' (also referred to as 'source communities', Peers and Brown 2003; see Jaarsman 2002 for discussion on the use and control of ethnographic materials; the return of photographic images, frequently referred to as 'visual repatriation', is discussed in Dudding 2005). Both Larson and MacDonald witnessed the impact of Firth's ethnography on Tikopia: in 1965

> [a]t least one Tikopia possessed a copy of 'We the Tikopia' and another of 'Social Change in Tikopia' … it was doubtful that any really understood these works, but the fact that they possessed them and showed keen interest in their contents should indicate that as their educational opportunities improve they will be eager to analyze them carefully.
>
> (Larson 1966: 146)

Larson's prediction was to come true. During her fieldwork between 1979 and 1980, Judith MacDonald recorded that Firth and his ethnographies were often referred to when she asked about traditional practices: for example, when asking a woman about childbirth the anthropologist was referred to a male nurse: 'I recorded a sixty minute tape of his account of traditional childbirth practices which ended with the statement, "At least, that's what Raymond says."' (MacDonald 1991:17). MacDonald was aware that some Tikopia not only possessed Firth's books, but shared and discussed the information in them. On another occasion she recorded statements 'which were couched in exactly the same words Firth had reported 50 years before'. She contemplated whether or not she was encountering the continuity of culture 'or whether Firth had fixed for all time, in the mind of readers of ethnography and the Tikopia themselves, the received version of Tikopia's belief and practice'. Tikopia were proud that Firth had recorded their cultural practices, and particularly so when they compared themselves to their Melanesian neighbours who remained 'unrecorded' (1991:17).

While Firth had already left copies of his books in Tikopia, he had also wanted to send prints of photographs he had taken of people, and indeed sent these in 1977 (Firth to Craven, 14 December 1977, LSE Firth Specimens 1.19.15). But he had been concerned about the preservation of these materials as well as who, in Tikopia, should take care of them and distribute them. Clearly Firth supported the return of objects, information and photographs because he saw that rapid social change had the potential to undermine the continued transmission of cultural knowledge between generations.

Firth made his views on the value and need for preservation of cultural heritage clear in 1973 in his presentation 'Development and the cultural heritage' at the University of the South Pacific, at a workshop titled 'Social Issues in Development Planning' (SPC and SPSoc.Sc.A housed at LSE Archives Firth 7.10.40; subsequently published as Firth 1980). Addressing an audience which he expected to consist largely of economists, he defined the word 'culture' in the phrase 'cultural heritage' in two ways: first, using what he termed an 'old definition', he described culture as encompassing the sum of cultural and social institutions; second, which he called the 'new definition', referred to symbolic systems, ways of 'expressing meaning through language, and through non-verbal actions'. These two ideas together combined pragmatic and symbolic elements: thus objects, actions and meanings were interdependent. 'Moreover, the meanings, the symbols, cannot exist alone. They need solid material and economic underpinning.' (LSE Archives Firth 7.10.40, pp. 3–4).

He explained to his audience that anthropologists think about 'how people relate to one another by using things – which are the symbols of their culture'.

> In the kind of traditional societies which many anthropologists have studied in the Pacific, the relations of young people with their elders are kept up by their using the same kinds of things, participating in actions with the symbols ... the cultural heritage is handed down by socialization, a basic process. Socialization is learning, but learning in society is by doing as much as by watching and listening.
>
> (LSE Archives Firth 7.10.40, p. 4)

Firth demonstrated his argument using the movement of gifts of food in Pacific societies as an example: gifts of food were 'a set of symbols representing an invisible network of relationships between people, very subtle, very delicate, with every parcel of food bearing a silent message'. Children learn this 'silent message' when eating food, hearing about food, collecting, cooking and carrying it. And so 'the culture of a people has a past and implies a future. It involves a committment [*sic*]. There is a heritage from the past, from one's elders; and the patterning tends to be reproduced, from one generation to another.' (LSE Archives Firth 7.10.40, pp. 4–5).

Radical changes, including those brought about by natural disasters, hold the potential to alter cultural patterns, and people, he argued, make choices about how their lives may change in response to the external circumstances that bring about that change. Therefore, cultural heritage must be seen as 'something which can change, has changed, and presumably will change as external circumstances alter' (LSE Archives Firth 7.10.40, p. 5).

For Firth's contemporary Pacific of 1973, cultural heritage functioned in three ways: firstly, as an identity marker which signalled difference (Firth cited the use of the word 'custom' in Solomon Islands); secondly, as 'a field of expression of values' which 'gives a form of communication to the people'; and lastly, as a 'marketable asset' (LSE Archives Firth 7.10.40, pp. 6–8).The development of ideas about cultural heritage was therefore related to the means through which people expressed changing social and personal values. The adoption of wage labour, for example, had introduced different ways of saving and different views on personal resources; while the process of urbanization had caused a shift in sensitivities to traditional social ties and values (LSE Archives Firth 7.10.40, p. 8).

For Firth, the ideas of 'traditional' life and 'modern' life were not best understood as two 'different frames of thinking', because people in the Pacific joined the two together all the time: their adoption and involvement of Christianity was cited as a case in point. Tradition was not therefore necessarily 'lost' as people changed their cultural practices (LSE Archives Firth 7.10.40, pp. 10–11).

> What I am arguing is the need for choice at two levels, at one level by individuals caught up in the process of development. And at another by those whose role it is to lead and take the major decisions on policy in this whole sphere. What is quite certain is that we cannot run a cultural heritage of any pure traditional kind, with its values intact, and at the same time expect to get full advantage of what we want from the modern developing economic system and its wealth of consumer goods and services.
>
> (LSE Archives Firth 7.10.40, p. 12)

Firth emphasized people's choices regarding what they chose to maintain and what they chose to give up, and it was the tensions inherent in these choices that made the transmission of cultural heritage problematic.

For example, if children were removed from the village to go to school, then the transmission of knowledge through oral means within the village and through participation in village activities would be truncated and thus insufficient to reproduce cultural practices. Therefore the '[p]roblems of recording become important, and also of interpreting to oncoming generations – and maybe to the world outside, so that other people can understand better why these things are important' (LSE Archives Firth 7.10.40, p. 12).

For Firth, anthropologists had a role within the project of recording and preserving which involved: recording custom and cultural heritage; collecting and analysing 'oral history'; collaborating with archaeologists in comparative historical interpretation; acting as cultural interpreters in general; and recording and preserving vernacular language (LSE Archives Firth 7.10.40, p. 13).

Firth's work on a Tikopia language dictionary with Ishmael Tuki (1985) and his recordings of Tikopia songs published with Mervyn Maclean (1990) reflect this stance: both have come to serve the purpose of preserving cultural heritage in an arena of social change in which the transmission of knowledge between generations through oral tradition can no longer be assured. The use of Firth's ethnographies by Tikopia, who now regard them highly, is perhaps an unintended consequence of Firth's ethnographic labours since 1928. In retrospect his books and his collection can also be understood as representations of connections, both between Firth and the Tikopia, and, as a means of transmission of cultural knowledge, between generations of Tikopia.

This book has demonstrated the multiple contexts in which objects can be interpreted, both in the past and in the present. Firth perceived the artefacts he collected through his anthropological theory, interpreting them as specimens of indigenous craft acquired as part of a 'scientific' programme to gather as much data as possible about Tikopia life. He was not particularly concerned with the aesthetic properties of objects (he felt that Tikopia aesthetics were best exemplified in musical and poetic composition). While he did not support an ethnological theory which associated artefacts with stages of evolutionary progress, he provided descriptive functional explanations of objects. But his ethnographies, which sought to describe highly complex economic, social and religious practices, have in turn provided a highly nuanced understanding of the objects he collected: while his functionalism de-emphasized the symbolic associations of artefacts, his writings have provided the means with which to comprehend their symbolic interpretations.

The history of interactions between Tikopia people and visitors to the island prior to Firth's arrival in 1928 demonstrated inter-island trading networks which required the building of sea-going vessels and the mastery of navigation. Experiences with European mariners, traders and missionaries also exposed Tikopia to broader cultural and economic influences. Nor were Tikopia people passive recipients of 'outside' influences, for they actively engaged with visitors and indeed, prior to Firth's arrival, welcomed many into their society.

This historical context helps us to comprehend Firth's relationships with the Tikopia and the way objects were used to facilitate their interactions. Considering how specific object types such as 'embodiments' mediated relationships between Tikopia people and their gods, and how other objects such as *maro* mediated relationships between people, we can see how Firth was drawn into Tikopia society through the exchange of the objects. While Firth was acquiring Tikopia artefacts, the Tikopia were, perhaps, acquiring him.

Firth's acquisition of objects such as 'embodiments' of the gods revealed processes of change in Tikopia which belie an unquestioned presumption of untouched 'traditional' practices extant in 1928. When Firth first arrived in Tikopia, parts of the population were adjusting to the presence of a new religion: Firth was witness to transformations that had been set in motion before his arrival by Christian missionaries and their island teachers. He continued to record social change on subsequent visits and this experience contributed to his view, expressed some fifty years later, of the importance of cultural heritage.

Firth's collection was made through acts of participation on his part and on the part of the Tikopia. Objects were not unethically obtained, although the parties involved may have had different interpretations of the transactions that occurred between them. In the request for repatriation of the Tikopia collection the artefacts mediated a different set of relationships: between the nation states of Solomon Islands and Australia. The repatriation process was not completed despite the good will of those involved and extensive preparations having been made for the return of the collection. The request had been initiated by an expatriate curator at the National Museum of Solomon Islands, who had been in liaison with Tikopia, but with her departure from the museum, so too departed the Tikopia's intermediary. While the files available do not explain why the return failed, it may have been that the request lacked ongoing support on behalf of the Tikopia, or indeed directly from them. The National Museum of Solomon Islands' emphasis in the 1980s was on the practical difficulties associated with repatriations, and further, on the need to have regard for the wishes of the collectors. The latter consideration adds another perspective to discussions concerning the significance of museum collections (see also Edwards and Stewart 1980; Foana'ota 1991, 1994, 2007; Lindstrom and White 1994a, b; Roe and Totu 1991; Totu and Roe 1991).

During the 1990s anthropology museums focused less on critical analysis of objects in their collection, and more on the promotion of museum collections in programmes which focused on making connections with communities of origin and providing access to objects now viewed as cultural heritage. This change of focus reflected the museum's transformation, at least in many settler societies, from 'research centre' to 'cultural resource'.

But Lindstrom and White have suggested that: 'Anthropology's task … is to explain the contemporary, end of the millennium popularity of discourses of culture, custom, and tradition by situating these in historical and political contexts' (1995:208). Using a museum collection as a tool in the investigation of the connection between cultural identity and social and cultural change, Firth's collection allows us to focus on historical and political contexts in a specific case, in parallel with the development of the concept of cultural heritage. Analysis of the collection has established its importance as an embodiment of Firth's relationship with the Tikopia, and revealed the symbolism of the objects in their original context of use. When Firth acquired 'objects of native craft', the objects he collected mediated and materialized social relations between himself and Tikopia, amongst Tikopia and between Tikopia and their gods. While Firth collected Tikopia, in the form of objects, ethnographies and sound, he is also implicated in the creation of this cultural heritage, along with the museums which now house these materials.

APPENDIX 1

Firth's 'Specimen List'

The information in this table draws from Firth's 'Specimen List' (Firth 1928). It records, in a running list based on the date acquired, how each object was transacted, from whom and its 'price'. The name of the donor or vendor reflects the spelling used by Firth on the Specimen List: the list lacks consistency and I have not attempted to standardize any names. The third column presents the description of the object presented by Firth, but it has been edited to facilitate clear understanding (thus for example, abbreviations have been removed). The fourth column lists the Tikopia language name for each object as given by Firth. Sometimes he did not list the local name (nor did he always translate the Tikopia name into English). How the objects were acquired and for what is listed in column five. Where I have been able to match each object to Firth's catalogue number, which appears on Wedgewood's (1930) catalogue listing, this number appears in the last column.

Text appearing in square brackets refers to interpretation of Firth's data; and where it follows Tikopia language names, provides translation of terms using the *Tikopia-English Dictionary* (Firth with Tuki 1985).

Date acquired	Name of the donor/vendor	Firth's description	Tikopia name	Method of acquisition	Cat. no.
28 July 1928	Clement	mat, ornamented border, large		acquired as a gift	
28 July 1928	Clement	circular pearl-shell ornament	*mata nipara*	acquired as a gift [possibly from Clement]	
29 July 1928	Pa te Kaumata	mat, ornamented border, large		acquired as a gift	
29 July 1928	Pa te Kaumata	bark-cloth mat	*māmi*	acquired as a gift	
29 July 1928	Pa Whenua Turaki	mat, ornamented, large		acquired as a gift	
29 July 1928	Pa Korokoro	mat, ornamented, small		acquired as a gift	
1 August 1928	Pa Rangi Tisa	mat, ornamented		acquired as a gift	
1 August 1928	Pa Raro Akau	bark-cloth	*māmi*	acquired as a gift	
1 August 1928	Pa Raro Akau	bone needle, old good specimen		acquired as a gift	
1 August 1928	Pa Raro Akau	coconut scraper		acquired as a gift	
2 August 1928		coral sinker	*foi punga*	picked up in [not legible]	
2 August 1928	Robert	waist mat	*kie*	purchased, amount not stated	
2 August 1928	Robert	waist mat	*fakaeroa*	purchased, amount not stated	
2 August 1928	Pa te Kaumata	sinnet beater, *toa* wood	*sasa kafa*	acquired as a gift	96.1
2 August 1928	Tari Matangi	sleeping mat, ornamented	*mēnga*	no detail recorded	
3 August 1928	Clement	breast ornament, old specimen	*tavi*	no detail recorded	
3 August 1928	Clement	sinnet coil	*kafa*	no detail recorded	

Date	Name	Description		acquisition	poss.
3 August 1928	Clement	sinnet, commencement of plait	*kafa*	no detail recorded	poss. 33.13
3 August 1928	Clement	husk for sinnet	*Raurino*	no detail recorded	
4 August 1928	Rakeitino	[bark-cloth] good piece	*mami*	acquired as a gift	
7 August 1928	John Munakina	child's grass toy	*fara balilisi*	no detail recorded	100.1
9 August 1928	Ariki Matā	[bowl] medium size, new	*kumete*	purchased with: 1 length of red calico; 6 fish-hooks	
10 August 1928	no name recorded	water bottle, coconut & *kafa* [sennit]		purchased with: 1 pipe; 1 stick of tobacco	
11 August 1928	Ellison	paddle work of Philip, gift of Ellison at *pungumu* of son	*fe*	acquired as a gift	11.2
11 August 1928	Ellison	paddle made by Philip, gift of Ellison at *pungumu* of son	*fe*	acquired as a gift	11.4
11 August 1928	Ellison	[sinnet] 1 coil, gift of Ellison at *pungumu* of son	*kafa*	acquired as a gift	
13 August 1928	Ellison	[sleeping mat] good specimen, gift on *punga umu*	*mēnga*	acquired as a gift	
13 August 1928	Ellison	[bark-cloth] good specimen, gift on *punga umu*	*māmi*	acquired as a gift	
13 August 1928	Ellison	*fakamaru* coloured *ango*, gift at *punga umu*	*maro toki*	acquired as a gift	
13 August 1928	Ellison	[man's waist cloth] 4 pieces coloured *ango*, gift at *punga umu*	*fakamaru*	acquired as a gift	

(continued) Date acquired	Name of the donor/vendor	Firth's description	Tikopia name	Method of acquisition	Cat. no.
22 August 1928	Ariki Tafua	[bag, turmeric] from *nuanga* [turmeric extraction] of Ariki Tafua	*kaka tauo*	no detail recorded	77.3
?? August 1928	no name recorded	adze blade, shell		purchased with: 2 fish-hooks	
24 August 1928	no name recorded	adze shell, modern haft	*toki tapu*	no detail recorded	
24 August 1928	Pa Nukuafua	for grating ango	*tuma*	purchased with: 16 fish-hooks	
24 August 1928	no name recorded	20 shell adze blades		purchased with: 24 fish-hooks	
24 August 1928	no name recorded	shell adze blades (broken) [no of items not specified]		purchased with: 4 fish-hooks	
24 August 1928	no name recorded	[breast ornament] good specimen	*tavi*	purchased with: 6 fish-hooks	
25 August 1928	no name recorded	tattooer's kit, with 4 chisels, cup, 2 strikers, bamboo tube of *refu*, *tuki* for mixing pigment; complete artefact		purchased with: 6 fish-hooks; 1 pipe	
25 August 1928	Pa Fenuifo [?]	good old club, shell cut	*raku taua*	purchased with: 1 plane iron; 1 string of beads	
25 August 1928	no name recorded	shell fish-hook shank	*pa maori*	purchased with: 1 fish-hook	
25 August 1928	no name recorded	2 shell ornament for wrist, large		purchased with: 2 fish-hooks	
	no name recorded	1 shell wrist orn.			

Date	Name	Description		Notes	
25 August 1928	no name recorded	20 shell adzes [*sic*] blades + 4 broken		purchased with: 22 fish-hooks	
25 August 1928	no name recorded	1 shell neck ornament.		purchased with: 1 fish-hook	
25 August 1928	Calet?	dart	*tika*	purchased with: 3 fish-hooks	20
27 August 1928	Mathiu	1 [headrest]	*urunga*	purchased with: 1 belt	
27 August 1928	James Firua	headrest	*urunga*	purchased for 1 *toki fakatu* [adze hung over the shoulder]	
28 August 1928	Pa te Kasumata	1 [sleeping mat]	*mēnga*	purchased with: 1 string of beads; 1 pipe	
28 August 1928	no name recorded	7 adze blades, shell		purchased with: 5 fish-hooks	
28 August 1928	Philip Seremata	1 funeral instrument, made of bamboo	*lopu*	not recorded	28.2
29 August 1928	Maifunga	1 *tika* dart with *fakatonga* [fibre ring on middle finger to assist in throwing dart] and *tālada* [? spelling not clear]	*tika*	purchased with: 1 plane iron	20
29 August 1928	Maifunga	1 net shuttle	*sika*	acquired as a gift	20
29 August 1928	Vaitere	bow		purchased with: 3 fish-hooks	10.7
29 August 1928	no name recorded	2 adze blades, shell		purchased with: 3 fish-hooks	
30 August 1928	no name recorded	7 adze blades, shell; plus 2 broken		purchased with: 7 fish-hooks	
30 August 1928	no name recorded	1 dance club	*paki*	purchased with: 8 fish-hooks	
30 August 1928	Daniel [not legible]	1 [headrest] old specimen	*urunga*	purchased with: 1 cotton belt	

(continued) Date acquired	Name of the donor/vendor	Firth's description	Tikopia name	Method of acquisition	Cat. no.
30 August 1928	no name recorded	1 [sinnet beater]	*sasa kafa*	purchased with: 3 fish-hooks	96.2
30 August 1928	no name recorded	1 top, with *uka* [cord, string]	*moa*	purchased with: 4 fish-hooks	99.1
30 August 1928	no name recorded	3 [darts]	*tika*	purchased with: 9 fish-hooks	20
3 September 1928	no name recorded	1 [taro grater]	*sina*	purchased with: 10 fish-hooks	88.3
3 September 1928	no name recorded	1 [taro grater]	*sina*	purchased with: 10 fish-hooks	88.2
3 September 1928	no name recorded	breast ornament	*tifa*	purchased with: 5 fish-hooks	
3 September 1928	no name recorded	[arrow] tipped human bone	*ngasau*	purchased with: 4 fish-hooks	
3 September 1928	no name recorded	2 shell adze blades, broken		purchased with: 1 fish-hooks	
3 September 1928	no name recorded	shark hook, old specimen	*kau*	purchased with: 20 fish-hooks	
3 September 1928	no name recorded	5 arrows, tipped human bone	*ngasau*	purchased with: 20 fish-hooks	
3 September 1928	no name recorded	1 [headrest]	*urunga*	purchased with: 10 fish-hooks	
3 September 1928	no name recorded	1 [headrest]	*urunga*	purchased with: 10 fish-hooks	
3 September 1928	no name recorded	1 betelnut mortar, pestle and *kuti* [illegible]; [*kuti* is a woman's hand net]	*soka*	purchased with: 1 pipe	
4 September 1928	no name recorded	[arrow] tipped human bone	*ngasau*	purchased with: 4 fish-hooks	
4 September 1928	no name recorded	1 dart with *fakatonga* [fibre ring on middle finger to assist in throwing dart]	*tika*	purchased with: 3 fish-hooks	20
6 September 1928	Pa Faranga Noa	1 net	*kuani*	purchased with: 6 fish-hooks	35.2

Date	Name	Description	Native name	Acquisition	No.
6 September 1928	Pa Te Kaumata	1 arrow, from Vanikoro, human bone		purchased with: 4 fish-hooks	
6 September 1928	Pokia	mortar	*soka*	purchased with: 1 pipe	8.12
6 September 1928	Pa ra[t] matini	1 [sleeping mat]	*mēnga*	purchased with: 1 length of calico; 1 fish-hook	
7 September 1928	Pa Rangi Furi	1 [bowl] for *roroi*, old specimen [for holding coconut cream, see 1.17 in Appendix 2].	*kumete*	purchased with: 1 plane iron	1.10
7 September 1928	Pa Rangi Furi	1 [bowl] for *roroi*, new [for holding coconut cream, see 1.17 in Appendix 2]	*kumete*	purchased with: 1 plane iron	1.9
7 September 1928	P[hilip?] Seremata	1 adze blade and 1 broken		acquired as a gift	
8 September 1928	Name not recorded	1 [kava bowl] cracked	*tau kava*	purchased with: 15 fish-hooks	2.2
8 September 1928	Pae Sau	1 [kava bowl] old specimen	*tau kava*	purchased with: 1 length of white calico; 40 fish-hooks; 2 pipes	2.1
8 September 1928	no name recorded	1 [net shuttle]	*sika*	purchased with: 5 fish-hooks	
8 September 1928	P[hilip] Seremata	shark hook, old specimen	*kau*	acquired as a gift	93-4
8 September 1928	P[hilip] Seremata	2 tattooer's chisels	*matau*	acquired as a gift	
8 September 1928	P[hilip] Seremata	3 finger-rings for girl	*ngasane*	acquired as a gift	
8 September 1928	P[hilip] Seremata	1 [basket]	*longi*	acquired as a gift	
8 September 1928	Pa Fetauta	1 [spear] old specimen	*tokotoko*	purchased with: 9 beads, small strings	16.1

(continued) Date acquired	Name of the donor/vendor	Firth's description	Tikopia name	Method of acquisition	Cat. no.
8 September 1928	Pa Niu Kaso	1 [headrest]	*urunga*	purchased with: 8 fish-hooks	4.32
8 September 1928	Pa Pangisis	1 roll [sinnet, valued property, used in canoe rigging, binding for rolls of tobacco] & Tikopia tobacco	*maia*	acquired as a gift	
9 September 1928	Pa Niu kapu	1 bowl for *renga* "Pu Rangi Tisa," old specimen, good [probably belonged to Pu Rangi Tisa]		Bowl and spear (below) purchased with: 1 axe	1.15
9 September 1928	no name recorded	1 [spear] good specimen, old. Pu Niukasu. [Probably belonged to Pu Niukasu]	*tokotoko*	Spear and bowl (above) purchased with: 1 axe	16.2
10 September 1928	Pa Nui kasu	1 club, short, old specimen	*tuki*	purchased with:10 fish-hooks	
10 September 1928	P[hilip] emata	3 finger-rings		acquired as a gift	46
11 September 1928	Pa Rongotau	[adze] blade	*toki fatu uri*	purchased with: 4 fish-hooks	
11 September 1928	Kauraro	adze blade, very large	*toki*	purchased with: 6 fish-hooks	
11 September 1928	Pa Raro Toa	[headrest]	*urunga*	purchased with: 9 fish-hooks ·	
11 September 1928	Pa Fetauta	[headrest]	*urunga*	purchased with: 9 fish-hooks	
11 September 1928	Pa Nuku Furi	t[urmeric cyclinder]	*umu te renga*	purchased with: 9 fish-hooks	7.5
11 September 1928	Pa Paiu	[taro grater] old specimen	*sina*	purchased with: 12 fish-hooks	

Date	Name	Description	Local name	Purchased with	No.
11 September 1928	no name recorded	[arrow] tipped in *tangata* [human being, person – human bone tip]	*ngasau*	purchased with: 8 fish-hooks	
11 September 1928	Tukurina Pa Rengorei	[Traditional small circular wrist ornament of clam shell – no longer worn]	*tanipara*	purchased with: 8 fish-hooks	
11 September 1928	Pa Rongorei	[bark-cloth beater]	*ike*	purchased with: 7 fish-hooks	9.8
10 September 1928	Pa Motuangi	1 [bonito hook], koroa ariki [valued property of the ariki]	*pa atu*	purchased with: 1 string of small beads; 2 pipes	44.13
10 September 1928	no name recorded	5 [arrows], tipped in *tangata* [human being, person – human bone tip]	*ngasau*	purchased with: 22 fish-hooks	
10 September 1928	Pa Te Kaumata	1 [bonito hook], ordinary	*pa atu*	purchased with: 8 fish-hooks	
10 September 1928	Pa Rangifuri	for grating *ango* [turmeric plant]	*tama*	purchased with: 3 strings of small beads	21.3
10 September 1928	Pa Mukara	1 waist mat & 1 *viki kumete* [little bowl]	*kie & kumete*	purchased with: 1 'tomahawk'	1.16
12 September 1928	Pa Rangifau	[pointed club, see 13.oo in Appendix 2]	*rakau taua*	purchased with: 4 strings of beads	13.14
12 September 1928	Tarivoka	[net shuttle]	*sika*	purchased with: 6 fish-hooks	
12 September 1928	Pa Raro Toa	[bark-cloth beater]	*ike*	purchased with: 7 fish-hooks	
12 September 1928	Kafatasi	[mortar for crushing betel]	*soka*	purchased with: 7 fish-hooks	
12 September 1928	Sefokisaki	spoon, European model		purchased with: 4 fish-hooks	3.9

(continued) Date acquired	Name of the donor/vendor	Firth's description	Tikopia name	Method of acquisition	Cat. no.
12 September 1928	Titus	[bowl] round, low	*kumete*	purchased with: 1 length of red calico; 3 fish-hooks	
12 September 1928	Samoa	[headrest]	*urunga*	purchased with: 1 pipe	4.30
12 September 1928	Samoa	[plaiting slab] [probably *papa feū raranga*, 90.2 see Appendix 2]	*fui raranga rakuu* [?]	purchased with: 7 fish-hooks	90.2
12 September 1928	Ariki Tafua	[bowl] for *susua* [?], good old specimen	*kumete*	not recorded	
13 September 1928	no name recorded	[dance club] rough specimen but well worn	*paki*	purchased with: 1 pipe	
13 September 1928	no name recorded	[dance club] rough specimen but well worn	*paki*	purchased with: 7 fish-hooks	
13 September 1928	no name recorded	[mortar for crushing betel] good sp, *pani* [mark of colour]	*soka*	purchased with: 7 fish-hooks	
13 September 1928	no name recorded	[headrest]	*urunga*	purchased with: 9 fish-hooks	
13 September 1928	Pa Taetae	4 [arrows] bone tipped	*ngasau*	acquired as a gift	
13 September 1928	Ellison	[cord, usually sinnet or hibiscus fibre; with a plait of 4 ply]	*uka matai*	acquired as a gift	
13 September 1928	Pa Nuku Tai	[headrest]	*urunga*	purchased with: 9 fish-hooks	
13 September 1928	Nukufuri, possibly from	[pounder] whalebone, for betel-mortar, old specimen	*tuki*	purchased with: 5 fish-hooks	

Date	Name	Description			Number
13 September 1928	Nukufuri, possibly from	adze blade, good specimen, shell	*toki*	purchased with: 3 fish-hooks	
13 September 1928	Nukufuri	[breast ornament], good old specimen	*tavi*	purchased with: 20 fish-hooks	48.18
13 September 1928	Fetauta	arrow, 2 pronged	*ngasau*	purchased with: 5 fish-hooks	
13 September 1928	Pa Nuku Nefu	bark-cloth	*mami*	purchased with: 5 fish-hooks; 2 pipes	
13 September 1928	no name recorded	[arrow] bone tipped	*ngasau*	purchased with: 4 fish-hooks	
13 September 1928	Pa Avakofe	[pounder] for betel *tafora* [? possibly of whale bone], good old specimen	*tuki*	purchased with: 2 fish-hooks; 3 strings of beads	
13 September 1928	no name recorded	3 adze blades		purchased with: 3 fish-hooks	
13 September 1928	no name recorded	[bowl] small, circular	*kumete*	purchased with: 15 fish-hooks	
13 September 1928	Ariki Tafua	2 bags [turmeric pigment]	*renga*	acquired as a gift	38.1 & .4
13 September 1928	Ariki Tafua	[sinnet] for *k[auma]futa*	*kafa*	acquired as a gift	
13 September 1928	Ariki Tafua	2 [stirrers]	*fe*	acquired as a gift	91.00
13 September 1928	Ariki Tafua	2 [tongs]	*ukofi*	acquired as a gift	91.00
13 September 1928	Ariki Tafua	1 [bowl] small	*kumete*	acquired as a gift	
13 September 1928	Pa Mukava	[coconut-grating stool]	*rakau saro niu*	acquired as a gift	
14 September 1928	Name not recorded	[cup] with wooden hook attached	*fangongi*	purchased with: 4 fish-hooks	3.7 [?]
15 September 1928	Pa Nuku Tai	[fibre-scraping slab]	*tama raru fau*	purchased with: 1 pipe	22.1
16 September 1928	Pa Taetae	shark noose		acquired as a gift	

(continued) Date acquired	Name of the donor/vendor	Firth's description	Tikopia name	Method of acquisition	Cat. no.
16 September 1928	Sia	necklet of beads & teeth		purchased with: 10 fish-hooks	
18 September 1928	Sa Sau	tooth		purchased with: 3 fish-hooks	
18 September 1928	Sa Sau	[mortar for crushing betel] old specimen	soka	purchased with: 5 fish-hooks	
18 September 1928	Pa Niu Kaso	[club pointed]	rakau taua	purchased with: 3 strings of beads	13.15
19 September 1928	Pa Raro Tonga	[breast ornament] old specimen	tavi	purchased with: 12 fish-hooks	48.9
15 September 1928	Pa Paiu	[breast ornament]	tavi	purchased with: 1 length of white calico	48.12 or .12
15 September 1928	Pa Mukava	[pearl-shell neck ornament]; old specimen brought by puna [grandparent] of Pa Mukava from Vanikoro	tifa	purchased with: 1 blue calico print	Poss. 52.40
19 September 1928	Pa Fenua Fara	[shark hook]	kau	purchased with: 11 fish-hooks	
19 September 1928	Pa te Kaumata	[coconut shell used for grating sago]	fangango saro ota	acquired as a gift	87.1
19 September 1928	Pa Ranga Tau	[adze, stone]	toki uri	purchased with: 6 fish-hooks	
19 September 1928	Paito Resiake	[?] of coconut shell [see saumo below; fakatikopia = in Tikopia fashion].	saumo fakatikopia	purchased with: 3 stings of beads, large	
19 September 1928	Taungivaka	[club, pointed]	rakau taua	purchased with: 1 length of white calico	
19 September 1928	Pa Mesara	[club]	tuki	purchased with: 1 length of white calico	

Date	Name	Description	Local name	No.	Purchase
19 September 1928	Pa Ronga Rei	[breast ornament]	*tavi*		purchased with: 10 fish-hooks
19 September 1928	no name recorded	14 shell adzes			purchased with: 18 fish-hooks
20 September 1928	Pa Rongo Taono (Frank)	[headrest]	*urunga*	4.27	purchased with: 9 fish-hooks
20 September 1928	Pa Fenua Fara	[headrest]	*urunga*	4.25	purchased with: 9 fish-hooks
20 September 1928	Paito Fare Kofe	[spear]	*tokotoko*	16.4	purchased with: 1 length of white calico
20 September 1928	Mathiu	2 [traditional small circular wrist ornament of clam shell – no longer worn]	*tanipara*		not recorded
20 September 1928	Philip [Seremata?]	2 [traditional small circular wrist ornament of clam shell – no longer worn]	*tanipara*		not recorded
20 September 1928	Pa Rangatau	[?] of coconut shell	*saumo*		purchased with: 3 string of beads
20 September 1928	Nau na Neve	[waist-mat made of pandanus]	*fakuro (kie)*		purchased with: 4 string of beads
20 September 1928	Paito Ariki Kafika	1 [possibly an arrow]	*Ngasare* [?] or *ngasau*		purchased with: 4 fish-hooks
20 September 1928	Ariki Kafika	adze [stone] good specimen	*toki uri*		purchased with: 7 fish-hooks
20 September 1928	Ariki Kafika	adze [stone] side broken	*toki uri*		purchased with: 1 pipe
20 September 1928	Pa Fongare Vai	[?]	*saumo*		purchased with: fish-hooks (not stated how many)
20 September 1928	Mathiu	[spear]	*tokotoko*		purchased with: 1 length of white calico
20 September 1928	Mathiu	[headrest]	*urunga*		purchased with: 9 fish-hooks
20 September 1928	Mathiu	[bark-cloth beater]	*ike*		purchased with: 8 fish-hooks

(continued) Date acquired	Name of the donor/vendor	Firth's description	Tikopia name	Method of acquisition	Cat. no.
20 September 1928	Pa Fenua Fara	[bark-cloth beater]	*ike*	*fakafaiki* [?]	
20 September 1928	Pa Paiu	[headrest]	*urunga*	purchased with: 9 fish-hooks	
20 September 1928	Pa Nuku Tauo	[breast ornament]	*tavi*	purchased with: 10 fish-hooks	
20 September 1928	no name recorded	[breast ornament] poor specimen	*tavi*	purchased with: 6 fish-hooks	
20 September 1928	Pa Nuku Tano	? [bucket-shaped cup, see 3.8 in Appendix 2]	*fangengo*	purchased with: 4 large fish-hooks	3.8
20 September 1928	Pa Fenua Fara	[bonito hook]	*pa atu*	purchased with: 1 length of white calico	44.12
20 September 1928	Rangi rikoi	[bowl]	*kumete*	purchased with: 1 length of white calico	
21 September 1928	Pa Nuku Afu	[bonito hook & bark beat]	*pa atu & ike*	purchased with: 1 length of white calico	
21 September 1928	Faranga Noa	[little bowl]	*kumete viki*	purchased with: 12 fish-hooks	1.18
21 September 1928	Pa Mesara	[man's bag]	*tanga*	purchased with: 5 large fish-hooks	
21 September 1928	Pa Koroatu	[netting shuttle]	*sika*	purchased with: 6 fish-hooks	12.6
21 September 1928	Pa Rangi Tisu	[bowl]	*kumete*	purchased with: 5 fish-hooks; 2 pipes	
21 September 1928	no name recorded	[pearl-shell neck ornament]	*tifa*	purchased with: 1 fish-hook	
21 September 1928	Pa Koroatu	[fish-hook shank]	*pa*	purchased with: 3 fish-hooks	
21 September 1928	Pa Tara Nuia	[pearl-shell neck ornament]	*tifa*	purchased with: 8 fish-hooks	
21 September 1928	Tiforau	[headrest]	*urunga*	purchased with: 9 fish-hooks	4.26
21 September 1928	Kavavaniu	[headrest]	*urunga*	purchased with: 9 fish-hooks	4.34
21 September 1928	Pa Tanga	[headrest]	*urunga*	purchased with: 9 fish-hooks	4.20

21 September 1928	Pa Fare Ata	[headrest]	*urunga*	purchased with: 9 fish-hooks	
21 September 1928	no name recorded	[headrest]	*urunga*	purchased with: 9 fish-hooks	
21 September 1928	no name recorded	[headrest]	*urunga*	purchased with: 9 fish-hooks	
21 September 1928	Tupungaru [?]	3 [arrows]	*ngasau*	purchased with: 12 fish-hooks	
21 September 1928	Pa Fenua Fara	1 [arrow]	*ngasau*	purchased with: 4 fish-hooks	
21 September 1928	Pa Marae Vaka	[breast ornament]	*tavi*	purchased with: 10 fish-hooks	
21 September 1928	no name recorded	[breast ornament]	*tavi*	purchased with: 7 fish-hooks	
21 September 1928	Paito Farefikai	[mortar for crushing betel]	*soka*	purchased with: 8 fish-hooks	8.8
21 September 1928	no name recorded	[mortar for crushing betel]	*soka*	purchased with: 7 fish-hooks	
21 September 1928	Totorofaka Tonga	[mortar for crushing betel] good specimen	*soka*	purchased with: 8 fish-hooks	8.7
21 September 1928	Pa Motuangi	[dance club]	*paki*	purchased with: 1 length of red calico	
21 September 1928	Pa Nuku Manongi	[breast ornament] of *fangongo* [coconut shell]]	*tavi*	purchased with: 6 fish-hooks	
22 September 1928	Pa Vaetoka	[headrest]	*urunga*	purchased with: 9 fish-hooks	4.18
22 September 1928	Pa Tani Anu		*sansio* [?]	purchased with: 6 strings of small beads beads	
22 September 1928	no name recorded	[fish-hook shank] good specimen	*pa*	purchased with: 12 fish-hooks	
22 September 1928	Pa Matatae	[bow]	*fana*	purchased with: 6 fish-hooks	10.8
22 September 1928	Pa Matatae	[rhythm beater]	*kau ta tē mako*	purchased with: 4 fish-hooks	95.1
22 September 1928	Pa Porima	[breast ornament]	*tavi*	purchased with: 5 fish-hooks	48.11
22 September 1928	no name recorded	[headrest]	*urunga*	purchased with: 9 fish-hooks	

(continued) Date acquired	Name of the donor/vendor	Firth's description	Tikopia name	Method of acquisition	Cat. no.
22 September 1928	Pa Te Kaumate	[headrest]	*urunga*	purchased with: 9 fish-hooks	4.38
22 September 1928	no name recorded	[dart]	*tika*	purchased with: 5 fish-hooks	20
22 September 1928	no name recorded	[cup for tattooing dye?]	*fangongo refu*	purchased with: 2 fish-hooks	
22 September 1928	Firua?	[lime container]	*kapia niu*	purchased with: 4 fish-hooks	
22 September 1928	Pa Farareu	[bark-cloth beater] good spec	*ike*	purchased with: 8 fish-hooks	9.12
22 September 1928	no name recorded	30 adze blades	*penu toki*	purchased with: 35 fish-hooks	
22 September 1928	no name recorded	[bowl]	*kumete*	purchased with: 11 fish-hooks	
22 September 1928	Pa Nuku o Manu	[bowl]	*kumete*	purchased with: 1 length of white calico	
22 September 1928	Pa Paiu	[bag, turmeric]	*kaka tauo*	purchased with: 1 razor	
22 September 1928	no name recorded	[arrow]	*ngasau*	purchased with: 4 fish-hooks	
22 September 1928	Pa to Kaumata	[hook]	*kau*	purchased with: 4 fish-hooks	94.1
22 September 1928	Pa Motuangi	[hook]	*kau*	purchased with: 4 fish-hooks	94.2
22 September 1928	Pa Taetae	mat, small		purchased with: 3 strings of beads	
23 September 1928	Pa Niu Kapu	[kava bowl]	*tau kava*	purchased with: small beads	2.3
23 September 1928	Pa Niu Kapu	[bark-cloth beater]	*ike*	purchased with: 9 fish-hooks	
23 September 1928	Pa Niu Kapu	[bark-cloth beater] new specimen	*ike*	acquired as a gift	9.11
23 September 1928	Pa Niu Kapu	[dance club]	*paki*	acquired as a gift	14.4
23 September 1928	Pa Niu Kapu	[net shuttle]	*sika*	purchased with: 6 fish-hooks	12.8
23 September 1928	Pa Niu Kapu	[net gauge]	*afa*	purchased with: 2 fish-hooks	

Date	Name	Description	Native term	Purchase	No.
23 September 1928	Pa Niu Kapu	[bonito hook]	*pa atu*	purchased with: 1 length of red calico	44.11
24 September 1928	Pa Rangi Furi		*rakau fetaaki*	purchased with: 1 length of red calico	
24 September 1928	Pa Rangi Furi	sinnet, prob belt	*maia*	purchased with: 15 fish-hooks	40.9
4 November 1928	Pa Rangi Furi		*tao*	purchased with: 1 adze	
4 November 1928 ?	Pa Rangifuri	[sleeping mat]	*mēnga*	purchased with: 1 knife	
4 November 1928 ?	Ariki Tafua	[sleeping mat]	*mēnga*	purchased with: 1 1 adze	
4 November 1928 ?	Fani Resiake	2 [fan?]	*iri*	purchased with: 8 sticks of tobacco	
4 November 1928 ?	Mairunga	[spear]	*tao fetuaki ota*	not recorded	
4 November 1928 ?	Mairunga	sling	*maka*	not recorded	
4 November 1928 ?	Ariki Tafua	1 *mēnga*, 1 *marotafi*, 8 *fakamaru* from pariki	*maro*	purchased with: 3 pieces of calico, 1 pocket knife	
	Pa Nitini	[club]	*tuki*	not recorded	
4 November 1928 ?	Captain of the *Southern Cross* [the Anglican Mission boat].	*mēnga* 5 [sleeping mat, given as presents to the Captain]	*mēnga*	Purchased with 7 knives	
4 November 1928 ?	Captain of the *Southern Cross* [the Anglican Mission boat].	*kie* 2 [waist mat, given as presents to the Captain]	*kie*	Purchased with a twelve-inch knife	
4 November 1928 ?	Pa Te Kaumata	[adze]	*toki tapu*	purchased with: a fourteen-inch knife	

(continued) Date acquired	Name of the donor/vendor	Firth's description	Tikopia name	Method of acquisition	Cat. no.
4 November 1928 ?	Jones of Vanikoro [a trader based on Vanikoro]	2 [turmeric cylinder]; given to Jones of Vanikoro in exchange for Santa Cruz loom	*renga*	purchased with: 2 fourteen-inch knives	
4 November 1928 ?	P[hilip] Seremata	[fish line]		purchased with: 1 twelve-inch knife	
4 November 1928 ?	Pa Teva	fish line	*matai*	purchased with: 1 sheath knife	
4 November 1928 ?	P[hilip] Seremata	fish float	*uta*	not recorded	
4 November 1928 ?	Pa Motuangi	bark-cloth	*màmi*	not recorded	
4 November 1928 ?	Pa Mukura	waist mat	*kie*	purchased with: 1 twelve-inch knife	
4 November 1928 ?	Sa Sau	[turmeric cylinder] small	*renga*	purchased with: 1 twelve-inch knife	
4 November 1928 ?	Pa Avakofe	[sleeping mat]	*mènga*	purchased with: 1 knife	

APPENDIX 2

The Firth Collection at the Australian Museum

The objects in Firth's 1928–9 collection are listed in the order they appear on the collection lists drawn up by Camilla Wedgewood (1930), followed by the registration number assigned by the Australian Museum. 'Not in AM' indicates that the object is not present in the Australian Museum, and may reside in another institution.

A second list (LSE Archives, Firth Specimens 1.2.5 titled 'Sent to Bishop Museum') lists a number of objects sent to the Bernice Bishop Museum, Honolulu. Presence on this list is marked by an asterisk (*), and where there is uncertainty, such as an irregularity in the identification numbers, this has been indicated with a question mark (?).

1.00 Bowls (*kumete*) used for ceremonial gifts at marriage, death, etc., as well as for ordinary household purposes

1.1	E84300	Food bowl *kumete* – unique specimen with legs; carved with steel tools. Made by Ariki Kafika several generations ago. Given as part of *malai* marriage gift from clan Kafika to clan Taumako for a woman from the latter. Obtained from Paito i Oliki. Only two such *kumete* were made.
1.2	E84869	*kumete*, long – given Pa Rangimaseke
1.3	E84380	*kumete*, food bowl
1.4	not in AM	*kumete*, food bowl, unusual shape
1.5	not in AM	*kumete*, for making turmeric – small size
1.6	not in AM	*kumete*, food bowl, broad shape
1.7	E84376	*kumete*, for holding coconut cream – unusual shape; made by Pu Resiake
1.8	not in AM	*kumete*, small, elliptical type, used for holding mud or lime for hair plastering
1.9	not in AM	*kumete*, round, type for holding coconut cream; new, made by Pa Rangifuri
1.10	E84291	*kumete*, same type as 1.09, from Pa Rangifuri
1.11	not in AM	*kumete*, old specimen, notched ornamentation; from Ariki Tafua, food bowl
1.12	not in AM	*kumete*, from Pa Paiu – food bowl
1.13	E84298	*kumete*, food bowl

1.14	E84378	*kumete*, food bowl – unusual type with foot
1.15	E84296	*kumete*, for making turmeric – old specimen called Pu Rangitisa, so named from the fact that he was its maker, some two to three generations ago. From Pa Niu Kapu.
1.16	E84297	*kumete*, for making turmeric – ordinary small type, from Pa Mukava
1.17	E84299	*kumete*, for holding coconut cream – *kumeti roroi* – small round bowl
1.18	E84809	*kumete*, small wooden bowl, used to hold lime or mud for dressing the hair. Probably from Santa Cruz group. From Paito Faranganoa

2.00 Kava bowls – *tau kava* – shallow in form with four feet close together

2.1	E84377	*tau kava* – old specimen obtained from Pae Sao, Pure of Ariki Tafua; has been in his family for generations
2.2	not in AM	*tau kava* – old specimen
2.3	E84290	*tau kava* – Pa Niu Kapu

3.00 Cups *fangongo kava* (kava cups), cut from half small coconut shell, not polished

3.1	E84804	*fangongo kava*
3.2	E84805	*fangongo kava*
3.3	E84806	*fangongo kava*
3.4	not in AM	*fangongo kava*
3.5	E84287	wooden cup with handle, modern specimen made in imitation of European ladle; used for drinking liquids; made by Pa Panapa
3.6	E84807	*fangongo kava*
3.7	not in AM	*fangongo*, cup for drinking, with wooden handle attached for hanging up when not in use
3.8	E84288	*fangongo*, made in the shape of a European bucket and probably copied from one on an early ship, but an old specimen of Tikopian workmanship, from Pa Nuku Tano
3.9	E84908	*puni* – a spoon – an old specimen made in imitation of an European tablespoon

4.00 Headrests, *urunga*, carved from wood in a variety of shapes; those of chiefs usually have long wings: used for sleeping and resting, the back or side of the head being laid as on a pillow

4.1	not in AM	*urunga* – small specimen on two feet; given by Pae Sao; his first piece of work
4.2	not in AM	*urunga* – unusual shape with stand; given by Pa Ngatitiu.
4.3	E84630	*urunga* – common type on single stand given by Pa Niukapu
4.4	Bishop Museum*	*urunga* – same type as 4.3; given by Pa Maniva [annotated with D close to collection number]
4.5	not in AM	*urunga* – type commonly used by chiefs with forked foot; the wings of this specimen have been cut; made by Pa Fangatau about 1890. [annotated with D close to collection number]
4.6	E84642	*urunga* – same type as 4.5, from Paito i Veterei

4.7	E84035	*urunga* – common type, new; made by Pa Rangifuri, notched ornamentation
4.8	Bishop Museum*	*urunga* – chief's type, made by Pa Avakofe, both feet forked, one mended by Pa Motuatu – an example of native repair work. [annotated with D close to collection number]
4.9	E84639	*urunga* – chief's type
4.10	E84019	*urunga* – shape adapted from a branch – given by Mairunga
4.11	E84033	*urunga* – common type, notched ornamentation
4.12	E84024	*urunga* – common type; with bulbous stand, given by Pa Fenua tara, cross on foot purely decorative, he is not a Christian
4.13	E84028	*urunga* – common type
4.14	E84034	*urunga*
4.15	E84633	*urunga*
4.16	BASEL	*urunga* – from Pa Funua Tara; Basel [crossed out on list]
4.17	E84025	*urunga* – from Paito Tanimua
4.18	E84638	*urunga* – from Pa Vae Toka
4.19	E84637	*urunga* – chief's type (*urunga nga ariki*) from Mairunga
4.20	not in AM	*urunga* – very unusual type – from Pa Taunga
4.21	not in AM	*urunga*
4.22	E84631	*urunga* – from Paito fetauta
4.23	E84632	*urunga*
4.24	E84026	*urunga*
4.25	E84030	*urunga* – from Pa fenua fara
4.26	E84021	*urunga* – from Ti forau
4.27	E84018	*urunga* – from Pa Rongo Taono
4.28	E84031	*urunga*
4.29	not in AM	*urunga* – from Pa Fare ata
4.30	not in AM	*urunga* – from the Samoa family
4.31	E84029	*urunga* – old specimen cut by father of Pu rangi rikoi, (the latter being about seventy years old)
4.32	not in AM	*urunga* – chief's type but with abbreviated wings, from Pa Niu Kaso
4.33	E84636	*urunga* – chief's type, old specimen
4.34	E84022	*urunga* – intermediate type with rudimentary wings; from Kavarauniu
4.35	BASEL	*urunga* – presented to Basel Museum für Völkerkunde
4.36	E84027	*urunga*
4.37	E84032	*urunga* – from Fetauta family
4.38	E84020	*urunga* – from Pa te Kaumata

5.00 Coconut grating stools, *rakau saro niu*; a seat on legs, the front one being forked; a serrated grater of coconut shell is tied to the projection in front

5.1	E84054	*rakau saro niu* – large specimen with broad seat
5.2	E84055	*rakau saro niu*
5.3	E87720	*rakau saro niu* – small specimen; old, slight decoration – an unusual feature

6.00 Canoe baler, *ta* – These much resemble the Maori type, but are not carved.

| 6.01 | not in AM | *ta* |

7.00 Cylinders for cooking turmeric, *taonga* or *umu renga*; these are of wood, usually decorated with notched designs. The workmanship of these varies considerably and specimens are valued by the natives according to the volume and finish of their interior; certain men are noted craftsmen in making these cylinders

7.1	E84795	*umu renga* – from Paito I Maranga one; the interior badly shaped in native opinion
7.2	E84796	*umu renga* – good specimen in native opinion, interior well hollowed
7.3	E84797	fine specimen, both in finish and design; it carries '*renga*' as natives say
7.4	E84794	*umu renga* – properly hollowed specimen
7.5	E84792	*umu renga* – from Pa nuku furi – a particularly small specimen
7.6	E84798	*umu renga* – from Pa Mesara [annotated with D close to collection number]
7.7	E84793	*umu renga* – from Ariki Tafua

8.00 Betel mortars, *soka*; usually made of *toa*, cassowarina [sic, probably Casuarina species] wood

8.1	not in AM	*soka* – old specimen, property of Ariki Kafika, Pu Mapusanga, given by his descendant Pa Tarai Raki
8.2	not in AM	*soka* – old specimen, property of Tarotu former Ariki Kafika, from his grandson pa Marakei
8.3	E84784	*soka* – bulbous shape – unusual
8.4	E84782	*soka* – with cleaning rag of piece of old net
8.5	E84785	*soka* – unusual bulbous shape
8.6	E84788	*soka* – large specimen, really a food mortar; used to pound canarium nuts and food for an old man; belonged to Pu Nukura, given by Pa Nukura his descendent
8.7	E84786	*soka* – a good specimen, from Paito Torofakatonga
8.8	E84790	*soka* – from Paito Farefikai
8.9	not in AM	*soka*
8.10	E84789	*soka* – old specimen, from Pae Sao
8.11	Bishop Museum*	*soka*
8.12	E84783	*soka* – large specimen with cleaning rag of *kuti* – net, from Pokia

8.13	E84780	*soka* – with cleaning rag of *kuti* net and a wooden pestle (*tuki*). The latter is new (today a piece of iron is used) and represents the old type; the mortar wood is *toa*; the pestle is *tiake*
8.13	E84627	*tuki – pestle*

9.00 Bark-cloth beaters, *ike*, of common Polynesian type

9.1	not in AM	*ike* – from Paito I Ratiare [annotated with D close to collection number]
9.2	E84358	*ike* – good specimen, from Pa Rangi maseke
9.3	E84361	*ike* – cylindrical, unusual shape from Pa Nuku-manongi
9.4	E84362	*ike* – small specimen, from Pa Nuku mangongi
9.5	not in AM	*ike*
9.6	In Basel	*ike* – Basel [entry crossed out and annotated with D close to collection number]
9.7	E84363	*ike*
9.8	E84577	*ike* – from Pa Rongo rei
9.9	not in AM	*ike* – from Pa Sao
9.10	E84360	*ike* – from Pa Nuku afua
9.11	Bishop Museum*	*ike* – a new specimen, from Pa Niu Kapu
9.12	E84359	*ike* – good specimen, from Pa Fara reu
9.13	E84364	*ike*

10.00 Bows, *fana*, usually made of *miro* wood by special craftsmen

10.1	E92199	*fana* – fine specimen, made by Pa Niuwaru, given by Pa Fenuatara in token of friendship.
10.2	E92200	*fana* – given by Pae Sao
10.3	E92198	*fana* – made by Pa Siamano, given by Pa Taraoro
10.4	E92203	*fana* – from Pa Maniva
10.5	E92196	*fana*
10.6	E92202	*fana*
10.7	E92197	*fana* – of *miro* wood – type used by youths, from Vaitere
10.8	E92201	*fana* – from Pa Matatae

11.00 Paddes – *foa* or *fe*; Tikopian paddles are of large rough type, suited to open sea work used also as ceremonial gifts by men

11.1	E85140	*foa* – gift on incision of Munakina to mother's brother
11.2	E85142	*foa*
11.3	E85014	*foa* – as 11.1
11.4	E85143	*foa* – large specimen

12.00 Netting shuttle, *sika* varying in siae according to mesh of net

12.1	E84683	*sika*
12.2	E84688	*sika* – [annotated with D close to collection number]
12.3	E84374	*sika*
12.4	E84684	*sika*

12.5	E84375	*sika*
12.6	E84689	*sika* – from Pa Koroatu
12.7	E84686	*sika*
12.8	E84687	*sika* – from Pa Niu kapu
12.9	E84685	*sika* – from Pa Rangifuri [annotated with D close to collection number]
12.10	E84690	*sika*

13.00 Clubs – of two main types, pointed *rakau taua* and short blunt *tuki*

13.1	E85062	*rakau taua*
13.2	E85059	*rakau taua* – old specimen, from Pa Ngatotiu
13.3	E85106	*rakua taua* – old specimen
13.4	E85064	*rakau taua* – carved by the father of Pa Ngatotiu, decorative design added later for dancing
13.5	E85058	*rakau taua*
13.6	E85061	*rakau taua*
13.7	E84651-1	parts of *tuki*, broken in killing steersman of a Santa Cruz canoe, about ten years ago; the crew was slaughtered in revenge for Tikopian youths lost at sea and said by the mediums to have been killed in Vanikoro; this specimen was used by Pa Orokofe and given by his brother Pa Papai-rau; Anutan type of *tuki* formerly belonged to Ariki Kafika who also is said to have killed a man with it.
13.8	E84651-2	as 13.7
13.9	E84896	*tuki* – from Pa Rangifuri – unique specimen of unusual shape and design
13.10	E84650	*tuki* – old specimen – about four generations – from Pa Faioa
13.11	E84652	*rakau taua* – model made by Seuku, boy of 12 years old
13.12	E84649	*rakau faka Nukuoro* – from Nukuoro, the land to the north-east of Tikopia; this specimen was brought back by a Tikopian on an early whaler
13.13	not in AM	*tuki* – ancient specimen, weapon of Pu Resiake, warrior who killed Kaitu; buried in a storm a decade ago, later dug up
13.14	E85107	*rakau taua* – old specimen, from Pa Rangi fau
13.15	E85060 or E85063?	*rakau taua* – from Pa Niu Kaso made by his father
13.16	not in AM	*rakau taua*
13.17	not in AM	*tuki*
13.18	E85065	*tuki*

14.00 Dancing bat, *paki*; used by men, made from *puka* or *mei* wood

14.1	E84657	*paki*
14.2	E84656	*paki* – old specimen, made by father of Pa Porima
14.3	E84658	*paki* – old specimen, from Paito Rangi fau
14.4	E84659	*paki* – from Pa Niu Kapu
14.5	E90652	*paki*

14.6	E84655	*paki*
14.7	E84654	made from a slab of European wood from Pa Nuku mosokoi
15.00		
15.1	E85147	pounder *tuki* – used in preparing food
15.2	not in AM	shark-killing club, *siki*, old specimen from Pae Sao
15.7	not in AM	shark-killing club [annotation on original list]

16.00 Spears, *tōkotoko* or *tao*; used in warfare and as staff by chief when visiting; usually barbed; made of *toa*, cassowarina [sic, probably Casuarina species] wood

16.1	E92184	*tōkotoko* – old specimen from Pa Fetauta
16.2	E92182	*tōkotoko* – old specimen from Pa Niukapu
16.3	E92183	*tōkotoko* – spear from Pa Nukumoanu
16.4	not in AM	*tōkotoko* – from Paito i Farekofe
16.5	E92159	*tōkotoko* – old specimen from Pa Rangifuri
16.6	E92185	*tōkotoko* – from Pa Tavi; this specimen is an embodiment (*fakatino*) of a sea diety Pu i te moana, belonging to Paito i Tavi; has been carved with steel tools, succeeding an earlier specimen, when the latter decayed
16.7	E92191	*tōkotoko* – very plain; from Pa Taraoro
16.8	E92192	*tōkotoko* – unusual type; coconut wood, from Pa Nukura
16.9	E90536	*tōkotoko* – fine specimen; from Pa Rangifuri – said to come from Anuta
16.10	E92158	*tōkotoko* – from Pa Tonga rutu
16.11	E92186	*tōkotoko*
16.12	E92193?	*tōkotoko* – religious emblem, embodiment (*fakatino*) of Pu Te Oneroa – a sea deity from Paito Niuwaru of Kafika
16.13	E92194	*tōkotoko* – made in Anuta – unfinished?
17.1	**E85144**	**Single stick, *tao fetāki*, made from mid rib of sago leaf**
18.1	**E92187**	**Fish spear with prongs, *mataika*, with bamboo shaft; prongs of betel wood**
19.1	**E92204**	**Whip thrower for *tika* dart, *tātata* from Mairunga**

20.00 Darts *tika* – head of cassowarina [sic, probably Casuarina species] wood (*toa*) and shaft of reed; usually thrown by hand

20.1	E84811-17	*tika* [registered as dart heads]
20.2	E84874-79	(A and B) a bundle of five *tika* and one extra [dart] head and three propelling rings (*fakatonga*)

21.00 Turmeric grater, *tama kuku ango* – tapering slab of wood with rough sinnet cord on which the turmeric is grated

21.1	E92156	*tama kuku ango* – from Paito i Fetu
21.2	E85146	*tama kuku ango*
21.3	E85145	*tama kuku ango* – old specimen, has been in the family of Ariki Tafua for several generations; the lashing is modern, from Pa Rangifuri

22.00	Fibre scraping slabs, *tama varu fau*	
22.1	E84665	*tama varu fau*
22.2	E84666	*tama varu fau* – very old specimen, for scraping hibiscus fibre for *tiri* net, from Pa Nuku tai
23.1	**E90660**	**Socket for bonito rod –** *futia*
24.1	**E84873**	**Fire stick for making fire by the 'plough' method** *sika afi* **– frequenty used by Tikopians; the rubber is called** *tau viroviro*
25.00	Woman's hand net, *kuti*	
25.1	not in AM	*kuti* – old specimen, mended twice, from Pa Sukumarae
26.00	Cleat, *matapiri*, far [*sic*]at bow of canoe for fastening stay of mast	
26.1	E90655	*matapiri*
27.00	Magic wand for restoring health to man who has slipped in a sacred place (*pongi*)	
27.1	E84391	*pongi*
28.00	Bamboo for sounding during ceremonial songs of the *seru*. (*Lopu*)	
28.1	E92205	*lopu*
28.2	E84647	*lopu* – from Seremata
29.00	Arrows, *ngasau*	
29.1	E92115 to E92121	7 *ngasau* – Vanikoran type
29.2	E92061 to E92068	8 *ngasau* – Tikopian type
29.3	E92106 to E92114 E92069 to E92105	Bundle of mainly *ngasau* (mainly Tikopian type)
30.00	Lime gourd, *kapia* – occassionally enclosed in sinnet bag	
30.1	E84718	*kapia* – in sinnet bag
30.2	E84724	*kapia* – in sinnet bag
30.3	E84719	*kapia*
30.4	E92056	*kapia* – a coconut (not gourd) for holding lime
31.00	Water bottle, *vai* – coconut in sinnet bag	
31.1	E84570	*vai*
31.2	E84569	*vai*
31.3	E84568	*vai*
32.00	Float for catching small fish in a loop (for holding bait, above) – *uta*	
32.1	E84433	*uta*
33.00	Sinnet *kafa* made from husk of green coconuts steeped in water, beaten and dried, rolled in short lengths on the thigh and plaited – used for deep sea fishing, house building and for ceremonial exchanges	
33.1	E84834	*kafa*
33.2	E84833	*kafa*
33.3	E84836	*kafa*

33.4	In Basel	*kafa* Basel [line crossed out annotated with D close to collection number]
33.5	E84835	*kafa*
33.6	E84832	*kafa*
33.7	E84837	*kafa*
33.8	E84830	*kafa*
33.9	not in AM	*kafa* – poor quality, used for lashing canoes
33.10	E84626	*kafa* – twisted not plaited, poor quality, used for canoe lashing
33.11	E84831	*kafa*
33.12	Bishop Museum[*]	*kafa*
33.13	not in AM	*kafa* – the beginning (*tamata*) of a piece, to show technique of manufacture
33.14	E84678	*rau rino*, coconut husk used for plaiting into sinnet, from Pa Motuangi

34.00 Hair circlet, *fau*, worn by women, made of hair of male relatives, especially husband, brother or father; cherished as an heirloom (*tauarofa*)

34.1	E84697	*fau*

35.00 Bag-net, *kuani* used for deep-sea fishing

35.1	not in AM	
35.2	E84306	from Pa Farnaga Noa

36.00 Rat trap, *tuparu*

36.1	E84713	spring variety
36.2	E84714	from Raga [Raga Island, Banks Islands, Vanuatu?], same principle as 33.1 [sic, probably 36.1] *vidi ngarivi* (*vidi*=trap, *ngarivi*=rat), presented by Miss Broughton
36.3	E84715	rat rattle from Raga, presented by Miss Broughton

37.00 Rope, *maia paka*, used for binding rolls of tobacco, rough quality, from inner bark of tree

37.1	not in AM	*maia paka* [annotated with D close to collection number]
37.2	not in AM	*maia paka*
37.3	not in AM	*maia paka*

38.00 Turmeric cylinders, *renga*, in bark-cloth wrappings (*kuru*); highly valued, buried with dead chiefs and used in ceremonial exchange

38.1	E84700	from Ariki Tafua
38.2	E84699	from Pa Korokoro
38.3	E84397	from Pae Sao
38.4	not in AM	from Ariki Tafua – large specimen generally reserved for chiefs

39.00 Net Gauge, *afa*, made of hardwood, polished with coral stone (*punga*)

39.1	E84693	*afa*
39.2	E84694	*afa*
39.3	E92058	*afa*

40.00 Rope of sinnet, *maia*; used indifferently as shark noose, *maia noa mango*, or occasionally as a man's belt, *tautu*, especially in war. The latter generally finer specimens.

40.1	E84769	*maia noa mango*
40.2	E84885	*maia noa mango*
40.3	E84770	*maia noa mango*
40.4	not in AM	*tautu*
40.5	E84628	*tautu*
40.6	in Basel	*tautu* Basel [crossed out and annotated with D close to collection number]
40.7	E84907	*tautu* [annotated with D close to collection number]
40.8	E84905	*tautu*
40.9	E84906	*tautu* – from Pa Rangifuri

41.00 Women's belt, *kafa fakafafine (tautu)*, always worn to hold up the skirt

41.1	E84669	twisted sinnet
41.2	not in AM	plaited and twisted sinnet
41.3	E84670	plaited; fine specimen
41.4	E84629	plaited; fine specimen
41.5	E84673	plaited
41.6	E84672	plaited; fine specimen

42.00 Fish line; the round plait type, termed *matai* and is usually made from *kari suka*, bark

42.1	not in AM	for *para*, *varu* and other large fish – *matai*
42.2	E84439	for *para*, *varu* and other large fish – *matai*
42.3	not in AM	ordinary deep-sea line, from Pa Faioa – *matai*
42.4	E84443	ordinary deep-sea line, from Pa Faioa – *matai*
42.5	E84441	ordinary deep-sea line, from Pa Faioa – *matai*
42.6	E84436	light line – *matai*
42.7	E84442	ordinary deep-sea line – *matai*
42.8	E84884	thick line for shark or *para* with iron hook attached, this forged in Tikopia – *matai*

43.00 Fish-line, *uka*, of twist, that of *kari suka* is stronger than the commoner *fau*

43.1	E84767	very thick, for large fish – *uka*.
43.2	E84444	very thin, for small fish – *uka* (of *fau*)
43.3	E84766	*uka* of type often used for net-making (of *fau*)
43.4	E84438	from *kari suka*
43.5	E84437	of *fau*
43.6	E84440	medium thinkness of *fau*

44.00 *Pa atu,* bonito hooks, used in fishing but also highly valued for ceremonial presentation, usually given only to chiefs in expiation of an offence. The *pa tu manga,* with barb of tortoise shell or whale bone affixed is essential for this purpose. The shanks (45.00), termed *pa* are much in use for neck ornaments. *Pa tu manga* are also thus used and are stuck in the ear lobes of dead people of rank.

44.1	E84584	*pa atu* – pearl-shell shank, tortoise-shell barb, from Pa Rarovi
44.2	E84582	*pa atu* – clam-shell shank, bone barb, from Pa Porima
44.3	E84585	*pa atu* – pearl-shell shank, tortoise-shell barb, fr –[no name recorded]
44.4	E84579	*pa atu* – pearl-shell shank, tortoise-shell barb; correct lashing, from Ariki Fangarere
44.5	E59459-5	*pa atu* – pearl-shell shank, tortoise-shell barb; from Ariki Kafika
44.6	E59459-3	*pa atu* – clam-shell shank, bone barb, unskilful lashing, from Pae Sao
44.7	Bishop Museum*	*pa atu* – pearl-shell shank, bone barb, from Pa Faioa
44.8	E84581	*pa atu* – pearl-shell shank, bone barb, good specimen from Pa Vainunu
44.9	E84580	*pa atu* – pearl-shell shank, tortoise-shell barb, from Pa Motuata
44.10	E59459-2	*pa atu* – pearl-shell shank, notched ornamentation, bone barb; beautiful old specimen
44.11	E59459-1	*pa atu* – shank of stone from Panapa Id; from [obtained from] Pa Nuikapu with *tanipara* wrist ornament attached
44.12	E84578	*pa atu* – from Pa Fenuafara; with lure of (?) bosun bird (*tavake*) feathers
44.13	E59459-4	*pa atu* – from Pa Motuangi

45.00 Neck ornaments of bonito-hook shank (v.44.00)

45.1	E84598	*pa* – pearl-shell, very large from Pa Motuata
45.2	E84476	*pa* – clam-shell
45.3	E84469	*pa* – pearl-shell
45.4	E84478	*pa* – clam-shell
45.5	E84472	*pa* – clam-shell
45.6	E84473	*pa* – pearl-shell
45.7	E84470	*pa* – clam-shell
45.8	E84475	*pa* – pearl-shell
45.9	E84471	*pa* – clam-shell
45.10	E84477	*pa* – pearl-shell
45.11	E84479	*pa* – of wood; shank new; barb of turtle shell, old; of interest since worn by boy after incision ceremony; hence coated with turmeric from his breast – worn by Seuku
45.12	E84474	*pa* – pearl-shell – poor specimen; shank probably made for barter; barb of pearl-shell – unusual but genuine

46.00 Finger-rings *ngasane* of coconut shell; made by girls; worn by girls and boys

46.1	E84565	*ngasane*
46.2	not in AM	*ngasane*
46.3	not in AM	*ngasane*
46.4	E84564	*ngasane*
46.5	not in AM possibly Bishop Museum[*]	*ngasane* – bunch of six rings

47.00 Ear-rings, *kango*

47.1	not in AM	made from handle of discarded tooth brush and regarded as valuable property, owing to its similarity to turtle shell – *kango*
47.2	E84561	*kango* – made in Tikopia, from turtle hauled up on fishing line, Santa Cruz model

48.00 Breast ornament of clam-shell discs, *tavi*, cf. Santa Cruz *ndavi*, Guadalcanal *ndavi*, N. Malaita *fui davi*

48.1	E92047	*tavi*
48.2	E84451	*tavi*
48.3	E84461	*tavi* – large specimen: from Pa Motuangi
48.4	E84448 & E84458	*tavi* – from Pa Marae raka
48.5	E92048	*tavi* – battered specimen, from Pa Sia mano
48.6	E84456	*tavi*
48.7	E84449	*tavi*
48.8	E84450	*tavi* – old specimen; good. From Pa Motuatu
48.9	E84455	*tavi* – old specimen; from Pa Rarotonga
48.10	E84453	*tavi* – old specimen
48.11	E92046	*tavi* – from Nau Porima
48.12	E84464	*tavi* – exchanged by the father of the present Ariki Tafua in Vanikoro; from Pa Paiu
48.12	E84463	*tavi*
48.13	E84454	*tavi*
48.14	E90644?	*tavi* – old specimen
48.15	E84452	*tavi* – from family of Ariki Tafua
48.16	E90644?	*tavi*
48.17	E84457	*tavi*
48.18	E84459	*tavi* – beautiful old specimen: from Pa Nukufuri
48.19	E84460	*tavi* – good old specimen, from Pa Faioa
48.20	E84462	*tavi* – shell partly ground down, not yet pierced, a *tavi* in the making

49.00 Wrist ornaments, small discs of clam-shell *mata nipara*

49.1	E84504-3	three *mata nipara* [two registered]
49.2	E84507-8	two *mata nipara*

49.3	E84521-26	six *mata nipara*
49.4	E84519-20	two *mata nipara*
49.5	E84505-6	one *mata nipara* [two registered]
49.6	E84529-35	seven *matanipara* including one of pearl-shell

50.00 Shell armrings *kalikau* – ground down from *trochus* shell, worn for dancing by men and women

50.1	E84509-10	two *kalikau*
50.2	E84511	one *kalikau*
50.3	Possibly sent to Bishop Museum*	one very large *kalikau* belonged to ancestor of Pa Porima, on whose arm it fitted tightly
50.4	E84527-28	*kalikau* – very large specimen [two registered]

51.00 Nose rings, *ngasane*, worn only by unmarried people

51.1	E84510	*ngasane* – of *murinere* [?] tortoiseshell, worn by Pae Sao – discarded on marriage
51.2	E84546	*ngasane* – four bone specimens – rare
51.3	E84545	*ngasane* – one bone specimen – rare
51.4	E84554	*ngasane* – five bone specimens – rare

52.00 Pearl-shell neck ornament, *tifa*

52.1	E84485	*tifa*
52.2	E84486	*tifa*
52.3	E84487	*tifa*
52.4	not in AM	*tifa* – very large specimen, brought by grandfather of [not recorded]
52.7	E84488	breast ornament of coconut shell made in imitation of one of pearl-shell (*tifa*)

53.00 *Rei*, ['cylindrical ornament of bead type, 2–3 cm long, of clam shell, Firth with Tuki 1985: 393

53.1	not in AM	three old specimens of *rei*, from Ariki Taumako
53.2	E84466	old specimen of *rei* – from Pa Nukura
53.3	E84467	three specimen of *rei*
53.4	E59460	one *rei* from Pa Siamano
53.5	E84468	one *rei*
53.6	E84595-97	three specimen of *rei*

54.00 Neck ornaments of whale tooth

54.1	E84608	Neck ornament of whale tooth – unique specimen. ['Ancestral specimen of Mapusanga family' crossed out]

55.00 Nose ornament, *tiu*, worn by young men and maidens – ostensibly sign of virginity

55.1	E84555	*tiu*
55.2	E84547-53	*tiu* – bundle of seven

56.00 Wrist ornament, *tui*, of shell

56.1	E84395	*tui* worn on the wrist by Pa Vetere, grandfather of present Ariki Taumako from Pa Motuata
57.1	**E84593**	**String of *tiu* shell ornaments**
57.2	E84586	old necklace of *tiu* shell, restrung on new cord

58.00 Beads of white *conus* shell (*supe*) called *korokoro*, rare

58.1	E84499	*korokoro* – from Pa Tariki tonga
58.2	E84587	*korokoro* – from Pa Sau ki rima
58.3	E84489	*korokoro* – from Pa Maniva
58.4	E84498	*korokoro* – from Pa Nukura

59.00 Beads of black coconut shell, *somo fangongo* – valued property

59.1	E84501	*somo fangongo* – Ellice Island type – from Pa Taraoro from his mother's *patio* [house]
59.2	E84496	*somo fangongo*
59.3	not in AM	*somo fangongo* – from Ariki Taumako
59.4	E84589	*somo fangongo*
59.5	E84493	*somo fangongo* – from Pa Motuata
59.6	E84490	*somo fangongo* – from Pa Rangi fakaino
59.7	E84491	*somo fangongo* – from Pa Tuama
59.8	E84495	*somo fangongo* – from Pa Maniva
59.9	E84502	*somo fangongo* – Ellice Isd type, from Pa Tongarutu
59.10	E84497	*somo fangongo* – from Pa Faioa
59.11	E84494	*somo fangongo* – from *paito* I Marangaone – with red and white shell beads (*supe*)
59.12	E84492	*somo fangongo*
59.13	E84590	*somo fangongo*
59.14	E84591	*somo fangongo* – from Pa Fongarevai
59.15	E84592	*somo fangongo* – from Pa Tanianu
59.16	Bishop Museum*	*somo fangongo* – made by Pu Resiake, grandfather of the owner Fani
59.17	E84500	*somo* – necklet of shell beads and ? imported dog's teeth

60.00 Tattooing implements

60.1	E84829	*matāu* adze sharpener – *vatuke* of sea-urchin spine.
60.2	E84825	*matāu* tattooing needle
60.3	E84826	*matāu* tattooing needle
60.4	E84827	*matāu* tattooing needle
60.5	E84828	*matāu* tattooing needle
60.6	not in AM	shell for cleaning out the teeth of the *matāu*
60.7	E84702-11	tattooer's kit (*te koroa tufunga ta tau*), complete, comprising: bag, three adzes, bamboo tube of *refu* (powder), pigment-cups, pestle, strikers; also water cup, mixing stick, spare bone for adze, and two *ratuke* (sharpeners)
60.8	not in AM	cup used by tattooer for holding and mixing pigment
60.9	not in AM	two tattooing adzes

61.00 Betel pestle, *tuki kamo*		
61.1	E84394	*tuki kamo* – old specimen of whale bone from Pa Nuku renga
61.2	E97774	*tuki kamo*
62.00 Bone needle, *sau*		
62.1	E84691	*sau* – old specimen of whale bone – very fine – for sewing fibre bags for turmeric etc. – unique specimen
63.1	not in AM	Sacreds shell trumpet, *pu*, *tapu* specimen, unique, from Mapusanga house, cleaned annually and blown, from Pa Tarairaki
64.1	E92060	Sacred whale-tooth necklet, *kasoa*, *tapu* specimen, unique from Mapusanga house, property of former Ariki Kafika, ?brought from Fiji
65.1	E84402	Shell *fuateka*, used as hook to hang up food baskets, from Paito i Raitiare
66.1	E84480	Shell ornament for breast
67.1	not in AM	Sacred adze, *toki tapu*; given by Pa Tekaumata; dug up from Ngatotiu house, used in canoe ceremonies, very [underlined two times] sacred, unique [given to Firth secretly, *manua toki*, very sacred – Firth 1967a:58]
68.1	E84820	Ball of coconut leaf, *pa tikitiki*
69.1	E84567	Shell for boring wood, *muriroa* (Terebra dimidiato) used before introduction of iron as canoe auger
70.00 Fans, *iri*, plaited from young coconut leaf (*sakilo*)		
70.1	not in AM	*iri*
70.2	not in AM	*iri*
70.3	not in AM	*iri*
70.4	E84355	*iri*
70.5	E84350	*iri*
70.5	E84356	*iri*
70.6	not in AM	*iri*
71.00 Hand-bags, *tanga* or *tāfeta*, made by men, used to hold betel and small implements of daily use		
71.1	E91719	*tanga*
71.2	E91726	*tanga* – from Pa Nuku Sau Kava
71.3	E91720	*tanga*
71.4	E84414	*tanga* – large specimen
71.5	E84725	*tanga* – from Pae Sao
72.00 Waist bark-cloths (*fakamaru*) worn by men, largely used for ceremonial gifts on all occasions, when they are folded in special ways and termed *maro* (see 82.02)		
72.1	E84113-17	bundle of six *fakamaru*
72.2	E84129-32	bundle of four *fakamaru*
72.3	E84133-35	bundle of three *fakamaru*

**73.00 Bark-cloth squares (*mami*) made from the inner bark of large trees; used
as skirts for women (*raroa*) or blankets (*kafu*) according to size and shape; used
ceremonially for gifts at incision etc. and regarded esoterically as a symbol of female
gods**

73.1	not in AM	one *mami* – fine specimen
73.2	E84109-11	bundle of four *mami*
73.3	E84125-28	bundle of four *mami*
73.4	not in AM	bundle of four *mami*
73.5	not in AM	bundle of four *mami*
73.6	E84108 and E84145.	bundle of four *mami*

**74.00 Food baskets, *longi*, of various styles; those finely made and stained with
turmeric are termed *raurau* for chiefs**

74.1	E84415	*longi*
74.2	E84731	*longi*
74.3	E84732	*longi*
74.4	E91723	*raurau*
74.5	E84416	*raurau*
74.6	Bishop Museum*	*raurau*
74.7	E84728	*raurau*
74.8	E91722	*raurau*
74.9	E84727	*longi*
74.10	E81721	*longi*
74.11	E84726	*longi*

**75.00 Mats (*mēnga*) of pandanus, used primarily for sleeping on, but also as a main
article of ceremonial exchange; normally decorated with a simple coloured band
along either edge, then termed *mēnga fakasikimero***

75.1	E84082	*mēnga fakasikimero*
75.2	E84073	*mēnga fakasikimero*
75.3	E84089	*mēnga fakasikimero* – decorated along one border only
75.4	E84072	*mēnga fakasikimero*
75.5	E84065	*mēnga* – no ornamentation
75.6	E84083	*mēnga* [crossed out]
75.7	E84085	*mēnga fakasikimero* – with odd red threads of ornamentation in the body of the mat
75.8	E84087	*mēnga fakasikimero* – unusual, with two simple red bands running lengthwise down the body of the mat; unique specimen
75.9	not in AM	*mēnga* – very large example, made by Nau Porima, presented to Paito i Nukufuti as gift to *tuatina* (mother's brother) on incision of the eldest son in Porima

75.10	E84090	*mēnga fakasikimero* – large mat of type used to present to *tuatina* (mother's brother) on incision having served as bed-mat for the boy; also used as special marriage gifts
75.11	E84066	*mēnga fakasikimero* – presented by Pa Fenuatara
75.12	E84067	*mēnga fakasikimero* – ornamentation along one border only – very fine plaiting
75.13	E84150	*mēnga fakasikimero* – has been used as sleeping mat
75.14	E84081	*mēnga fakasikimero* – rather coarse plait
75.15	E84071	*mēnga fakasikimero* – decorated on one side only; light coloured dye
75.16	E84086	*mēnga fakasikimero*
75.17	E84069	*mēnga fakasikimero*
75.18	E84091	*mēnga*
75.19	E84149	*mēnga fakasikimero* – decorated on one side only
75.20	not in AM	*mēnga fakasikimero* – small specimen [record crossed out]
75.21	E84068	*mēnga fakasikimero* – good, well plaited specimen
75.22	not in AM	*mēnga* – for exchange
75.23	not in AM	*mēnga fakasikimero* – decorated one side border, finely plaited
75.24	not in AM	*mēnga fakasikimero* – for exchange
75.25	E84088	*mēnga* – for exchange
75.26	E84070	*mēnga fakasikimero* – for exchange
75.27	not in AM	*mēnga fakasikimero* – two bands of decoration along one border
75.28	E84080	*mēnga fakasikimero* – band along either end
75.29	not in AM	*mēnga*, small, made by Anutan woman resident in Tikopia [record crossed out]

76.00 Kit, kete – for carrying food, fish, water-bottles etc., plaited from coconut leaf

76.1	E84734	*kete*
76.2	E84733	*kete*
76.3	E84417	*kete*

77.00 Bag of coconut fibre, kākā, used for holding sago (koko) or edible turmeric (tauo)

77.1	E84420	*kākā*
77.2	not in AM	*kākā* – full of *tauo*
77.3	not in AM	*kākā* – from Ariki Tafua
77.4	E87775	*kākā* – sewn sheet of coconut fibre used as a filter in turmeric making

78.00 Dance ornaments, made for the occasion, of leaves and flowers

78.1	not in AM	neck ornament of white *tiare* blossom – *kassoa tiare*
78.2	E84401	neck ornaments of shredded turmeric leaves – *kassoa rau ango*
78.3	E84698	head circlets, *fau* – of shredded dracaena leaf (*ti*)
79.1	**E84413**	**Fish bag, *tanga*, of coconut leaf – coarsely plaited**

80.00 Waist–mats (*kie*) – these are of Anutan type but many are now made by Anutan women married to husbands in Tikopia; these mats are plaited from fine pandanus fibre and some examples are ornamented with an overlaid stitch from the inner bark of a tree, dyed red; they are worn in dancing, especially by men of rank; they are not used in ceremonial exchange

80.1	E84148	fine example decorated along both edges (*kie*)
80.2	E84078	*kie*
80.3	E84076	a very large specimen; simple fringe decoration along one edge; unusual (*kie*)
80.4	E84077	*kie* – very finely woven
80.5	E84147	unusually large specimen (*kie*)
80.6	E84079	*kie* – normal type with decorated lower border and plain coloured band along upper border
80.7	E84146	*kie* – very fully ornamented along edges as well as along lower and upper borders

81.00 Waist-mats (*fakaro*) of pandanus, of rather coarser make than *kie*; usually decorated with a simple coloured band along borders; sometimes more elaborate, with *kie* ornamentation

81.1	E84075	*fakaro* – with slight *kie* ornmentation
81.2	E90651	*fakaro* – normal type
81.3	E84675	*fakaro* – with narrow band on reverse side; on obverse side *kie* ornamentation
81.4	E84674	*fakaro* – normal type
81.5	E84074	*fakaro* – made by an Anutan woman living in Tikopia (wife of Pa Niukaso)

82.00 Ceremonial offerings (*maro*)

82.1	E84096	ceremonial offering to canoe gods of bark-cloth, including *mami* (bark-cloth squares) and *maro tafi* (bark-cloth dyed with turmeric); given by Pa Nuku Renga
82.2	In Macleay Museum	ceremonial gift (*maro*) of bark-cloth, including seven *fakamaru* (waist bark-cloths) and one *maro tafi* (bark-cloth dyed with turmeric)
82.3	not in AM	ceremonial gift (*maro*) of bark-cloth, including five *fakamaru* (waist bark-cloths)

83.00 Bark-cloth, stained with turmeric (*marotafi*); used as waist cloths by men and to 'top off' *maro* (ceremonial gifts and religious offerings of bark-cloth)

| 83.1 | not in AM | bundle of four *marotafi* |
| 83.2 | E84097 to E84100 | bundle of three *marotafi* |

| **84.1** | **E62591** | **Canoe, *vaka*, single outrigger, small specimen – usual sea-going type of bow and stern piece** |

85.00 Shell adze-heads

85.1	E64071.1	shell adze-heads – *toki* (in box)
85.1	E64071.2	shell adze-heads – *toki* (in box)
85.2	E64052	large shell adze-head

| 85.3 | E64070 | large shell adze-head, *toki tapu*? |
| 85.4 | E84886 | *toki tapu*, hafted |

86.00 Stone adze-heads (*toki*) made in Tikopia?, more valued than shell, rare (however, see Firth 1959)

86.1	E64073	*toki uri* – (black)
86.2	E64072.2	*toki uri*
86.3	not in AM	*toki uri*
86.4	E64072.3	*toki uri*
86.5	not in AM	*toki uri* – from Pa Rongatao
86.6	E64074	*toki uri* – from Ariki Kafika
86.7	E64072.1	*toki uri*
86.8		*toki tapu–* [record crossed out]

| **87.1** | **E84572** | **Coconut shell used for grating sago – *fangango saro ota*** |

88.00 Taro graters, *sina* – often made of soft wood, generally breadfruit, studded with pieces of iron wire (formerly with fish bone)

88.1	E84663	*sina* – old specimen dating from early days of introduction of iron, from Paito Pau
88.2	E84664	*sina* – old specimen but with iron points, from Maraetanu
88.3	E84662	*sina* – old specimen but with iron points, from Maraetanu

| **89.1** | **E85066** | **_Kofe_, a wooden knife made some years ago by Pa Rangifuri, in imitation of a religious emblem in the sacred _paito_ of Niukapu, since decayed on the introduction of Christianity; it is said that such implements were used for felling banana stems and are of genuine Tikopia type** |

90.00 Plaiting slabs (*papa feú raranga*) used as a flat surface on which to plait mat; owned by women

| 90.1 | E84695 | *papa feú raranga* – old specimen of *kauariki* wood, from Reseake family |
| 90.2 | E84696 | *papa feú raranga* – old specimen; from Paito Samoa |

91.00 Objects used for making turmeric (*renga*) including two pairs of tongs (*ukofi*) for handling hot stones in the oven; two stirrers (*fé*) for stirring the liquid in the cylinder; supports for holding up the coconut fibre in the filter – all made of coconut rib – from Ariki Tafua (13:IX:28), obtained during the turmeric season

91.1	E84898 to E84899	*ukofi*, tongs
91.2	E84900 to E84901	*fé*, stirrers
91.3	E84902 to E84903	supports for holding fibre in the filter

| **92.1** | **E84904** | **Digging implement used for taking the loose soil from deep holes made for holding house posts; made on the spot for each house built** |

93.00 Shark-hooks of wood (*kau*) – sometimes made in one piece, sometimes with wooden barb lashed on – now replaced by iron hooks

| 93.1 | not in AM | *kau* – old specimen |

93.2	not in AM	*kau* – old specimen
93.3	not in AM	*kau* – old specimen, bearing marks of teeth – original lashing made by Pu Resiake I
93.4	E84765	*kau* – old specimen, made by Pu Resiake I, new barb lashing by his descendant Seremata

94.00 Wooden hooks (*kau*) used for hanging up food baskets and other articles in the house

94.1	not in AM	*kau* – from Pa te Kaumata
94.2	Bishop Museum*	*kau* – from Pa Motuangi

95.1	E84883	**Stick used for beating a sounding board during a dance (two are used) – *kau ta tē mako***

96.00 Wooden tools used for beating sinnet

96.1	E84373	*sasa kafa* – of *toa* wood (casuarina), formerly a piece of a spear, from Pa te Kaumata
96.2	E84372	*sasa kafa* – from Pa rangi rikoi

97.00 Net floats (*futa*) made of bread-fruit (*mei*) used on *tiri* (seine) nets

97.1	E84432	from Pa Mairunga
97.1	E84431	from Pa Mairunga

98.1	E92504	**Stick for cleaning out inside of a coconut to make a water bottle (*Te sisi saro vai*); in former days a fragment of shell (*sisi*) was used at the tip instead of a piece of iron; from Pa Taitai**
99.1	E84819	**Top (*moa*) with its spinning cord (*uka*), from Pu Rangi rikoi**
100.1	E84821	***Kali lisi* – a grass toy representing a lizard (*kali lisi*) made by Munakina, a boy of 9 yrs**
101.1	E84594	**A tooth, said to be that of *tafora* (?porpoise or dolphin) – *nifo tāfora*, belonged formerly to Paito Pae Sao for some long time**
101.2	E84465	*nifo tāfora* –?porpoise or dolphin
102.1	E84818	**Fruit of the barringtonia (*te futu*) used in the game of *tupe***
103.1	E64053	**? a sling stone**

APPENDIX 3

Names of individuals who gave objects to Firth

The information presented here was compiled from information provided by Ishmael Tuki [IT], Frieda Tuki [FT] and from Firth's ethnographies

Title	Name	Clan	AM reg. no.	Firth's no.	Remarks
	Fani	Taumako		59.16	grandfather of Fani is Pu Resiake, who made the item
	Kavarauniu (?)	?	E84022	4.34	[IT]
	Maraetanu	?	E84662	88.3	
	Maraetanu	?	E84664	88.2	
	Munakina	father from Banks Island	see E85140	see 11.01	
	Munakina	father from Banks Island	E84821	100.1	9 years old
	Pokia	?	E84783	8.12	rejected suitor see (Firth 1983:451)
	Seremata*	Taumako	E84647	28.2	? [IT] Seremata a Christian of Taumako
	Seremata*	Taumako	E84765	93.4	probably from Resiake family, made by descendant of Pu Resiake, Seremata
	Seuku	Taumako	E84762	45.11?	his son is in Kira Kira [IT] son of Pa Fetu (Firth 1983:394).
	Seuku	Taumako	E84652	13.11	individual name, 12 years old, son of Pa Fetu (Firth 1983:394).
		Taumako		13.13	belonged to Pu Resiake
	Ti forau?	Taumako?	E84021	4.26	bachelor of Rangitisa House

Title	Name	Clan	AM reg. no.	Firth's no.	Remarks
	Vaitere	Taumako	E92197	10.7	should be Vaiterei, craftsman of Taumako, deceased [IT]; but appears as Vaitere son of Pa Niukapu (Firth 1983:406)
	Arakofe	Kafika			same house as Mapusanga
Pa	Avakofe	Taumako		4.8	family living in KiraKira; of Kafika, contrary to Firth [IT]; important man of rank (Firth 1967:111).
Pa	Faioa	Taumako		44.7	
Pa	Faioa	Taumako	E84439	42.3	
Pa	Faioa	Taumako	E84497	59.10	
Pa	Faioa	Taumako	E84650	13.10	
Pa	Faioa	Taumako	E84460	48.19	
Pa	Fangatau	Fangerere		4.5	family now living in Kira Kira [IT]
Ariki	Fangerere	Fangerere	E84579	44.5	
Paito	Faranga noa	Kafika	E84809	1.18	family now living in Kira Kira [IT/FT]
Pa	Faranga noa	Kafika	E84306	35.2	family now living in Kira Kira [IT]
Pa	Fare ata	Kafika		4.29	family now living in Kira Kira [IT]
Pa	Fare reu	Kafika	E84359	9.12	now Faleleu, family now living in Kira Kira [IT]
Paito	Farefikai	Kafika	E84790	8.8	deceased, married to woman living in Kira Kira. Most of family now in Russells or Vanikoro [IT]
Pa	Fenoa tara	Kafika?	E84066	75.11	possibly Pa Fenuatara, son of Ariki Kafika, (Firth 1967a:299)
Pa	Fenua fara	Tafua	E84030	4.25	'Afara' contemporary [IT]

Title	Name	Clan	AM reg. no.	Firth's no.	Remarks
Pa	Fenua fara	Tafua	E84578	44.12	
Pa	Fenuatara	Kafika	E92199	10.1	made by Pa Niuwaru, Kafika, also spelt Fenuatara, important man of rank (Firth 1967c:111)
Pa	Fenuatara	Kafika	E84024	4.12	photo in songs book, important man of rank (Firth 1967c:111); not a Christian (4.12)
Pa	Fenuatara	Kafika	E84713	36.1	photo on songs book, important man of rank (Firth 1967c:111)
Pa	Fenuatara	Kafika		4.16	photo on songs book, important man of rank (Firth 1967c:111)
Pa	Fetauta	Kafika	E92184	16.1	
	Fetauta	Kafika	E84032	4.37	family now living in Kira Kira [IT]; in Marinoa house (Firth 1983:61)
Paito	Fetauta	Kafika	E84631	4.22	family now living in Kira Kira [IT]
Pa	Fongarevai	Tafua	E84591	59.14	[IT]
Paito	i Farekofe	?		16.4	
Paito	i Fetu	Taumako	E92156	21.1	same family as Manivam in Kira Kira [IT]
Paito	i Maranga one	Tafua	E84494	59.11	
Paito	i Maranga one	Tafua	E84795	7.1	these types more widely made now
Paito	i Oliki	Taumako?	E84300	1.1	family living in Kira Kira [IT]; clan info in Firth 1967a:136; but see also Kumete notes
Paito	i Ratiare	Tafua		9.1	family now living in Vanikoro [IT]
Paito	i Ratiare	Tafua	E84402	65.1	
Paito	i Veterei	Taumako	E84642	4.6	family now living in Kira Kira [IT]

Title	Name	Clan	AM reg. no.	Firth's no.	Remarks
Ariki	Kafika	Kafika		44.5	
Ariki	Kafika	Kafika		85.6	
Pa	Koro atu	Taumako	E84689	12.6	mother's father's brother still alive [FT] in Kira Kira [IT]
Pa	Korokoro	Tafua	E84699	38.2	family now living in Kira Kira [IT]
	Mairunga	Taumako	E92204	19.1	
	Mairunga	Taumako	E84637	4.19	family now living in KK [IT]
	Mairunga	Taumako	E84019	4.10	family now living in KK [IT]
Pa	Mairunga	Taumako	E84431	97.1	
Pa	Mairunga	Taumako	E84432	97.2	
Pa	Maniva	Taumako	E84489	58.3	
Pa	Maniva	Taumako	E84495	59.8	
Pa	Maniva	Taumako	E92203	10.4	
Pa	Maniva	Taumako		4.4	family now living in KK [IT]
Pa	Maniva	Taumako	E84489	58.3	
Paito	Mapusanga	Kafika	E92060	64.1	from Mapusanga house
Pa	Marae raka	?	E84448, E84458?	48.4	clan? [IT]
Pa	Marakei	Kafika		8.2	former property of Tarotu, former Ariki Kafika; donor is his grandson; brother of Pa Tonga rutu [IT]
	Marunga	Kafika			not in collection
Pa	Matatae	Tafua	E92201	10.8	died, wife alive and in Makira; bishop is of this family [IT]
Pa	Mesara	Tafua	E84798	7.6	
Pa	Motuangi	Kafika		44.13	(Firth 1967b:181)
Pa	Motuangi	Kafika		94.2	(Firth 1967b:181)
Pa	Motuangi	Kafika	E84678	33.14	(Firth 1967b:181)

Title	Name	Clan	AM reg. no.	Firth's no.	Remarks
Pa	Motuangi	Kafika	E84461	48.3	(Firth 1967b:181)
Pa	Motuata	Taumako	E84580	44.9	also spelt Motu ata
Pa	Motuata	Taumako	E84395	56.1	item worn by Pa Vetere, grandfather of 'present' Ariki Taumako
Pa	Motuata	Taumako	E84450	48.8	
Pa	Motuata	Taumako		45.1	
Pa	Motuata	Taumako		4.8	family now living in Kira Kira [IT]
Pa	Motuata	Taumako	E84493	59.5	
Pa	Mukava	Tafua	E84297	1.16	family now living in Kira Kira [IT]
Pa	Ngatotiu	Taumako		4.2	family now living in Kira Kira [IT]
Pa	Ngatotiu	Taumako	E85059	13.1	deceased
Pa	Ngatotiu?	Taumako	E85064	13.4	item carved by Pa Ngatotiu's father
Pa	Niu Kapu	Taumako		9.11	family of IT's wife, in Kira Kira [IT]
Pa	Niu Kapu	Taumako	E84630	4.3	Lily's family, family living in Kira Kira
Pa	Niu Kapu	Taumako	E84290	2.3	Lily's family, family living in Kira Kira
Pa	Niu Kapu	Taumako	E84687	12.8	same family as Pa Koro atu; father? mother's father?
Pa	Niu Kapu	Taumako	E84659	14.4	sometimes spelt Niu Kapu/Niu Kapu
Pa	Niu Kapu	Taumako	E92182	16.2	
Pa	Niu Kapu	Taumako	E84296	1.15	Lily's family, living in Kira Kira [IT]
Pa	Niu Kaso	Taumako		4.32	family living now in Kira Kira [IT]
Paito	Niu Kaso	Taumako	E84074	81.5	made by Anutan woman, wife of Pa Niukaso, but given by her or him?, hence *paito*

Title	Name	Clan	AM reg. no.	Firth's no.	Remarks
Pa	Niu Kaso	Taumako	E85060 or E85063	13.15	made by father
Pa	Niuwaru	Kafika			see E92199; 10.1
Paito	Niuwaru	Kafika	E92193	16.12	
Pa	Nuikapu	Taumako		44.11	also spelt Nui Kapu
Pa	Nuku afua	Kafika	E84360	9.10	house gone [IT]
Pa	Nuku furi	Tafua	E84792	7.5	family now living in Kira Kira [IT]
Pa	Nuku mosokoi	Tafua	E84654	14.7	[IT]
Pa	Nuku Sau Kava	?	E91726	71.2	IT's house, father's family's name [IT]
Pa	Nuku tai	Kafika	E84666	22.2	same family as Tavi [IT]
Pa	Nuku-manongi	Fangerere	E84362	9.4	family living in Kira Kira [IT]
Pa	Nuku-manongi	Fangerere	E84361	9.3	family living in Kira Kira [IT]
Pa	Nukufuri	Tafua	E84459	48.18	brother of A.Tafua [IT]
Paito	Nukufuti?	Taumako		75.9	
Pa	Nukumoanu	Kafika	E92183	16.3	not recognized by I Tuki [IT], kin of Pa Rangifuri (Firth 1965:284, 1967c:110)
Pa	Nukura	Taumako	E92192	16.8	
Pa	Nukura	Taumako	E84788	8.6	belonged to Pu Nukura, in Kira Kira [IT]
Pa	Nukura	Taumako	E84498	58.4	
Pa	Nukura	Taumako	E84466	53.2	
Pa	Nukurenga	Taumako	E84394	61.1	(Firth 1967a:93)
Pa	Nukurenga	Taumako		82.1	(Firth 1967a:93)
	Pae Sao	Tafua	E84377	2.1	family now living in Kira Kira [IT]
	Pae Sao	Tafua	E84789	8.10	also spelt Pao Sao, now living in Kira Kira [IT]

Title	Name	Clan	AM reg. no.	Firth's no.	Remarks
	Pae Sao	Tafua		44.6	family now living in Kira Kira [IT]
	Pae Sao	Tafua		51.1	
	Pae Sao	Tafua		10.2	
	Pae Sao	Tafua		4.1	family now living in KK [IT]
Paito	Pae Sao	Tafua	E83594	101.1	
	Pae Sao	Tafua	E84725	71.5	
	Pae Sao	Tafua		9.9	also spelt Pae Sao, family now living in Kira Kira [IT]
	Pae Sao	Tafua	E84397	38.3	family now living in Kira Kira [IT]
	Pae Sao	Tafua	E85147	15.1	
Paito	Paiu	Tafua	E84663	88.1	
Pa	Paiu	Tafua		1.12	family now living in KK [IT]
Pa	Paiu	Tafua	E84463, E84464	48.12	Pa Nukufuri, Pa Rangorei and Pa Paiu are brothers to Ariki Tafua
Pa	Papai-varu	Kafika	E84651	13.8	used by Pa Orokofe, brother to Pa Papai-varu, formerly belonged to Ariki Kafika, Pa Mapusanga also a brother
Pa	Porima	Kafika		50.3	
Nau	Porima	?	E92046	48.11	
Pa	Porima	Kafika	E84582	44.2	
Pa	Porima?	Kafika	E84656	14.2	made by father of Pa Porima
Pa	Rangi fakaino	Kafika	E84490	59.6	brother of Tavi, family now living in Kira Kira [IT]
Paito	Rangi fau	Taumako	E84658	14.3	
Pa	Rangi fau	Taumako	E85107	13.14	family now living in Kira Kira [IT]

Title	Name	Clan	AM reg. no.	Firth's no.	Remarks
Pa	Rangi maseke	Kafika	E84358	9.2	house possibly gone [IT]; Pa Rangimaseke, heir to Pa Tavi (Firth 1967:361, 385, 393)
Pa	Rangi rikoi	Taumako	E84819	99.1	ritual elder of Taumako, old, travelled to 'white man's' land (Firth 1983:62)
Pu	Rangi rikoi	Taumako	E84029	4.31	
Pa	Rangi rikoi	Taumako	E84372	96.2	
Pa	Rangifuri	Tafua	E84906	40.9	
Pa	Rangifuri	Tafua	E84685	12.9	no. 2 chief, deceased
Pa	Rangifuri	Tafua	E84896	13.9	
Pa	Rangifuri	Tafua	E84035	4.7	family now living in Kira Kira [IT]
Pa	Rangifuri	Tafua	E84291	1.10	family now living in Kira Kira [IT]
Pa	Rangifuri	Tafua		16.9	
Pa	Rangifuri	Tafua	E85066	89.1	
Pa	Rangifuri	Tafua		1.9	family now living in Kira Kira [IT]
Pa	Rangifuri	Tafua	E85145	21.3	
Pa	Rangifuri	Tafua	E92159	16.5	
Pa	Rangimaseke	Taumako	E84869	1.2	family now living in Kira Kira [IT]
Pa	Rangitisa	Taumako			an important man of rank (Firth 1967c:110)
Pa	Rarotonga	Taumako	E84455	48.9	related to Niukapu and Koroatu [IT]
Pa	Rarovi	Kafika	E84584	44.1	elder of Kafika (pictured Firth with McLean 1990:69) [IT]
Pu	Resiake	Taumako	E84376	1.7	[IT]
Paito	Resiake	Taumako		93.3	probably from Resiake family, made by Pu Resiake
Paito	Resiake	Taumako	E84695	90.1	

Title	Name	Clan	AM reg. no.	Firth's no.	Remarks
Pa	Rongatao	?		86.5	possibly Pa Rongotau, mission teacher (Firth 1965:249)
Pa	Rongo rei	Tafua	E84577	9.8	deceased, brother is Joseph Manu-tai, lives in Honiara, house (grandson) now living in Kira Kira, 48.12 [IT]
Pa	Rongo Taono	Kafika		4.27	family now living in Kira Kira [IT] (Firth 1983:61)
Paito	Samoa	Samoa	E84696	90.2	
Paito	Samoa	Samoa		4.30	
Pa	Sau ki rima	Tafua	E84587	58.2	house gone [IT]
Pa	Siamano	Kafika	E92048	48.5	
Pa	Siamano	Kafika		53.4	
Pa	Siamono	Kafika			see E92198; 10.3
Pa	Sukumarae	Kafika		25.1	[IT]
Pa	Sukuporu	Tafua	not rel	not rel	an important man of rank (Firth 1967c:111)
Ariki	Tafua	Tafua		38.4	
Ariki	Tafua	Tafua	E84900	91.3	
Ariki	Tafua	Tafua		1.11	
Ariki	Tafua	Tafua	E84899	91.2	
Ariki	Tafua	Tafua		77.3	
Ariki	Tafua	Tafua	E84700	38.1	
Ariki	Tafua	Tafua	E84898	91.1	
Ariki	Tafua	Tafua	E84452	48.15	from the family of the Ariki Tafua
Ariki	Tafua	Tafua	E84901	91.4	
Ariki	Tafua	Tafua	E84903	91.6	
Ariki	Tafua	Tafua	E84902	91.5	
Ariki	Tafua	Tafua	E84793	7.7	
Pa	Taitai	Taumako	E92054	98.1	of Rangi rikoi family [IT] (Firth 1983:62)

Title	Name	Clan	AM reg. no.	Firth's no.	Remarks
Pa	Tanianu	Kafika	E84592	59.15	brother of Nakutei, now living in Kira Kira [IT]
Paito	Tanimua	Tafua	E84025	4.17	
Pa	Tarai Raki	Kafika		8.1	former property of Ariki Kafika, Pu Mapusanga
Pa	Tarairaki	Kafika		63.1	from house of Mapusanga, Kafika
Pa	Taraoro	Fangerere	E92191	16.7	
Pa	Taraoro	Fangerere	E84501	59.1	
Pa	Taraoro	Fangerere	E92198	10.3	house gone [IT]
Pa	Tariki tonga	Taumako	E84499	58.1	family now living in Kira Kira, brother of Pa Vetere [IT]
Ariki	Taumako	Taumako		53.1	
Ariki	Taumako	Taumako		59.3	
Pa	Taunga	Kafika		4.20	family now living in Kira Kira [IT]
Pa	Tavi	Kafika	E92185	16.6	family now living in Kira Kira [IT]
Pa	te Kaumata	Taumako	E84020	4.38	family now living in Kira Kira [IT], same family as Ngatotiu
Pa	te Kaumata	Taumako		67.1	also spelt Tekaumata
Pa	te Kaumata	Taumako		94.1	
Pa	te Kaumata	Taumako	E84373	96.1	
Pa	Tonga rutu	Kafika	E84502	59.9	
Pa	Tonga rutu	Kafika	E92158	16.10	brother of Marakei and Pa Vainunu [IT]
Paito	Torofaka tonga	Kafika	E84786	8.7	family now living in Kira Kira [IT]
Pa	Tuama	?	E84491	59.7	? [IT]
Pa	Vae Toka	Kafika	E84638	4.18	family now living in Kira Kira [IT]

Title	Name	Clan	AM reg. no.	Firth's no.	Remarks
Pa	Vainunu	Kafika	E84581	44.8	family now living in Kira Kira [IT]; Pa Vainunu, Pa Tongaruta and Pa Marakei all brothers [IT]

APPENDIX 4

Tikopia objects held in public collections collected prior to 1928

Key: BM, British Museum; MAA, Museum of Archaeology and Anthropology, University of Cambridge; PITT, Pitt Rivers Museum, University of Oxford; AUCK, Auckland Institute and Museum. The name of the collector is followed by the year of collection, or if appearing in square brackets, the year appearing in the museum's accession records.

Name	No.	Name	Item	Description
Sir Walter Calverley Trevelyan (1797 – 1879) [1871]	BM OC.7402		adze head, basalt	
Revd John Jennings, [1898]	MAA Z 10905		shell necklace	22 well matched shells, 24 cm long
	PITT B.1.104	*pa*	pendant shank	purchased
William Halse Rivers, 1908	MAA Z 00290 (2)		horn ring	
	MAA Z 141 A/B		shells (2)	
Revd Durrad, 1910	AUCK 13798	*paki*	dance paddle	
	MAA Z 11092		shark line?	double-braided fibre
	MAA Z 10896	*kuani*	bag net	deep-sea fishing
	MAA Z 11098	*kuani*	bag net	deep-sea fishing
	MAA Z 10943	*kafa fakafafine*	belt women's	
	MAA Z 11091		shark line	double-braided fibre
	MAA Z 10914	*pa*	fish-hook complete	
	MAA Z 10913	*pa*	fish-hook complete	
	MAA Z 10912	*pa*	fish-hook complete	

Name	No.	Name	Item	Description
Revd Durrad, 1910 (continued)	MAA Z 10918		tattoo bowl	
	MAA Z 10919	*matau*	tattoo needle	
	MAA 1912 E 22 (63)	*te titi*	belt shell	also used as currency?
	MAA Z 11090	*uka*	fishing line	type of twist
	MAA Z 10902		wrist ornament	2 shells on fibre
	MAA Z 10916	*pa*?	pendant shank	clam-shell
	MAA Z 10898		coconut strainer	
	MAA Z 11101	*kalikau*	armlet	
	MAA Z 10903		wrist ornament	2 shells on fibre
	MAA Z 11093 (12)	*kalikau*?	ear rings	
	MAA Z 10920	*kalikau*	armlet	trochus shell
	MAA Z 11097	*somo fangongo*?	necklace	of brown clam-shell beads. worn by women
	MAA Z 11094	*ngasane*	ear rings	
	MAA Z 10922	*tifa*	breast ornament	
	MAA Z 20921	*tifa*	breast ornament	'toppes island'
	MAA Z 10904	*pa atu*?	pendant fish-hook	turtle shell
	MAA Z 11102		basket	
	MAA Z 10917	*pu*	sacred shell trumpet	
	MAA Z 10900	*iri*	fan	coconut leaf
	MAA?	*iri*	fan	coconut leaf

Name	No.	Name	Item	Description
Revd Durrad, 1910 *(continued)*	MAA 1912 E 22 (57)		toy trumpet	
	MAA Z 10944		toy	shells on rope
	MAA Z 10940	*umu (renga)*	turmeric container	
	MAA Z 10910	*ukofi*	tongs	
	MAA Z 10915	*pa?*	pendant shank	pearl-shell
	MAA Z 10897	*kafa*	rope, building	also exchange money
	MAA Z 10947	*vai*	coconut water container	
	MAA Z 10942	*fangongo kava*	kava cup/ ceremonial food bowl	of wood, not coconut
	MAA Z 11088		Basket	
	MAA Z 11089		Basket	
	MAA Z 11099	*tanga*	bag for lime box etc	men's bag
	MAA Z 10941	*kapia*	lime container	
	MAA Z 10937	*soka*	betel mortar	
	MAA Z 10911	*sika*	netting shuttle	
	MAA Z 11095	*kaka*	funnel / filter	coconut fibre
	MAA Z 11096	*kaka*	bag of bark-cloth...	
	MAA 1912 E 22 (27)	*urunga*	headrest chiefs	
	MAA Z 10901		shell scraper	
	MAA Z 10934		cup with handle	

Name	No.	Name	Item	Description
Archdeacon Comins	BM 1912.0708.7		club	plain [1912]
	AUCK 9067		chief's hair	purchased in 1918
Bishop Wood [donated in 1916]	AUCK 12992		canoe, *rakaitonga*	built by Pu Auekofe for Te Ariki Taumako etc.
Revd William Chamberlain O'Ferrall [1920]	MAA 1920.487	*iri*	fan	
	MAA 1920.485	*iri*	fan	
	MAA 1920.484	*iri*	fan	
Thomas Wheeler, [donated 1924]	AUCK 9611		sleeping mat	
Browne, [1927]	AUCK 10710		coconut grating stool	
Captain Burgess, of the *Southern Cross* [1927]	AUCK 18466	*bogutu*?	club	
	AUCK 18467	*bogutu*?	club	
	AUCK 18468	*boguto*?	club	
	AUCK 18462	*bogutu*?	club	
Captain Burgess, of the *Southern Cross* [1928]	AUCK 1885		canoe sail	now on sacred canoe
	AUCK 3830		stone adze	

REFERENCES

Archives
Anglican Church of Melanesia Archives, Honiara

Godfrey, R. 1928. 1928 Synod Trip. Diary of the Revd Richard Godfrey, priest
of the Melanesian Mission, Item 19, transcribed T. Brown, 2011.
anglicanhistory.org?oceania/godfrey_synod1928. Accessed 13 February
2014.

The Melanesian Mission, 1926. The Story of the Melanesian Mission. Transcribed
T. Brown, 2009. anglicanhistory.org/oceania/story_melanesia1926.
Accessed 13 February 2014.

London School of Economics
Archive Reference Firth 7.10.4 'Firth, ANRC, Objects to BM, Letters
from Tikopia'.

Firth to Radcliffe-Brown, 20 January 1927.

Firth to Radcliffe-Brown, 10 April 1927.

Firth to Radcliffe Brown, 21 September 1927.

Firth to Radcliffe Brown, Application for Grant to the Australian National
Research Council.

Firth to Radcliffe-Brown, 17 October 1928.

'Firth Cultural Heritage', 30 November 1973, seminar titled 'Development and the
Cultural Heritage. Some reflections from the South Pacific'

Archive Reference Firth 1.9.15 'Firth Specimens'
Craven to Firth, 27 September 1976.

Firth to Craven, 7 October 1976.

Firth to Craven, 14 December 1977.

Specht to Firth, 19 October 1978.

Mitchell Library, Sydney
Selwyn, G. 1857. Melanesian Mission. Two Letters and Melanesian Mission
Reports, Mitchell Library, Sydney.

Russell, B. 1830–1833. Mss. Journals. Originals in Mitchell Library, Sydney.
Typescript and Xerox copies in Alexander Turnbull Library, Wellington.

Sydney University Archives

Australian National Research Council Papers, AP Elkin papers, University of Sydney Archives, P130/40/7.

Radcliffe-Brown, A.R. 1928. Letter to A.J. Gibson, 28 November.

Radcliffe-Brown, A.R. 1929. Letter to A.J. Gibson, 12 April.

Gibson, A.J. 1928. Letter to Radcliffe-Brown, 14 December.

Gibson, A.J. 1929a. Letter to Radcliffe-Brown, 20 February.

Gibson, A.J. 1929b. Letter to Radcliffe-Brown, 13 April.

Australian Museum Archives

Bolton, L. 1985. Report on the Acquisition of the Museum of Australia Collection. Note to File, Sydney University Files, Australian Museum.

Hipsley, E.H. 1959. Letter to Deputy Crown Solicitor, 9 October. National Museum of Australia documents held at the Australian Museum.

Oakes, L. 1988. Report on the University of Sydney Collection, unpublished report held in the Anthropology Division at the Australian Museum.

Preiss, L. 1980. Draft Report. Concerning the Physical Condition of the Raymond Firth and James Spillius Collection: and Recommendations for Procedures to be considered, and for the Packing of the Collection, for its Return to the Solomon Islands. Materials Conservation Student, Canberra College of Advanced Education, January to February. Unpublished document held in the Sydney University File, Anthropology Division, The Australian Museum.

Specht, J. and L. Bolton. 1988. Minutes of Meeting, 6 May 1988, University of Sydney File, Anthropology Division, The Australian Museum.

Wedgewood, C. 1930. Catalogue of Specimens Collected from Tikopia by R.W.Firth 1928–1929. Copy held in the Raymond Firth files, in the University of Sydney Collection files in the Anthropology Division, The Australian Museum. Original held at Macleay Museum, University of Sydney.

The University of Sydney file, 1988. Documents from the National Museum of Australia, held in the Anthropology Division, The Australian Museum, Sydney.

Bonshek personal archive

Firth, R. 1928. Specimens. Copy of handwritten document listing items acquired
    and date. Original held with Professor Firth.

Manuscript source

Richards R. (ed) Tikopia: First Foreigner Visitors – a resource book for Tikopians.
    Manuscript, 2005. Courtesy of the editor.

Published material

Allen, N. 1998. Maori vision and the imperialist gaze. In T. Barringer and T. Flynn
    (eds) *Colonialism and the Object*, pp. 144–52. London: Routledge.

Anderson, C. 1990. Australian Aborigines and museums – A new relationship.
    Curator 33(3):165–79.

——— 1995a. The economics of sacred art: The uses of a secret collection in the
    South Australian Museum. In C. Anderson (ed.) *Politics of the Secret*
    (Oceania Monograph 45), pp. 1–42. Sydney: Oceania Publications.

——— (ed.) 1995b. *Politics of the Secret* (Oceania Monograph 45). Sydney:
    Oceania Publications.

Anon. 1828. *Barque Alfred from Port Jackson as a Whaling Voyage to the
    Northward*. Cambridge University Library, Official Publications.

——— 1839. Ship news. Horrible massacre. *Sydney Gazette* 37 (4126, 22 January).

——— 1931. Summary of lecture presented by Dr. Raymond Firth at the Annual
    General Meeting of the Anthropological Society of New South Wales,
    March 17, 1931. *Mankind* 1(1):3–4.

Appadurai, A. 1986. Commodities and the politics of value. In A. Appadurai (ed.),
    The Social Life of Things, pp. 3–63. Cambridge: University Press.

Bayly, G. 1885. *Sea-Life Sixty Years Ago*. London: Kegan Paul, Trench & Co.

Bennett, J.A. 1987. *Wealth of the Solomons. A History of a Pacific Archipelago,
    1800–1978* (Pacific Islands Monograph Series). Honolulu: University of
    Hawaii Press.

Bolton, L. 1993. Finding the right model: Museums, cultural centres and cultural
    heritage management in the Pacific. *Bulletin of the Conference of
    Museum Anthropologists* 24:35–40.

Bonshek, E. 2004. Ownership and a peripatetic collection: Raymond Firth's Collection from Tikopia, Solomon Islands. In V. Attenbrow and R. Fullagar (eds), *A Pacific Odyssey: Archaeology and Anthropology in the Western Pacific. Papers in Honour of Jim Specht* (Records of the Australian Museum, Supplement 29), pp. 37–45. Sydney: Australian Museum.

Burney. J, 1967. *A Chronological History of the Discoveries in the South Seas* (vol. 2). Amsterdam: N. Israel.

Campbell, S.F. 1983. Attaining rank: A classification of kula shell valuables. In W.J. Leach and E. Leach (eds), *The Kula. New Perspectives in Massim Exchange*, pp. 229–48. Cambridge: University Press.

Chapman, M. 1991. Pacific Island movement and socioeconomic change: Metaphors of misunderstanding. *Population and Development Review* 17(2):263–92.

Clark, G. 2003. Indigenous transfer of La Pérouse artefacts in the southeast Solomon Islands. *Australian Archaeology* 57:103–111.

Clifford, J. 1988. *The Predicament of Culture.* Cambridge, Mass.: Harvard University Press.

——— 1997. *Routes. Travel and Translation in the Late Twentieth Century.* Cambridge, Mass.: Harvard University Press.

Codrington, R.H. 1969. *The Melanesians: Studies in their Anthropology and Folklore.* Oxford: Clarendon Press.

Cohen, P.S. 1967. Economic analysis and economic man: Some comments on a controversy. In R.W. Firth (ed.), *Themes in Economic Anthropology*, pp. 91–118. London: Tavistock.

Coote, J. 1987. Notes and queries and social interrelations: An aspect of the history of social anthropology. *Journal of the Anthropological Society of Oxford* 18(3):255–72.

Council of Australia Museums Association. 1993. *Previous Possessions, New Obligations: Policies for Museums in Australia and Aboriginal and Torres Strait Islander Peoples.* Melbourne: The Council.

Craig, B. 1996. Samting Belong Tumbuna: The Collection, Documentation and Preservation of the Material Cultural Heritage of Papua New Guinea. Ph.D. dissertation, Flinders University of South Australia.

Dillon, P. 1829a. *Narrative and Successful Result of a Voyage of the South Seas, Performed by Order of the Government of British India, to Ascertain the Actual Fate of La Pérouse's Expedition, Interspersed with Accounts of the Religion, Manners, Customs and Cannibal Practices of the South Sea Islanders, Vol. 1.* London: Hurst, Chance and Co.

——— 1829b. *Narrative and Successful Result of a Voyage of the South Seas, Performed by Order of the Government of British India, to Ascertain the Actual Fate of La Pérouse's Expedition, Interspersed with Accounts of the Religion, Manners, Customs and Cannibal Practices of the South Sea Islanders, Vol. 2.* London: Hurst, Chance and Co.

Dudding, J. 2005. Visual repatriation and photo-elicitation: Recommendations on principles and practices for the museum worker. *Journal of Museum Ethnography* 17:218–31.

Dumont d'Urville, J.S.C. 1987. *An Account in Two Volumes of Two Voyages to the South Seas by Captain (later Rear-Admiral) Jules S.C.Dumont d'Urville of the French Navy to Australia, New Zealand, Oceania 1826–1829 in the Corvette Astrolabe and to the Straits of Magellan, Chile, Oceania, South East Asia, Australia, Antarctica, New Zealand and Torres Strait 1837–1840 in the Corvettes Astrolabe and Zélée, Vol. 1: Astrolabe 1826–1829* (trans. and ed. H. Rosenman). Carlton: Melbourne University Press.

Durrad, W.J. 1913. A Tikopia vocabulary. *Journal of the Polynesian Society* 22:86–95, 141–8.

——— 1922. The depopulation of Melanesia. In W.H. Rivers (ed.), *Essays on the Depopulation of Melanesia*, pp. 3–24. Cambridge: University Press.

——— 1926. A Tikopia vocabulary: Compiled mainly from materials collected by the Revd W.J. Durrad. *Journal of the Polynesian Society* 35:267–89.

——— 1927. A Tikopia vocabulary: Compiled mainly from materials collected by the Revd W.J. Durrad. *Journal of the Polynesian Society* 36:1–20, 99–117.

Earle, A. 1832. *A Narrative of a Nine Months' Residence in New Zealand in 1827; Together with a Journal of a Residence in Tristan D'Acunha, an Island Situated Between South America and the Cape of Good Hope. Augustus Earle, Draughtsman to his Majesty's Surveying-ship 'the Beagle'.* London: Longman, Rees, Orme, Brown, Green, and Longman.

Edmundson, A. 2013 For Science, Salvage, & State. Official Collecting in Colonial New Guinea. PhD Thesis, Research School of Humanities and the Arts, Australian National University, Canberra.

Edwards, E., C. Gosden, and R. Philips (eds) 2006. *Sensible Objects: Colonialism, Museums and Material Culture.* Oxford: Berg.

Edwards, R. and J. Stewart (eds) 1980. *Preserving Indigenous Cultures. A New Role for Museums* (Papers from a Regional Seminar Adelaide Festival Centre 10–15 September 1978). Canberra: Australian Government Publishing Service.

Eoe, S.M. and P. Swadling (eds) 1991. *Museums and Cultural Centres in the Pacific.* Port Moresby: Papua New Guinea National Museum.

Eyo, E. 1994. Repatriation of cultural heritage: The African experience. In F.E.S. Kaplan (ed.), *Museums and the Making of 'Ourselves': The Role of Objects in National Identity,* pp. 330–50. London: Leicester University Press.

Fabian, J. 1998. Curios and curiosity: Notes on reading Torday and Frobenius. In E. Schildkrout and C.A. Keim (eds), *The Scramble for Art in Central Africa,* pp. 79–108. Cambridge: University Press.

Feinberg, R. 1981. *Anuta: Social Structure of a Polynesian Island.* Provo, Utah: The Institute for Polynesian Studies.

——— 1988. *Polynesian Seafaring and Navigation: Ocean Travel in Anuta Culture and Society.* Kent, Ohio: The Kent State University Press.

Firth, R. 1925a. The Korekore Pa: An ancient Maori fortress. *Journal of the Polynesian Society* 34(1):1–18.

——— 1925b. The Maori career. *Journal of the Polynesian Society* 34(4):277–91.

——— 1925c. Maori storehouses of today. *Royal Anthropological Institute of Great Britain and Ireland* 55:363–72.

——— 1925d. Economic psychology of the Maori. *Royal Anthropological Institute of Great Britain and Ireland* 55:340–62.

——— 1926a. Wharepuni: A few remaining Maori dwellings of the old style. *Man* 26:54–9.

——— 1926b. Proverbs in native life, with special reference to those of Maori, 1. *Folklore* 37(2):134–53.

——— 1926c. Proverbs in native life, with special reference to those of Maori, 2. *Folklore* 37(3):245–70.

——— 1927. Maori hill forts. *Antiquity* 1(1):66–78.

——— 1930a. Marriage and classificatory system of relationship. *Royal Anthropological Institute of Great Britain and Ireland* 60:235–68.

——— 1930b. Report on research in Tikopia. *Oceania* 1(1):105–17.

——— 1930c. Totemism in Polynesia. *Oceania* 1(3):291–321.

———— 1930d. Totemism in Polynesia. *Oceania* 1(4):377–98.

———— 1934. The meaning of dreams in Tikopia. In E. Evans-Pritchard and C.G. Seligman (eds), *Essays Presented to C.G. Seligman*, pp. 63–74. London: Kegan Paul, Trench, Trubner Co.

———— 1936a. Bond friendship in Tikopia. In L.H.D. Buxton (ed.), *Custom is King: Essays Presented to R.R. Marett on his Seventieth Birthday June 13, 1936*, pp. 259 –69. London: Hutchinson's.

———— 1936b. *We, the Tikopia: A Sociological Analysis of Kinship in Primitive Polynesia* (1st edn). London: Allen and Unwin.

———— 1937. Anthropology and the study of society. In J.E. Dugdale (ed.), *Further Papers on the Social Sciences: Their Relations in Theory and Teaching*, pp. 75–90. London: Le Play House Press.

———— 1939. *Primitive Polynesian Economy* (1st edn). London: Routledge.

———— 1940. The analysis of *mana*: An empirical approach. *Journal of the Polynesian Society* 49:483–510.

———— 1947. Bark cloth in Tikopia. *Man* 47:69–72.

———— 1951. Notes on some Tikopia ornaments. *Journal of the Polynesian Society* 60:130–3.

———— 1952a. Anthropological fieldwork in the Solomons. *British Solomon Islands Society, Transactions* 1:1–4.

———— 1952b. Notes on the social structure of some south-eastern New Guinea communities. Part 1 Mailu. *Man* 52:65–7.

———— 1952c. Notes on the social structure of some south-eastern New Guinea communities. Part 2 Koita. *Man* 52:86–9.

———— 1954 Anuta and Tikopia: symbiotic elements in social organization. *Journal of Polynesian Society* 63:87-131.

———— 1958. Social anthropology as science and as art. William Evans Special Lecturer in the University of Otago. Paper delivered before the Australian and New Zealand Association for the Advancement of Science during their 32nd meeting at Dunedin. Dunedin: University of Otago.

———— 1959a. Ritual adzes in Tikopia. In J.D. Freeman and W.R. Geddes (eds), *Anthropology in the South Seas – Essays Presented to H.D. Skinner*, pp. 149–50. New Plymouth: Thomas Avery and Sons.

———— 1959b. *Social Change in Tikopia: Restudy of a Polynesian Community after a Generation*. London: Allen and Unwin.

——— 1960a. A Polynesian aristocrat. In J.B. Casagrande (ed.), *In the Company of Man*, pp. 1–14. New York: Harper & Brothers.

——— 1960b. Tikopia wood working ornament. *Man* 60:17–20.

——— 1961. *History and Traditions of Tikopia*. Wellington: The Polynesian Society.

——— 1965. *Primitive Polynesian Economy* (2nd edn). London: Routledge & Kegan Paul.

——— 1966a. *Malay Fishermen: Their Peasant Economy* (2nd edn). London: Routledge & Kegan Paul.

——— 1966b. Twins, birds and vegetables: Problems of identification in primitive religious thought. *Man* 1(1):1–17.

——— 1967a. *The Work of the Gods in Tikopia* (2nd edn). London: The Athlone Pres.

——— 1967b. An analysis of *mana*: An empirical approach. In R.W. Firth (ed.), *Tikopia Ritual and Belief*, pp. 174–94. London: George Allen & Unwin.

——— 1967c. Bond friendship. In R.W. Firth (ed.), *Tikopia Ritual and Belief*, pp. 108–15. London: George Allen & Unwin.

——— 1969. Extraterritoriality and the Tikopia chiefs. *Man* 4(3):354–78.

——— 1970a. *Rank and Religion in Tikopia: A Study in Polynesian Paganism and Conversion to Christianity*. London: George Allen & Unwin.

——— 1970b. Tikopia string figures. *Royal Anthropological Institute Occasional Papers*, 29.

——— 1973a. Food symbolism in a pre-industrial society. In R.W. Firth (ed.), *Symbols Public and Private*, pp. 243–61. London: George Allen & Unwin.

——— 1973b. Tikopia art and society. In A. Forge (ed.), *Primitive Art and Society*, pp. 25–48. London: Oxford University Press.

——— 1974. Faith and scepticism in Kelantan village magic. In W.R. Roff (ed.), *Kelantan: Religion, Society and Politics in a Malay State*, pp. 190–224. Kuala Lumpur: Oxford University Press.

——— 1975. An appraisal of modern social anthropology. *Annual Review of Modern Social Anthropology* 4:1–25.

——— 1978. Sex roles and sex symbols in Tikopia society. *Kroeber Anthropological Society Papers* 57/58:1–19.

———— 1980. Let the hundred flowers bloom: culture, language and the arts. In Sione Tupouniua, R. Crocombe and C. Slatter (eds), *The Pacific Way: Social Issues in National Development*, Suva: South Pacific Social Sciences Association.

———— 1983 [reprint of 2nd edn 1957]. *We the Tikopia. A Sociological Study of Kinship in Primitive Polynesia.* California: Stanford University Press.

———— 1988. Malinowski in the history of social anthropology. In R. Ellen, E. Gellner, G. Kubica and J. Mucha (eds), *Malinowski between Two Worlds: The Polish Roots of an Anthropological Tradition*, pp. 12–42. Cambridge: Cambridge University Press.

———— 1990. Encounters with Tikopia over sixty years. *Oceania* 60(4):241–9.

———— 1992. Art and anthropology. In J. Coote and A. Shelton (eds), *Anthropology, Art and Aesthetics*, pp.15–39. Oxford: Clarendon Press.

———— 1996. The founding of the Research School of Pacific Studies. *Journal of Pacific History* 31(1):3–5.

Firth, R.W. with M. McLean. 1990. *Tikopia Songs: Poetic and Musical Art of a Polynesian People of the Solomon Islands.* Cambridge: Cambridge University Press.

Firth, R.W. with I. Tuki (Pa Rangiaco). 1985. *Tikopia English Dictionary. Taranga fakatikopia ma taranga fakainglisi.* Auckland: Auckland University Press.

Foana'ota, L.A. 1991. Solomon Islands National Museum. In S.M. Eoe and P. Swadling (eds), *Museums and Cultural Centres in the Pacific*, pp. 95–102. Port Moresby: Papua New Guinea National Museum.

———— 1994. Solomon Islands National Museum and Cultural Centre Policy. In L. Lindstrom and G.M. White (eds), *Culture, Kastom, Tradition: Developing Cultural Policy in Melanesia*, pp. 95–102. Fiji: Institute of Pacific Studies, University of the South Pacific.

———— 2007. The future of indigenous museums: The Solomon Islands case. In N. Stanley (ed.), *The Future of Indigenous Museums: Perspectives from the Southwest Pacific*, pp. 38–46. Oxford: Berghahn Books.

Fox, C. 1967. *The Story of the Solomons.* Taroaniara, British Solomon Islands: D.O.M. Publications.

Frankenberg, R. 1967. Economic anthropology: one anthropologist's view. In R.W. Firth (ed.), *Themes in Economic Anthropology*, pp. 47–89. London: Tavistock.

Freedman, M. 1967. Preface. In M. Freedman (ed.), *Social Organization. Essays presented to Raymond Firth*, pp. vii–ix. London: Frank Cass & Co.

Furst, H.J. 1989. Recording ethnographic collections: the debate on the return of cultural property. In S. Pearce (ed.), *Museum Studies in Material Culture*, pp. 97–100. London: Leicester University Press.

Galla, A. 1997. Indigenous peoples, museums, and ethics. In G. Edson (ed.), *Museum Ethics*, pp. 142–55. London: Routledge.

Gell, A. 1998. *Art and Agency: An Anthropological Theory*. Oxford: Clarendon Press.

Gosden, C. and C. Knowles. 2001. *Collecting Colonialism: Material Culture and Colonial Change*. Oxford: Berg.

Gosden, C. and F. Larson. 2007. *Knowing Things: Exploring the Collections at the Pitt Rivers Museum, 1884–1945*. Oxford: University Press.

Harris, M. 1968. *The Rise of Anthropological Theory: A History of Theories of Culture*. London: Routledge & Kegan Paul.

Henare, A., M. Holbrand and S. Wastell (eds) 2007. *Thinking Through Things: Theorising Artefacts Ethnographically*. London: Routledge.

Humphrey, C. and S. Hugh-Jones. 1992. Introduction: barter, exchange and value. In C. Humphrey and S. Hugh-Jones (eds), *Barter, Exchange and Value. An Anthropological Approach*, pp. 1–19. Cambridge: Cambridge University Press.

Institut für den Wissenschaftichen Film. 1993. *Firth on Firth: Reflections of an Anthropologist*. VHS videocassette, 47 mns. Institut für den Wissenschaftichen Film, Gottingen, Germany.

Jaarsman, S. 2002. *Handle with Care: Ownership and Control of Ethnographic Materials*. Pittsburgh: University of Pittsburgh Press.

Jack-Hinton, C. 1969. *The Search for the Islands of Solomon, 1567–1838*. London: Oxford University Press.

Jones, A. 1993. Exploding canons: the anthropology of museums. *Annual Review of Anthropology* 22:201–20.

Kaeppler, A.L. 1989. Museums of the world: stages for the study of ethnohistory. In S. Pearce (ed.), *Museum Studies in Material Culture*, pp. 83–96. London: Leicester University Press.

Kavanagh, G. 1989. Objects as evidence or Not? In S. Pearce (ed.), *Museum Studies in Material Culture*, pp. 125–37. London: Leicester University Press.

Keesing, R. and R. Tonkinson, (eds) 1982. *Reinventing Traditional Culture: The Politics of kastom in Island Melanesia. Mankind* 13(4) Special issue.

Kirch, P.V. 1986. Exchange systems and inter-island contact in the transformation of an island society: the Tikopia case. In P.V. Kirch (ed.), *Island Societies. Archaeological Approaches to Evolution and Transformation*, pp. 33–41. Cambridge: Cambridge University Press.

—— 1996. Tikopia social space revisited. In J. Davidson, G. Irwin, F. Leach, A. Pawley and D. Brown (eds), *Oceanic Culture History: Essays in Honour of Roger Green*, pp. 257–74. New Zealand Journal of Archaeology Special Publication.

Kirch, P.V. and D.E. Yen. 1982. *Tikopia: The Prehistory and Ecology of a Polynesian Outlier* (Bulletin of the Bernice Bishop Museum 238). Honolulu: Bernice Bishop Museum Press.

Kopytoff, I. 1986. The cultural biography of things: commoditization as process. In A. Appadurai (ed.), *The Social Life of Things*, pp. 64–91. Cambridge: Cambridge University Press.

Kreps, C. 2007. The theoretical future of Indigenous museums: concept and practice. In N. Stanley (ed.), *The Future of Indigenous Museums. Perspectives from the Southwest Pacific*, pp. 223–34. Oxford: Berghahn Books.

Küchler, S. 1987. Malangan: art and memory in a Melanesian Society. *Man* 22(2):238–55.

Laracy, H.M. 1969. The first mission to Tikopia. *Journal of Pacific History* 4:105–9.

Larson, E.H. 1960. A Modern Plantation System: Tikopian Socio-Economic Organization in the Russell Islands. Ph.D. thesis, University of Oregon.

—— 1966. *Nukufero: A Tikopian Colony in the Russell Islands.* Eugene, Oregon: Department of Anthropology, University of Oregon.

—— 1968. Tikopian labour migration to the Russell Islands. *Journal of the Polynesian Society* 77(2):163–76.

—— 1977. Tikopia in the Russell Islands. In M.D. Lieber (ed.), *Exiles and Migrants in Oceania* (Association for Social Anthropology in Oceania Monograph 5). Honolulu: University of Hawaii Press.

Lawson, B. 1994. *Collected Curios: Missionary Tales from the South Seas.* Montreal: McGill University Libraries.

Layton, R. (ed.), 1989. *Who Needs the Past? Indigenous Values and Archaeology.* London: Unwin Hyman.

Liep, J. 1990. Gift exchange and the construction of identity. In J. Siikala (ed.),
    Culture and History in the Pacific, pp. 164–83. Helsinki: Transactions of
    the Finnish Anthropological Society 27.

Lindstrom, L. and G.M. White. 1994a. Cultural policy: an introduction. In
    L. Lindstrom and G.M. White (eds), *Culture, Kastom, Tradition:
    Developing Cultural Policy in Melanesia*, pp. 1–18. Suva: Institute of
    Pacific Studies, University of the South Pacific..

——— (eds) 1994b. *Culture, Kastom, Tradition. Developing Cultural Policy in
    Melanesia*. Suva: Institute of Pacific Studies, University of the South
    Pacific.

——— 1995. Anthropology's new cargo: future horizons. *Ethnology* 34(3):201–9.

Linnekin, J. and L. Poyer 1990. Introduction. In J. Linnekin and L. Poyer (eds),
    Cultural Identity and Ethnicity in the Pacific, pp.1–16. Honolulu:
    University of Hawaii Press.

MacDonald, G.F. and S. Alsford. 1995. Canadian museums and the representation
    of culture in a multicultural nation. *Cultural Dynamics* 7(1):15–36.

MacDonald, J. 1991. Women of Tikopia. Ph.D. thesis, University of Auckland, New
    Zealand.

——— 2000. The Tikopia and 'What Raymond said'. In S. Jaarsma and M.
    Rohatynskyj (eds), *Ethnographic Artifacts: Challenges to a Reflexive
    Anthropology*, pp. 107–23. Honolulu: University of Hawaii Press.

——— 2002. Obituary: Sir Raymond Firth. *Oceania* 72(3):153–5.

Mackay, J. 1887. Tucopia. *Proceedings and Transactions of the Royal Geographical
    Society of Australasia, Queensland Branch* 2(2):81–5.

Mauss, M. 1990. *The Gift: The Form and Reason for Exchange in Archaic Societies*
    (trans. W.D. Hall). London: Routledge.

McBryde, I. (ed.) 1985. *Who Owns the Past?* Melbourne: Oxford University Press.

McLear, D. 1996. First Peoples, museums and citizenship. In T. Bennett, R. Trotter
    and D. McLear (eds), *Museums and Citizenship: A Resource Book*, pp.
    79–113. South Brisbane: Queensland Museum.

Messenger, P.M. (ed.) 1989. *The Ethics of Collecting Cultural Property. Whose
    Culture? Whose Property?* Albuquerque: University of New Mexico
    Press.

Miller, D. 1994. *Material Culture and Mass Consumption*. Oxford: Blackwell
    Publishers.

——— (ed.) 2005. *Materiality*. Durham, N.C.: Duke University Press.

Milner, G.B. 1969. Siamese twins, birds and the double helix. *Man* 4(1):5–23.

Monberg, T. 1971. Tikopia color classification. *Ethnology* 10(3):349–58.

——— 1975. Informants fire back: a micro-study in anthropological methods. *Journal of the Polynesian Society* 84(2):218–24.

——— 1996. The Bellonese: High, low – and equal. Leadership and change on a Polynesian outlier in the Solomon Islands. In R. Feinberg and K.A. Watson-Gegeo (eds), *Leadership and Change in the Western Pacific: Essays Presented to Sir Raymond Firth on the Occasion of his Ninetieth Birthday*, pp. 187–204. London: The Athlone Press.

Mulvaney, J. 1985. A question of values: Museums and cultural property. In I. McBryde (ed.), *Who Owns the Past?* pp. 86–98. Melbourne: Oxford University Press.

National Museum of Australia. 2008. Collections Development Plan, Version 1.2, 24 November. www.nma.gov.au/__data/assets/pdf_file/0017/1448/Collections_development_plan_1.2_2008.pdf. Accessed 26 February 2013.

O'Keefe, P.J. and L.V. Prott (eds) 2011. *Cultural Heritage Conventions and other Instruments: A Compendium with Commentaries.* Builth Wells: Institute of Art and Law.

O'Hanlon, M. and R. Welsch (eds) 2000. *Hunting the Gatherers: Ethnographic Collectors, Agents, and Agency in Melanesia.* Oxford: Berghahn Books.

Pannell, S. 1995. The cool memories of *Tjurunga*: a symbolic history of collection authenticity and the sacred. In C. Anderson (ed.), *Politics of the Secret*, pp. 108–22. Sydney: Oceania Publications.

Parkin, D. 1988. Interview with Raymond Firth. *Current Anthropology* 29 (2): 327–42.

Pearce, S. 1989. Museum studies in material culture. In S. Pearce (ed.), *Museum Studies in Material Culture*, pp. 1–10. London: Leicester University Press.

——— 1994. *Interpreting Objects and Collections.* London: Routledge.

Peers, L. and A. Brown. 2003. *Museums and Source Communities: A Routledge Reader.* London: Routledge.

Pendergrast, M. 2000. *Tikopian Tattoo.* Auckland: Auckland Museum.

Peterson, N., Allen, L. and Hamby, L. (eds) 2008. *The Makers and Making of Indigenous Australian Museum Collections.* Carlton, Victoria: Melbourne University Press.

Prott, L. (ed.) 2009. *Witnesses to History. A Compendium of Documents and Writings on the Return of Cultural Objects.* Paris: UNESCO.

Prott, L. and P.J. O'Keefe. 1989. *Law and the Cultural Heritage. Vol. 3. Movement.* London: Butterworths.

Prott, L. and J. Specht. 1986. *Protection or Plunder? Safeguarding the Future of Our Cultural Heritage.* Papers of the UNESCO Regional Seminar on the Movable Cultural Property Convention, Brisbane, Australia. Canberra: Australian Government Publishing Service.

Quanchi, M. and Cochrane, S. 2007. *Hunting the Collectors: Pacific Collections in Museums, Art Galleries and Archives.* Newcastle: Cambridge Scholars Publishing.

Queirós, P. 1904. *The Voyages of Pedro Fernandez de Quiros 1596 to 1606* (trans. C. Markham), vol. 1. London: Hakluyt Society.

Radcliffe-Brown, A.R. 1952a. On social structure. In A.R. Radcliffe-Brown (ed.), *Structure and Function in Primitive Society*, pp.188–204. London: Cohen & West.

——— 1952b. On the concept of function in social science. In A.R. Radcliffe-Brown (ed.), *Structure and Function in Primitive Society*, pp. 178–87. London: Cohen & West.

——— 1952c. Social sanctions. In A.R. Radcliffe-Brown (ed.), *Structure and Function in Primitive Society*, pp. 205–11. London: Cohen & West.

Riley, B. 1991. Western Province Cultural Affairs Office, Gizo, Solomon Islands. In S.M. Eoe and P. Swadling (eds), *Museums and Cultural Centres in the Pacific*, pp. 152–3. Port Moresby: Papua New Guinea National Museum.

Rivers, W.H. 1906. Totemism in Polynesia and Melanesia. *Journal of the Royal Anthropological Institute of Great Britain and Ireland* 39:156–80.

——— 1914a. *The History of Melanesian Society. Vol. 1.* Cambridge: Cambridge University Press.

——— 1914b. *Kinship and Social Organization.* London: Constable.

——— 1922. *Essays on the Depopulation of Melanesia.* Cambridge: Cambridge University Press.

——— 1926. The ethnological analysis of culture. In W.H. Rivers, *Psychology and Ethnology* (ed. G.E. Smith), pp. 120–40. London: Kegan Paul, Trench, Trubner & Co.

Roe, D. and V. Totu. 1991. The Aola case: widening the debate, Guadalcanal, Solomon Islands. In S.M. Eoe and P. Swadling (ed.), *Museums and Cultural Centres in the Pacific*, pp. 138–47. Port Moresby: Papua New Guinea National Museum.

Rosenman, H. 1992. *Two Voyages to the South Seas ... Jules S.-C. Dumont D'Urville*. Melbourne: University Press.

Saunders, B. 1995. Kwakwaka'wakw museology. *Cultural Dynamics* 7(1):37–68.

Schaffarczyk, S. 2008. The Papuan Official Collection: The Biography of a Collection at the National Museum of Australia. Ph.D. thesis, Australian National University.

Schildkrout, E. and C.A. Keim 1998. Objects and agendas: re-collecting the Congo. In E. Schildkrout and C.A. Keim (eds), *The Scramble for Art in Central Africa*, pp. 1–36. Cambridge: University Press.

——— (eds) 1998. *The Scramble for Art in Central Africa*. Cambridge: University Press.

Specht, J. and C. Maclulich. 1996. Changes and challenges: The Australian Museum and Indigenous communities. In P.M. McManus (ed.), *Archaeological Displays and the Public*, pp. 27–49. London: Institute of Archaeology, University College London.

Spieser, F. 1913. *Two Years with the Natives in the Western Pacific*. London: Mills and Boon.

Spieser, F. 1922. Decadence and preservation in the New Hebrides. In W.H. Rivers (ed.), *Essays on the Depopulation of Melanesia*, pp. 25–61. Cambridge: University Press.

——— 1990. *Ethnology of Vanuatu: An Early Twentieth Century Study* (trans. D.Q. Stephenson). Crawford House Publishing, Bathurst.

Spillius, J. 1957a. Natural disaster and political crisis in a Polynesian society: an exploration of operational research (part one). *Human Relations* 10(1):3–27.

——— 1957b. Natural disaster and political crisis in a Polynesian society: An exploration of operational research (part two). *Human Relations* 10(2):113–25.

——— 1957c. Polynesian experiment: Tikopia Islanders as plantation labour. *Progress* 46–47:91–6.

Stanley, N. (ed.) 2007. *The Future of Indigenous Museums: Perspectives from the Southwest Pacific*, pp. 223–34. Oxford: Berghahn Books.

Stanton, J., B. Meehan, V. Attenbrow, A.H. Mian, B. Reynolds, R. Robins, E. Wishart, C. Anderson, J. Clark and R.J. Watt.(eds) 1990. Positions and policies of museums in Australia on human skeletal remains. *Australian Archaeology* 31:52–60.

Stratham, P. and R. Erickson (eds), 1998. *A Life on the Ocean Wave: The Journals of Captain George Bayly, 1824–1844*. Carlton: Melbourne University Press.

Stocking, G.W. 1984. Radcliffe-Brown and British Social Anthropology. In G.W. Stocking (ed.), *Functionalism Historicized: Essays on British Social Anthropology. History of Anthropology, Vol. 2*, pp. 131–91. Madison: University of Wisconsin Press.

——— (ed.) 1985. *Objects and Others: Essays on Museums and Material Culture*. Madison: University of Wisconsin Press.

Stone, R.P. 1960. *Kalori: Newsletter of the Museums Association of Australia* 20:2–3.

——— 1968. The Australian Institute of Anatomy. *Kalori: Newsletter of the Museums Association of Australia* 33:16–19.

Strathern, M. 1988. *The Gender of the Gift: Problems with Women and Problems with Society in Melanesia*. Berkeley: University of California Press.

——— 1990. Artefacts of history: events and the interpretation of images. In J. Siikala (ed.), *Culture and History in the Pacific*, pp. 25–40. Transactions of the Finnish Anthropological Society 27. Helsinki: Finnish Anthropological Society.

Thomas, N. 1989a. The force of ethnology: Origins and significance of the Melanesia/Polynesia division. *Current Anthropology* 30:27–34.

——— 1989b. *Out of Time: History and Evolution in Anthropological Discourse*. Cambridge: Cambridge University Press.

——— 1991. *Entangled Objects: Exchange, Material Culture, and Colonialism in the Pacific*. Cambridge, MA: Harvard University Press.

——— 2010. *Islanders: The Pacific in the Age of Empire*. New Haven: Yale University Press.

Tilley, C. (ed.) 1990. *Reading Material Culture: Structuralism, Hermeneutics and Post-Structuralism*. Oxford: Basil Blackwell.

Tilley, C., W. Keane, S. Küchler, M. Rowlands and P. Spyer (eds) 2006. *The Handbook of Material Culture*. London: Sage Publications.

Treadaway, J. 2007. *Dancing, Dying, Crawling, Crying: Stories of Continuity and Change in the Polynesian Community of Tikopia*. IPS Publications: University of South Pacific.

Totu, V. and D. Roe. 1991. The Guadalcanal Cultural Centre, Solomon Islands: keeping custom in the 1980s. In S. Eoe and P. Swadling (eds), *Museums and Cultural Centres in the Pacific*, pp. 113–31. Port Moresby: Papua New Guinea National Museum.

Warren, K.J. 1989. A philosophical perspective on the ethics and resolution of cultural property issues. In P.M. Messenger (ed.), *The Ethics of Collecting Cultural Property: Whose Culture? Whose Property?*, pp. 1–25. Albuquerque: University of New Mexico Press.

Weiner, A. 1985. Inalienable wealth. *American Ethnologist* 12:210–27.

——— 1988. *The Trobrianders of Papua New Guinea*. Fort Worth: Harcourt Brace Jovanovich.

INDEX

Textual differences in the spelling of Tikopia names have been retained in the index. Page numbers in *italic* refer to illustration captions.